PRAISE FOR ON THE ROCKS

"One of the most important lessons anybody could learn about this business is in this story."

—Jennifer English, James Beard Award Winner, Founder of *Food & Wine Radio Network*, Editor at Large *Proof Magazine*

"*On the Rocks* is a must-read for anyone thinking of starting a business. It's a poignant memoir detailing the trials and tribulations of running a restaurant. But beyond that, it's a heartwarming true story of love, determination, and family loyalty in the best of times and worst of times. . ."

—Stefanie Kratter, Senior Talent Producer for CNBC's *The Exchange* and *Power Lunch*

"*On the Rocks* takes readers back in time so much so that they will feel like they are sitting at a table inside The Primadonna. It's quite a tale—you don't want to miss this one."

—JoAnne Klimovich Harrop, the *Tribune Review* and Forthcoming Author of "*a daughter's promise*"

"I challenge anyone to not fall in love with Joe Costanzo and his family in this heartwarming, heartbreaking, and often hilarious narrative about a man who followed his dreams against all odds, but never forgot the importance of kindness, generosity, and humility. The in-depth behind-the-scenes look at building a highly successful restaurant from nothing and meeting the cast of characters that surround it is not only entertaining, but educational and shocking as well. Don't miss this one!"

—Amanda Raymond, Director and Producer at 13 Curves Production

"*On The Rocks* is a page-turning look at the rise and fall of an Italian American restaurateur... The most fascinating parts of his story are how he excelled in his culinary dreams to an unimaginable level; the quirky real-life cast of characters who frequented The Primadonna; the dos and don'ts—especially the cautions—of running a restaurant and hospitality empire; and food critic Mike Kalina's critical sphere of influence. For anyone who is nostalgic for the Italian American restaurateur culture à la 'Big Night,'... this book is for you."

—Jennifer Ciotta, *Corporate Flight Attendant* podcast

"All my life I've been fascinated by compelling characters that embody duality. Palmer and her coauthor Robbins deliver a must-read that you won't be able to put down. You can feel the love, the warmth, the forgiveness, and the undeniable passion the authors poured into the book..."

—Marilyn R. Atlas, Literary Manager, Producer, and Coauthor *Dating Your Character*

"Rich and delicious like a fine Italian meal... A chronicle of the timeless challenges of pursuing a dream while laboring to balance practicalities, poignantly captured and masterfully written, the tale of the larger-than-life Joe Costanzo Jr. and the rise and fall of the award-winning Primadonna Restaurant is a deeply satisfying read."

—Anjel B. Hartwell, The Wealthy Life Mentor, Nine-Time Award-Winning Podcast Host

"*On the Rocks* may seem like a standard biography on the surface, but Maria C. Palmer and Ruthie Robbins inhabit the voice of Joseph Costanzo in a book that attempts to disrupt the literary form to bring us a de facto memoir of a quintessential late twentieth-century restaurateur..."

—Thérèse Nelson, Chef, Writer, Founder BlackCulinaryHistory.com

"As a chef, I can relate to the highs and lows of working in the industry. The way the authors tell the story in such rich, vivid details got me emotionally invested in each character and made me feel like a lucky fly on the wall of The Primadonna."

—Mimi Lan, Michelin-trained Chef @TheTasteCurator, Ambassador @MAPPimpact

"*On the Rocks* is an intimate invite to slip into a half-lit booth at The Primadonna's bar and get swept up into a delectable story of family, food, American dreams, and the building of an institution that not only anchors a neighborhood but also offers everyone a seat at the table. . . It's also a heart-wrenching reminder that the hunger that makes us can also break us—but only if we allow it . . ."

—Josephine Caminos Oría, Founder, La Dorita Cooks and Author, *Sobremesa: A Memoir of Food and Love in 13 Courses*

"A truly personal story revolving around food, family, and the family we choose. You'll be drawn to the almost bigger than life personality of Joe Costanzo... Every win and loss centers around creating a community..."

—Jessie-Sierra Ross, Blogger and Author of *Straight to the Hips and Baby*

"*On the Rocks* chronicles . . . the impact Joe Costanzo's ambitious business had on the community of McKees Rocks, a rough and tumble town a stone's throw from Pittsburgh, and his family, a devoted clan of Italian American women who supported his vision through thick and thin. This gritty memoir . . . presents the good, the bad, and the ugly just as he remembered it, exhibiting the full range of humanity one experiences while chasing their dreams."

—Melissa E. Marinaro, Director, Italian American Program, Senator John Heinz History Center

". . . This story captured my attention with the first sentence and never let up until the last word—I couldn't put it down! I am in complete awe of the immense amount of unconditional love, vulnerability, determination, resilience, and forgiveness displayed by Joe and his entire community of family, friends, customers, business associates, and even inmates! . . ."

—Linda Carvelli, author of *Perfectly Negative* and biggest supporter of Foglia restaurant in Bristol, Rhode Island

"This book provides more education than any Ivy League degree ever could, telling the story of a self-made man who quickly rose to the top and had it all, only later to find himself seemingly losing it all. Yet, somehow, he found a way to keep it all together through the strength of his character along with the love of his wife and family. A must-read for learning how to navigate entrepreneurship as well as life!"

—Edward J. Maritz, EdD

"A riveting journey of culinary passion: *On the Rocks* delights the senses. . . It is an inspirational tale of ambition, perseverance, and the power of food to bring people together. It celebrates the human spirit, reminding us of the fragility of success and the immense toll it can take on not only ourselves but our family. I wholeheartedly recommend this book to anyone who appreciates a well-crafted tale that blends culinary delights with the captivating journey of a remarkable man."

— Sandra L. Rostirolla, Award-Winning YA Author of THE CECILIA SERIES and MAKING FRIENDS WITH MONSTERS

"This memoir tells of the grit and determination required in realizing one's dreams; but it is also a tale of unconditional love, kindness, authenticity, benevolence, and the importance of family."

—Elora Canne, author of *En Route: The Best Is Yet to Be*, Founder of Nonfiction Network

"It's colorful, gritty; it's *Cheers* with an edge, and you are going to cry at the end, so there's no reason not to pick this up."

—Alicia Pozsony, radio host of *Resilient YOU!* On iHeartRadio, Spotify, and Power98.5

". . . I was struck by the mythic aspect to Joe's ascent, fall, and reemergence. In some ways it mirrors Icarus's fall from the heavens, yet on another level it reads more like the Phoenix that rises from the ashes. . . I found myself rooting for him even when I thought *no, don't do that*! It speaks to each of us as it lays bare our desire to succeed and leave something lasting behind . . ."

—David Rigo, Professor, Interior Architecture at Chatham University, and Long-Time Employee at The Primadonna

"*On The Rocks* is a feast of relentless ambition with generous sides of benevolence, betrayal, and naivete. As you follow Joe Costanzo through his unlikely rags-to-riches-to-rags story, you'll alternate wondering, *How did he accomplish all that?* with *What was he thinking?*

—Mary Gin Starkweather, Dog Ears Writers, Buffalo, NY

MORE PRAISE FOR JOE COSTANZO AND THE PRIMADONNA

"The Primadonna Restaurant rivals any good Italian restaurant in NYC."

—Danny Aiello, Hollywood Actor

"Joe Costanzo, The Dodgers and all Italians are GREAT!"

—Tommy Lasorda, Former Major League Baseball Pitcher, Coach, and Manager of the Los Angeles Dodgers

"I always felt stories like Joe Costanzo's and The Primadonna Restaurant are so important to tell."

—Rocky Bleier, Former Pittsburgh Steeler NFL Player

". . . All the more credit to Joe for having achieved such success in attracting people to come there because McKees Rocks otherwise was not a destination place. . . . Joe was a very friendly, natural, unassuming, unpretentious individual who was dedicated to his work and committed to making his customers happy by being a gracious, warm, and generous host. . ."

—Dr. Cyril Wecht, American Forensic Pathologist Who Headed the JFK, RFK, Sharon Tate, JonBenet Ramsey, and Other Famous National and International Cases

"Joe came out of nowhere. The fact that he wanted to open up a place in one of the most unlikely towns ever is one of the most amazing feats. Joe had a vision in taking this little restaurant from the minor leagues to the major leagues. I wish everyone would have had an opportunity to go there. It is a shame it all ended the way that it did."

—Bob Priddy, Former fifteen-year MLB Player for the Pirates, Giants, Senators, White Socks, Angels, and Braves

"Joe was a great ambassador, not only for his restaurant, but for the food business in general. When sports figures, celebrities, and athletes came to town, everyone wanted to go to The Primadonna to eat. Joe made everyone feel like they were special, and he deserved every bit of success he had at The Primadonna Restaurant."

—Gerry Dulac, Sports Journalist for the *Pittsburgh Post-Gazette*

"The Primadonna Restaurant reminds me of a throbbing NYC restaurant, where the very frenzy of the place is as enticing as the cuisine."

—Mike Kalina, Former Dining Critic for the *Pittsburgh Post-Gazette* and *NY Daily News* Syndicated Columnist

"I'm from McKees Rocks. It's a rugged blue-collar town, and Joe always wanted to look out for everyone. He always treated you the right way. When I won the title, I would go to The Primadonna once or twice a week... It doesn't surprise me that Joe's story is going to be a book; it would surprise me if it wasn't."

—Paul Spadafora, Former IBF Lightweight Champion of the World

"Joe made that restaurant. He loved that place so much that when you walked in, you felt like you were walking into their home and sitting down at their dining room table. That's how Joe made you feel. This story is every man's story; this is every man's dream."

—Rep. Anita Kulik, Pennsylvania State Representative of the 45th District

"Everyone knew Joe. He was just that guy to talk to. He was a big hit in my family for dinners. You walked in, and everyone knew your name—it was like *Cheers* with a twist."

—Rachael Rennebeck, Cohost *YaJagoff!* Podcast and 92.9 FM Pittsburgh

"I distinctly remember limousines lining up outside there on a frequent basis. You would never really know which famous person was in there."

—John Chamberlin, Cohost *YaJagoff!* Podcast and 92.9 FM Pittsburgh

"Joe did have to fire me for making him look bad, which was the highest mortal sin at The Primadonna. It was 100 percent my fault, and I never held it against him. As I went on to work at other restaurants, no one came close to the passion that he had on that 5-Fork corner of the Rocks."

—Kirk Mousessian, Former Dishwasher at The Primadonna

"... I saw that place transform over the years from a small little restaurant to an internationally acclaimed restaurant, where you had to wait two hours to get a seat. You would do it, not only because the food was tremendous, but you did it because Joe was tremendous..."

—Joseph Kulik, Attorney and Early Customer of The Primadonna

"That restaurant was more than just a workplace. It was a place where I felt appreciated, welcomed, and genuinely loved. I am forever grateful."

—Jessica Hill, Former Server at The Primadonna

"Joe genuinely made you feel appreciated. So often I would thank him for something, and he would reply, 'No, no . . . thank *you*.' That simple phrase is so powerful and memorable, I have been using it on regular basis for almost thirty years."

—Chris Singel, Long-Time Employee of The Primadonna Restaurant

"Joe Costanzo in many ways is like an abacus! He can be louder than expected, he at times can be misunderstood, but the one thing you can bank on is he can always be counted on!"

—Mark Kautzman, Long-time Employee of The Primadonna Restaurant

"I will have the spaghetti con sausage . . . thanks for the zucchini!"

—Ernie Ricci, Ricci's Italian Sausage

"I grew up at the Primadonna. Both my parents grew up in the Rocks, so going to the Primadonna was a no-brainer. . . Joe treated you like family because you were to him."

—Kris Pritchard and The Pritchards

"... We may never be able to take the full measure of how much of a positive impact Joe has made, but we can appreciate his very human story and raise a glass to toast a family and community legacy that will be celebrated for generations to come."

—Daniel Gerson, Regular Customer at The Primadonna Restaurant

"Joe is a genius in the restaurant industry. What he did for his restaurant was totally innovative. At the time, people really didn't understand what he was doing, but that was part of the beauty. He was packed every day open until close just by his marketing concepts."

—Charlie Pellegrini, Owner/Manager of F. Tambellini Restaurant, Pittsburgh, PA

"During my time in Pittsburgh, I found The Primadonna Restaurant. . . Joseph Costanzo, Jr. . . . was nothing like any other restaurateur that I had met. I moved to NYC and then San Francisco, CA. I could not find one restaurant in either of these famous cities for food and dining that was better than The Primadonna."

—Bob Glickstein, Author and Software Engineer

"There were only three restaurants with the Distinguished Restaurants of North America (DiRoNA) Award in Western PA—the Carlton, which I owned, the Hyeholde, and The Primadonna. Joseph Costanzo, Jr. was the greatest front of the house owner that I have ever seen . . . I would train all of my front of the house staff . . . by sending them to The Primadonna to observe how Costanzo operated his well-oiled-machine and worked his magic with the customers."

—Kevin Joyce, Owner of The Carlton Restaurant, Pittsburgh, PA

On the Rocks: The Primadonna Story
by Maria C. Palmer and Ruthie Robbins
© Copyright 2023 Maria C. Palmer and Ruthie Robbins

ISBN 979-8-88824-027-4

All rights reserved. No part of this publication may be reproduced, stored in a retrieval system, or transmitted in any form or by any means—electronic, mechanical, photocopy, recording, or any other—except for brief quotations in printed reviews, without the prior written permission of the author.

Published by

köehlerbooks™

3705 Shore Drive
Virginia Beach, VA 23455
800-435-4811
www.koehlerbooks.com

ON THE ROCKS

The Primadonna Story

MARIA C. PALMER

and RUTHIE ROBBINS

VIRGINIA BEACH
CAPE CHARLES

For Donna (Mom) and Joe (Dad)

The intangibles that enabled me to achieve my greatness also contained the seeds to my destruction.
—Joseph Costanzo, Jr.

AUTHORS' NOTES

On the Rocks is an unusual book. Although the story is told in the first-person narrative voice of Joseph Costanzo, Jr., he is not the author. Joe's daughter, Maria Costanzo Palmer, began to write the original version in her own voice in 2007. In 2016, Maria reached out to her former English teacher and long-time friend, Ruthie (Dines) Robbins, and they began to collaborate closely with feedback from Ruthie's writers' group in Buffalo, NY. A successful crime fiction author in the group, Lissa Redmond, suggested that Maria and Ruthie try telling the story in Joe's voice. It not only worked, but the book became fun to write because of Joe's colorful personality. With his blessing, Joe shared his recollections and memorabilia throughout the writing process.

This is Joe's story, but it is also Maria's story. As Joe's daughter, Maria witnessed every aspect of the story from evolving vantage points as she grew up in the restaurant. It is also Ruthie's story, a "Rocks girl" who grew up on the street where the Primadonna sat, met most of the adults in the story when they were still children, and was one of Joe's earliest customers when he was serving only a dozen dinners a night.

Most of this story took place long ago, and humans are unreliable narrators. Our attempts at fact-checking have proven this. Nevertheless, we did our best to tell the story with integrity and truth, minus the necessary steps we took to protect the innocent (and sometimes the guilty).

The beauty of the story is that The Primadonna flourished without the help of TikTok, YouTube, Instagram, Facebook, cell phone pics, influencers, viral videos, pop-up ads, or even Yelp reviews. Although The Primadonna had become a destination restaurant, customers would not have been able to use a GPS to get there. It is relatively easy today to promote anything through social media, but Joe's success came from patiently and ceaselessly building relationships, one at a time. He did so as the welcoming, highly visible proprietor of the restaurant, but he also did so behind the scenes with business cards, in-person social visits, handshakes, phone calls, and his specialty—old-fashioned letter writing. Word-of-mouth was the restaurant's greatest marketing tool and remains the most authentic proof of the exceptionality of the restaurant.

Finally, the ways in which people interact with each other have changed. The yelling and harsh language that happened not only in the workplace but also in schools and homes was especially rampant in the restaurant industry. We understand that the ways in which some things were handled would never be tolerated today. Instead of compromising the integrity of the story, we chose to pull back the curtain and unveil even the parts that we would rather were distant memories.

THE ROCKS

Have you ever thought about what story you might tell about yourself if you had the chance? Would it ring true to those who knew you well? Or would you maybe polish it to shine like a brand-new BMW, making yourself seem glossier or larger than you really were? Or would you choose to tell the whole truth with all its flaws amid the moments of greatness? Well, I'm Joseph Costanzo, Jr., and that's what I've been thinking about because I've got a great story to tell you. I'll tell you *most* of it; the rest involves other people who might not appreciate their deeds being made public or whose memories I don't want to tarnish. I'll do my best to bridge those little gaps, but the main events involve me or my family. I can tell you all about those.

If the title of this book, *On the Rocks*, made you think the story has something to do with drinks served over ice cubes, you would be right. I managed a bar and restaurant where there were plenty of drinks served on the rocks and plenty of sticky situations that came with the territory. But let's put that on ice for now.

If you thought *On the Rocks* indicated something or someone was experiencing difficulties and was likely to fail, you would also be right.

You might not know, however, that the "Rocks" also refers to McKees Rocks, a town of about 6,000 people occupying one square mile straight down the Ohio River from downtown Pittsburgh. The bordering township of Stowe is home to about the same number of people, but for all practical purposes, the two little towns are generally referred to as the "Rocks" (or "Rox") collectively.

My family wasn't from the Rocks, but we sometimes drove there on Saturdays to spend an afternoon. Bakeries, meat markets, pharmacies with soda fountains and penny candy, fruit and vegetable markets, shoe stores, and more populated Broadway and Chartiers Avenue, two ideal streets for shopping that met at a ninety-degree angle. I have vivid recollections of those childhood trips: staring at the medicinal leeches in a jar near the cash register at Leftkowitz's Pharmacy; stopping cold on the sidewalk the first time I heard the Beach Boys' "Good Vibrations," blaring out of a record store's speakers; gently picking up pastel-dyed peeps at Eastertime from under the heat lamps at G. C. Murphy's; trying on suits taken from thick plastic zip-up casings hanging in The Children's Shop; and wondering why there were live chickens and an occasional turkey in the window of Jacobs Poultry, never guessing that the poultry was slaughtered and plucked to order or that the waiting chickens provided the store's fresh eggs. And I vaguely remember being inside Mary Lea Dairy, a busy deli that mainly sold lunchmeat but maintained a few tables for breakfast or lunch customers. I would never have believed that years later I would become the proprietor of a restaurant, The Primadonna, in that very same space.

We would usually end the day on Chartiers Avenue, where our parents would give us a few minutes to go downstairs to the toy section at G. C. Murphy five and dime. Every kid knew how to save a few cents to buy a set of jacks or a comic book on such occasions. Then we'd head across the street to Isaly's, where it was always Skyscraper cones for the kids and Krispy Klondikes for my parents.

Between the two retail areas on a small side street stood Mancini's Bakery, famous for Italian bread that is still delivered fresh daily to stores and restaurants around Pittsburgh. We'd all get out of the car to experience the incomparable aroma inside the bakery. This was always our last stop, and if we were lucky, we'd get warm loaves right out of the ovens. My brother, sister, and I would take turns sticking our noses into the white paper bags, inhaling and savoring the smell of the fresh loaves.

Pre–and post–World War II McKees Rocks was a popular place for my parents' generation to meet and date. They often talked about the huge ice rink behind the business district on Chartiers Avenue that drew crowds from all over. The Veterans of Foreign Wars Post, Pulaski Club, Italian Sons & Daughters of America, the Moose Lodge, and other such social clubs had well-stocked bars and beers on tap, hosting popular big-band style dances. There were two movie theaters and a couple of busy bowling alleys, along with many "beer gardens."

The Rocks sustained six Roman Catholic churches and their schools, each built and supported by different ethnicities. Along with those churches came bingo, pierogi kitchens, spaghetti dinners, and rummage sales. We loved when our parents took us to church festivals in the Rocks, with the whirring of the betting wheels that slowed to a clickety-clack, pick-a-ticket chances at winning stuffed animals, and roasters full of homemade ethnic food, from stuffed cabbages to German potato salad or pasta fagioli, depending on the church. There were several Protestant churches and one synagogue as well, and a happy life with a full calendar could be lived within the boundaries of the Rocks.

The Rocks boasts a lot of famous people for its two square miles. Some of the more distinguished include Justice Michael A. Musmanno, presiding judge at the Nuremberg trials, and John Kasich, former governor of Ohio and presidential hopeful in the 2016 primaries. "But wait! There's more—" is what McKees Rocks native Billy Mays, former renowned TV pitchman for OxiClean, would've said here. Cartoonist Jeff Smith, creator of the popular *Bone* comics, was born in the Rocks. The Rocks repeatedly produces champion sports teams with all-star athletes, many of whom turn pro, contributing significantly to Western Pennsylvania's reputation as a breeding ground for athletic talent. Damar Hamlin, the Buffalo Bills beloved #3 who suffered a cardiac event on the field, was from the area. His designated daycare charity that received nearly $9 million in donations as he fought for his life in the hospital sits right across the alley from the building that was once my restaurant.

There is historical evidence that Roy Washington, John F. Kennedy, Al Capone, and the Three Stooges all spent time in the Rocks. And get this—so did Jamie Lee Curtis, Danny Aiello, Pat Sajak, Cyril Wecht, Michael Keaton, Franco Harris, Smokin' Joe Frazier, and many other celebrities. I can attest to this personally because they came to my restaurant.

Around the same time that new malls began to draw shoppers from downtown Pittsburgh's Golden Triangle, the suburbs lured young families from the Rocks. New housing boomed on former farmland a mile or so up the hill in Kennedy Township, and a modern strip mall began to steal business from the Rocks's merchants. It wasn't long before businesses were boarded-up and retail shops were turned into accounting firms or dentist offices. A few businesses hung on, but as the vacancies left gaps in families' needs, McKees Rocks was no longer a destination for anyone but the locals.

1

I remember the first Saturday night in seventeen years that I didn't go to the restaurant. I had planned to go in. I showered and dressed in white shirt and dress slacks, pulled together by my favorite tie, but when four o'clock arrived, I paced the house like a caged animal, deliberating every insignificant detail of my brand-new status. Should I leave now or wait until later? Would I just walk in or stand in line outside with the customers? Should I have dinner, sit at the bar, or just hang out? I'd turn the radio on for a distraction and then turn it back off because it annoyed me. In a mirror, I noticed the nervous perspiration under my arms and changed my shirt. Hours passed; more than once I grabbed something to eat in case I decided not to eat at the restaurant. My wife and daughters ran out of encouraging things to say, replacing their attempts with sympathetic looks. I needed to see the people I had grown so close to, and I knew they wanted to see me. I felt like the restaurant was where I belonged, but I just couldn't go there. I couldn't bear it. That night was the lowest point, the point from which I was forced to reluctantly adapt to my new circumstances.

Unable to sleep, I lay awake until the sun rose, rehashing my decisions and wondering, *How the hell did I get here?*

I'll give you the short version of my history—the things you might wonder about later if I don't. I grew up in the Greenfield neighborhood in the city of Pittsburgh in a modest house. My parents were Italian immigrants. My father owned a cocktail lounge, Le Mardi Gras, in the upscale neighborhood of Shadyside, and my mother was a hardworking housewife whose duties centered on cooking.

We lived simply and frugally. We rarely went out to dinner and didn't go on vacations, which might have been different if my father weren't so in love with his cars. Displayed in the alley between houses were a light blue and white '57 Chevy, a gold 1970 Cadillac El Dorado with black leather interior, a dark blue 1968 Oldsmobile Cutlass, a lime green 1976 Chevy Montecarlo, a light blue 1969 Oldsmobile Toronado, and a tan 1962 Chevy Impala. My father had this odd ritual where he would move each car daily. Every morning he would choose a new place to park each car, as though he were saying, "You are my favorite today; you are not." His true favorite, however, was the '57 Chevy, a massive, sleek, Batmobile-like machine with "wings" on each side of the trunk that enabled it to simulate flight even at speeds under 35 mph. It seems incongruous that he displayed his wealth in this way when the rest of his life was one of slipping quietly under the radar, but he did. In 1973, while still in college, I took a job with the United States Postal Service, working from 6 o'clock in the evening until 2:30 in the morning while attending classes during the day. My wife Donna was working as a flight attendant for Allegheny Airlines. With both of us working, we were fortunate to be able to save money. We married in 1974 and settled temporarily in an apartment complex.

In 1977, we moved from the apartment to a functional house. The house was about twenty years old, located in Ingram, a working-class area of Pittsburgh. Over the years, we poured a lot of money and sweat into the place, upgrading with central air, a patio in the backyard, and a toolshed. We replaced the windows and put on a new roof. We thought that this is where we would be forever.

Donna became pregnant in 1980, but she was not sure whether

she would continue working. She loved the job, and it paid well. She had three months of maternity leave during which she had to decide.

When our daughter Maria was born in 1981, our whole lives changed for the better. We were caught up in the incomparable joy of being new parents. While it was a happy time, Donna was also drained and frail, having lost a good bit of weight. Looking back, she probably experienced post-partum depression, but we didn't know anything about that at the time. Giving up the job seemed the best choice. Donna is quite adaptable, and her new priority was our baby. When we added one person and subtracted one job, however, money was tight. Even so, we didn't really consider anything a struggle, just a different way of living.

"Joe! Joe!" called Miss Lavonne from her window. She had been watching out so she could offer me a glass of cold water.

"You're the best, Miss Lavonne." I gulped down half the glass in three seconds. "That really helps." I guzzled the rest and repeated, "That really helps."

A few blocks away, I found a sign taped onto the mailbox next to Miss Marguerite's front door: "JOE—KNOCK LOUD." I knocked, and Marguerite scuttled to the door holding banana bread wrapped in foil.

"Hi, Miss Marguerite. That sign on the door isn't for me, is it?"

"Yes, it is, Joe," she assured, handing me the still-warm loaf. "That's for your family, Joe. It's too hot to cook, I know, but I gotta do somethin' with my days."

"Aww, Miss Marguerite. That's so kind. So kind."

Around the corner, I'd have to gently break free from Mr. Brezinski, who would talk to me all day about WWII if I let him.

My mailbag felt heavier in the summer heat, but the monotony of the job diminished when the weather allowed me to interact with the people I served. I filled my pockets each day with Double Bubble and doled out pieces to any of the kids who came up to me. I noted the simple things that would make someone's day a little better, but it wasn't totally unselfish; I also enjoyed being known and liked wherever I went.

There were three basketball courts in the projects that were full if the weather was even half decent. As I walked near the court filled with pre-teen boys one summer morning, several of the boys stopped and waved with their loud, sing-songy, "Hi, Joe!" They looked like they were having a quick huddle about whether to stop the game to score some bubble gum, but I put down my sack of mail and hustled to them instead.

"Any three against me!" I shouted as I grabbed the ball.

The boys quickly identified their three best players, and the game was on. I was crushing them. When the score was twelve to four, I called timeout and reminded everyone that I had to get back to work. The boys were surprised at my skill.

"Five more minutes," they pleaded.

"Tomorrow," I promised, "I'll play five of you at once. A whole team against me." I started to walk away but then remembered and turned back to give each a piece of gum. "I almost forgot," I told them.

"We almost forgot, too," said a boy named Michael.

As I walked from mailbox to mailbox, I would daydream about winning a huge lottery and sharing some of the money with my acquaintances from the projects. When I saw a *HELP WANTED* sign in a window or a job posting in the Want Ads section of the newspaper, I thought about whether the job might be good for one of my unemployed postal customers. I embraced the people on my route as part of my life, and they returned the warmth.

My shift ended at three o'clock, and I made it a point to hurry home each afternoon. When *Reading Rainbow* came on TV, little Maria knew it was time for Daddy to come home, and she would wait at the window.

Donna opened the door and gave me a kiss while Maria instantly wrapped her arms around my leg, holding tight. "Daddy. I missed you."

I picked Maria up and give her a big hug, followed by a piggyback ride around the house. "Where to, my princess?" I asked.

Maria shouted, "To the castle!"

This was our routine. Maria delighted in coming up with different destinations, and I'd always feign shock and come up with an obstacle. Today it was, "The *castle*? But what about the dragon?" Then we'd run around the house laughing as we acted out the scenario.

"Everything go okay today, Joe?" asked Donna.

"Same as every other day, love," I replied.

Donna constantly worried about my safety because a disproportionate number of the city's crimes came from the housing projects where I delivered the mail. "Do you realize that you're the only uniformed person walking around that project without a gun?" she asked many times.

I always told her, "I carry the welfare checks; no one is messing with me."

Not only was I not at all apprehensive about working in a neighborhood known for drugs and gun violence, but the opportunity to befriend my postal customers was the saving grace of the job. People fascinated me, and I was able to build relationships quickly, simply by taking a genuine interest in each person I met. This neighborhood was more appealing to me than an upper-class section of town; I was able to connect with people whose unspoken boundaries (or whose perceptions of mine) would likely have prevented us from ever getting to know each other. It was gratifying to me that I was accepted, and I aimed to endear myself to everyone on the route.

What did bother me, however, was the mundane nature of the job. Some people might have been satisfied with a secure middle-class income and predictable work schedule. All I had to do was to deliver the mail responsibly, which I did. Job security and benefits were ideal. I had no work to bring home evenings or weekends and no myriad of worries like my father had running Le Mardi Gras lounge in Shadyside.

"How's the sewing going, Donna? Did you get any further?"

"I finished the body, but I wasn't sure what to do with the face. Or the clothing."

"Can you finish by tonight?"

"I'll have to, won't I? Joe, I just don't understand why you try so hard to promote the post office. It's not like they don't have any business."

"But they miss so many opportunities, Donna."

"It's not your problem, Joe. You're a mail carrier, not the postmaster general. Let him worry about it."

The "problem" with the job was not the job, but my own tendency to think big. Really big. I came to the postal field with the attitude that I was not only going to do my job well, but I would also somehow revolutionize the US Postal Service. From the first day on the job, I was brimming with marketing ideas that would transform the USPS into more of a brand and less of a service.

That night, Maria woke up from a bad dream and came running into our room to find her pregnant mom hovering over an outdated sewing machine while I dictated directions. "Donna, make him friendly-looking with big eyes and a smiley mouth."

Maria looked down and saw what looked like a deflated Sparky, the fire-hydrant-turned-dog that stood in the middle of our front yard. When we moved into our house, I had turned the fire plug eyesore into the neighborhood conversation piece with a little ingenuity and paint. "Can I hold him?" Maria asked.

Before Donna could answer, I asserted, "No, you can't touch him. He's for work." Then I softened and hugged Maria tightly. "Let me guess. You can't sleep again? Are those monsters back?"

"Yes. They are up in the attic."

"Let's go up, honey. I'm going to show you that there are no monsters."

"Dad, there *are* monsters. We can't go up there."

I got a flashlight from the kitchen. Holding it in my left hand, I scooped Maria up with my right arm and yelled down to Donna, "He needs to be wearing a uniform."

"All right, all right. I'm still working on his face," she shouted back.

I did the same thing I had done several times before. With Maria in my arms, I illuminated every corner of the attic, shining the light high and low to show her that there were no monsters. I held her tenderly and felt like I was holding the greatest treasure in the world.

2

On Thursday (my normal day off), I replaced my usual postal uniform with a suit and tie. Emphasizing and reemphasizing key words, I was practicing a speech while Donna was half-listening over the sizzle of eggs and bacon. Then I was off to the downtown headquarters, carrying an easel and what looked like a large costume. I was about to present Zippy, the first mascot of the United States Postal Service.

I shut the door but then ran back in and said, "Give me a kiss for good luck, girls." They sweetly obliged.

Donna prayed that today would be different. She had been there before and had seen me get so excited about an idea, only to be shot down.

"I'll see you after the meeting for dinner at Fusco's."

Fusco's was a local Italian restaurant that we frequented. It was in the middle of McKees Rocks, which had by this time become a town that was struggling to keep afloat (as was the restaurant). We loved coming to Fusco's because every time we came, not only was the food good, but it was pretty much a private dining experience—the perfect place to bring kids. Chef Nick Fusco always came to the table, and we shot the bull about life, family, and how business was going.

Nick knew that I had grown up in the bar business, so we had that bond, although I understood less about it than he thought I did. A combination of societal norms and the type of business my father ran had kept us kids distant, even for those times. In truth, many fathers of bygone days had an air of mystery. If you ask men of a certain age what they know about their fathers, they often reach an impasse. I was raised in the era when the father went away to work, spoke little or not at all about his job, and spent even less time cultivating a true heartfelt relationship with his children. Added to that, lounge hours were the hours when most families would be spending time together. My father slept during the day and went to work soon after we came home from school. There was also a firm but unspoken agreement among adults that children should not see or hear anything that would contribute to their "growing up too fast." My father's lounge, with its scantily clad dancers and drinks aplenty, was off limits to his family. Even as we kids left our teens, my father was probably not comfortable sharing his secrets of success in a business whose nature conflicted with our somewhat sheltered Catholic upbringing.

Donna and Maria got to Fusco's first, anxiously awaiting my arrival. I guess I had noticeably less pep in my step, even to Maria. Donna knew right away that the meeting must not have had the outcome we had hoped for.

"Daddy, what's wrong?"

"Nothing, sweetie. I brought you a present." Behind my back, I had Zippy.

"Can I keep him?"

"Yes, absolutely. I won't be needing him anytime soon."

"Joe, what happened?" asked Donna, concerned.

"I gave it my best. I talked *at* them, though. Nobody showed any real interest. They said there were already people working on the zip code campaign on a national level."

Donna hugged me as we sat down to enjoy some family-style pasta that, like always, didn't disappoint. Some people turn to alcohol to soothe their nerves; I turn to food.

As always, Nick came over to say hello, and Maria held up her new stuffed animal.

"Wow, he has a uniform on just like your dad's. Aren't you lucky?"

I interjected, "Yeah, at least *someone* likes Zippy."

"Rough day at work, Joe?" Nick asked.

"It's beginning to become more the norm lately. I have so many ideas that would help the post office, but they don't appreciate them. I can't get through to anyone."

"Joe, that's not exactly true," Donna chimed in. "They love your ideas."

"Even if that's true, it's obviously not getting me anywhere."

"Joe, I have just the thing that might pick up your spirits," said Nick. "Come on back with me; I want to show you the new oven I got." I didn't think seeing Nick's new oven would lift my spirits, but I politely accommodated.

"I'd love to see it, Nick." I got up and left the girls at the table.

As we walked into the kitchen, Nick's demeanor changed. "Joe, I have some news of my own. I'm moving to Myrtle Beach."

"Wow, that's big news! Congrats, Nick. Who's going to run this place?"

"I don't know . . . maybe *you*?"

I chuckled. "Listen, I have a good thing at the post office. I really can't complain. I just get these big ideas sometimes, and the post office is such a huge bureaucracy that I can't get them to the right people."

"Joe, I know you aren't happy there. I needed to put this out there. Think about it. If you are interested, please let me know."

3

With Nick Fusco's suggestion that I buy his place, I rejoined my family, but all that was on my mind was that the space around us could be the setting of my reimagined future. A future where I would not have to answer to anyone else. A future where I could put my marketing degree to work. A future where I could put all my gusto into something of my own. A future where I could own a restaurant and make people happy with the kind of food that made me happy.

Food is central in Italian culture. My non-Italian friends used to joke around that when they came to my family's home, they ate more on the fly than they did at holidays with their families. My mom always had something that she could whip up on a moment's notice, and I was the happy beneficiary of a great cook. Luckily, because of how active I was, it never showed. I was always slender and athletic, although I could eat with the best of them. In addition, I enjoyed the social aspect of sharing a meal. Perhaps this was why the idea of owning a restaurant seemed so perfect—like Cinderella finding the glass slipper. I was instantaneously determined to make this happen. Now all I had to do was to convince my wife and the rest of the family, which wouldn't be easy.

On the drive home, I mustered up enough courage to approach Donna.

"So, Don, ever dream that there is something else for us?"

Donna looked confused. Where I was always the dreamer, my wife stood ready to give a dose of reality. She loved me, no doubt, but she was always looking out for our future and the stability of the family.

"What do you think about owning a restaurant? Fusco told me his is for sale."

"A *restaurant*? Joe, right now you are making a stable income at the post office, and we have a mortgage, a four-year-old child, and a baby on the way. Are you crazy?"

Donna knew firsthand how hard things were. She had given up her well-paying airline job to raise a family, and she was the one who budgeted our income and paid the bills. In addition, she wasn't generally a risk-taker.

I decided it was best to do what I do the worst—shut my mouth. There would be another time for this, but it had to come soon. Fusco's place was up and running, ready to step right in. What if someone else wanted to run a business from that building? It didn't have to be a restaurant. Convincing Donna would be an uphill battle, but the opportunity wouldn't be open forever.

That Sunday, like most other Sundays, we headed over to my parents' house for a traditional pasta dinner. This seemed like a good time to bring up buying the restaurant. I thought that perhaps strength in numbers could help my case with Donna. After all, my father must have had the same dream that I did before he opened Le Mardi Gras. He was in the business, and my family would see the possibilities more clearly than Donna had.

As we all sat down to dinner, I thought it would be the perfect time to bring up owning a restaurant. I had already talked to my mother on the sly, but this had to be discussed in the open. In the tradition of most Italian families, my father would be the person whose approval was most important.

I did my best to appear confident and upbeat. "Hey, I'm giving some serious thought to buying a restaurant that's for sale in the Rocks. It has a lot of potential."

My father sat up straighter and widened his eyes. He remained silent at first, but I could tell by his fixed stare and set jaw that he strongly disapproved.

"A restaurant?" questioned my sister Diane. "You don't even cook."

"I would hire a chef. I think an upscale Italian restaurant would be welcome on that side of town," I replied, trying to sound nonchalant while my heart pounded to the tense vibe in the room.

"The Rocks? Who do you have in mind for clientele—the meth dealers or the bookies?" Diane laughed, pleased with her own attempt at a joke.

From across the table, family members took turns taking jabs at me.

"Are you *nuts*?"

"You have a young child and a baby on the way."

"You need to get your head out of the clouds."

"In McKees Rocks, of all places? Hahaha..."

When my father finally spoke, the rest of the room fell silent. He looked right at me as he spoke slowly and firmly, index finger raised in warning. "I cannot support you on this crazy idea. I will not lend you one dime, and when it all fails, which it will, I will not bail you out. I will sit back and watch it happen. I will never let your kids starve, but I will let you lose your house on principle."

No one was prepared for the gravity of my father's response. We quickly finished our meal, mostly in silence, except for the women unsuccessfully attempting small talk to help smooth over the awkward quiet. Amid everyone's disbelief, however, the fire inside of me just kept on burning stronger.

When I had told my mother about the restaurant earlier in the week, she mentioned a small inheritance from her deceased father that she would give me to help build the bar. I didn't know about this money and didn't ask for anything, but that's the kind of woman my mother was. Her thoughts immediately turned to ways she could help her family. My father somehow got word of her intentions to help me and made sure I never saw a cent of the money. I understood enough to pretend I forgot all about it.

The Zippy story was just one example of how I had no voice in the United States Postal Service. Having my own place and being my own boss was too appealing. I just *had* to do it, and my family's harsh words just further fueled the fire. My place was going to be better than my father's. Yes, there would be high-class martinis, but there would also be exceptional food, and lots of it.

Donna began to understand. She saw that there was little chance of moving up in the post office and knew that I needed a career where I could put my creativity to work. Donna had many talents of her own that could be directed toward a restaurant. A stellar flight attendant, Donna could train others in the art of serving. She also knew how to keep her cool no matter what the situation, a valued skill in working with the public. Over the next few weeks, Donna warmed up to the idea. I called Nick Fusco.

"Nick, this is Joe Costanzo."

"Hey Joe, how ya doing? Need a reservation?"

"Yes! I'm coming down tonight for a celebration."

"Yeah? I heard about the baby. Congratulations!"

"Yes, thanks. Kelly Costanzo was born on the twenty-first of May, and she's doing great. We're all doing great. However, tonight we're celebrating something else."

"Okay?"

"I'm buying your place, Nick."

We met with Nick a few times over the next many weeks before working out an agreement. Donna and I had a lot to consider. To buy the restaurant, we'd have to refinance our house, which had been paid off. I didn't want to open an upscale restaurant without a bar, so I'd have to dip into my USPS independent retirement. In my thirteen years at the post office, I'd put fifteen thousand dollars into the account—exactly the amount I needed to install a bar.

We signed the papers in August of 1985 but knew it would take months to transfer the liquor license. During this time, I kept my job at the post office. We now had a mortgage on our home again and a rent payment for the business. I went to the restaurant most days after my postal shift, taking care of the many details needing to be addressed before we opened—from choosing a menu to painting the walls and everything in between. Nothing was as enjoyable as it could have been because I could only work on the business after work, Donna could have used my help with the girls, and we both needed sleep, desperately.

In addition to renovations, there were so many other details to take care of. We needed a name. The obvious default name "Costanzo's" was already taken by a place downtown. Wanting to project a refined image in a not-so-refined part of town, I decided to name the place after the classiest person I knew—my wife. I did some research and found that the phrase *prima donna* in Italian meant "first lady." No other name could have been a more perfect fit. I installed a solid oak front door with a giant P on it, complemented by a new awning to give the entrance a classy look. The Primadonna was ready.

Donna oversaw our finances, directing every dollar during this time. Without her, this transition would not have worked. Without me, however, we would not have taken things to the next level. There was nothing in my mind that made me think the new business venture might fail. When you are thirty-two years old, you take chances and don't mull over possible consequences. My confidence was unwavering.

I remember a trip to the supermarket where Donna cautioned me not to pick up anything "extra." On the drive home, she said, "Joe, if they raise the rent on the restaurant by one dollar, we'll go bankrupt."

"You're worried that they will raise our rent?" I asked.

"Yeah, I am."

"Don't worry, love. Within a year, we'll own the building." I was that sure of myself.

4

The Primadonna officially opened for business precisely at four o'clock on February 20, 1986. Daylight turns to darkness quickly in winter, so I remember it as a frigid, serene night. Looking out of the window, it might have been a cozy scene if I hadn't been hoping for a flurry of customers rather than the flurries of snow swirling around the empty streets.

At eleven o'clock, the official closing of the dining room, I dismissed my small crew. They left with pats on the back and words of consolation—"It's a Thursday. Tomorrow will be better," and "Not the right weather for an opening."

After being open for eight hours without any customers, a scruffy man dressed in an oversized winter coat walked through the door of The Primadonna. As my first customer walked back through the swinging doors to the bar, I picked up a clean glass and pretended to be busy washing it. The customer walked around the small space, carefully surveying each nook as if looking for something.

"Sir, can I help you?" I asked.

The man didn't flinch. Like a dog, he was on a mission to sniff out the place. After several minutes, he reached his destination, hovering over a barstool.

"Budweiser. We *are* in a bar, right?"

"That's right, sir. This is a bar." There was no money left to spend, so I only bought a few bottles of liquor for that first night, but I did stock the most popular beers. I poured the Budweiser into a frosty mug and set it down on the countertop of the bar.

"Didn't this place used to be called Fusco's? The rumor on the street is, some young schmuck bought it and wants to make it a restaurant."

"Welcome to The Primadonna Restaurant," I replied.

"What's your name, kid?"

"Joe. Joe Costanzo, Jr."

"Jerry."

I offered my hand, and Jerry shook it weakly.

Silence filled the room as Jerry continued to drink his beer. It was hard to be friendly to a stranger who had the audacity to walk into my place and call me a schmuck. A glass slipped through my hand and broke, and I bent down to pick up the pieces.

"Hey, Joe, do you have a menu?"

Popping up from the floor, I reached into my back pocket, pulled out a menu, and placed it in front of Jerry, who seemed less than impressed. Jerry quickly finished his drink and put down a couple of dollars. As he got up to leave, he slammed his mug down, the sound echoing in the empty bar.

As he walked toward the door, Jerry looked over his shoulder and asked, "Hey, are you from the Rocks?"

"No, sir."

Smirking, Jerry added, "I've lived in here all my life, and there ain't no one who has survived here that ain't from here. It won't ever happen for you. You aren't a Rocks guy."

"Thanks, sir, for coming in."

That guy really floored me. I wondered what he meant by saying no one could make it here if they weren't from the Rocks. What was a Rocks guy supposed to be? Confused and irritated, I went back to my clock-watching. I calculated the number of hours of sleep I would get that night. I had compromised with Donna and promised to keep my day job until this place became financially sound. Working full-time during the day as a postal carrier and then coming to the restaurant for another ten-hour shift was not easy, but it kept the peace at home as well as an assured income, so I was willing to make the sacrifice.

The Primadonna had a sign on the front window with the hours—4:00 p.m. until 2:00 a.m. I was a man of principle, so even with no customers, I was determined to stick to the hours on the sign. Alone, I kept looking to the clock and then the door, which was about as fun as watching paint dry.

At one o'clock the most beautiful thing happened. Another customer walked in.

5

Family isn't always defined by blood—there is also "family." The only common criteria for this definition of family are that the people really want you to be in their lives and you want them to be in yours. I can't describe the restaurant without talking about the customers and employees who became *that* kind of family and helped to make The Primadonna the great place that it was. After all, *Cheers* wasn't just Sam Malone—Diane, Woody, Coach, Norm, Cliff, Carla, Frasier, Lilith, Rebecca, and all the rest made up the personality of the bar.

I already talked about the very first customer to come through The Primadonna's door on that snowy opening night in February 1986, pessimistically predicting that I wouldn't make it in the Rocks. My second and only other customer on that lonely night eventually turned out to be the first member of our Primadonna family.

The late-night customer was a thin man with a small frame and strawberry blond hair, maybe still in his thirties, dressed for the cold in jeans and layers under his coat. Since I'd only had one other customer that night, I really didn't expect anyone else to come in at that hour, but I was determined to stick to the hours I had advertised—4:00 p.m. to 2:00 a.m.

As he entered the bar area, I extended my hand. "Hey, how are you? Welcome. Joe Costanzo, Jr."

"Chuck Richards," he said as we shook hands.

"What'll you have?"

"I'll have a Budweiser."

Although there was something bashful about Chuck's demeanor, it was less awkward to engage in conversation than it was to turn my back with just the two of us in the building. He seemed comfortable talking once I began. What I really wondered was what had brought him in at such a late hour on a snowy night, but I didn't ask.

"Some night for opening a restaurant, eh?" I remarked with a chin nod toward the window that referenced the weather.

"I didn't even realize there was a bar here. I just noticed," he commented. Having said that, I knew he hadn't come in as a result of my ads in the local paper.

"We just opened. Today. I would appreciate it if you would spread the word."

I learned a little about my new customer as he drank his beer. Chuck was an only child, a Vietnam vet, and he was from the Rocks. He worked on different construction jobs when he could but wasn't regularly employed. He took care of his mother.

As Chuck got close to the end of his beer, I popped open another Budweiser and set it down. "This one's on me."

Chuck looked confused, then gratefully replied, "Thank you. This has never happened to me in the Rocks."

"What's that?" I asked.

"No one has ever given me anything. Thank you very much." With his hands on each side of the beer bottle, palms up and shoulders raised, Chuck gestured his disbelief.

I just smiled and said, "Enjoy!"

As Chuck left, I thanked him and said I hoped to see him again soon. He replied, "You will."

Chuck became my first regular customer. He came in often—every night when he was between construction jobs. We got in a lot of talk time in those early days before things got busy. We talked about current events, goings on in the Rocks, and his time in Vietnam. He talked about never feeling the same after being exposed to Agent Orange during the Vietnam War. Frequent headaches, unusual symptoms, and worries that he had "something worse" plagued him constantly. He showed terrible distaste for and distrust of the government. As he opened up more, I remember consciously feeling like Sam Malone on *Cheers* or Isaac Washington on *The Love Boat*. He awoke an awareness in me that I had another important role to fulfill if The Primadonna was going to be a success—Chuck unknowingly added "good listener" to my job description. This wasn't difficult for me because I found everyone to be fascinating. The less they were like me, the more fascinating they were.

Over time, we all got to know Chuck well as a gentle, unassuming soul who had found a home with us. Somewhere along the line, one of us added an *ie* to his name as a sign of endearment, and it stuck. Everyone has a place where they belong, and Chuckie Richards belonged at The Primadonna bar.

6

There were reasons why the naysayers who thought the business would never succeed always included the fact that it was in the Rocks. Not only do bars sometimes attract people at their lowest points, but this whole town was also at one of its lowest points—a volatile combination. Over time, the restaurant attracted a lot of great people, but the bar side also had its fair share of alcoholics, local drug dealers, men cheating on their wives, generally rowdy persons, and a few "untouchables" who triggered the heebie-jeebies in even the most unflappable of the local police. There were plenty of scary White guys in the Rocks.

When the restaurant first opened, I saw an old Greenfield buddy of mine when I was picking up supplies in the Strip District. He said, "Joe, I heard you opened up a place in the Rocks. Did you ever hear of a guy named Smarra? Clem Smarra?"

"Can't say I have. Why?"

"If you ever run into him, don't get on his wrong side. He's known all over town. Rumor has it that groups of badasses from different neighborhoods would go to the Rocks and look for him to fight."

"Fight about what?" I asked.

"Just fight. I don't know whether there were bets involved or just bragging rights. This guy is a legend, though. I heard that one night he fought twelve different guys. Anyway, I heard someone say *Broadway*. Isn't that where your place is located? Just look out."

That wasn't my only warning. One quiet night at the restaurant, an older man came in, probably in his eighties, having transferred buses to get to The Primadonna from the infamous McKees Rocks "Bottoms." The Bottoms was physically located right below the rest of McKees Rocks, accessible via various ramps. In recent decades, however, that part of town also took on a lowermost connotation related to the goings on in the area—numbers rackets, prostitution, and thugs for hire—although a few legit businesses still stood. When I checked on how his meal was, the man motioned to another chair at the table and said, "Have a seat," as though it were *his* place.

The man, Roy, told me that he came in because he loved Italian food and hadn't had any homemade since his sister died. He overheard someone at the drugstore saying The Primadonna had great food at good prices. He then proceeded to give me a grandfather-like lecture on moving the business.

Roy advised, "I'd get out of the Rocks if I was you. One of my best friends drove a tow truck, and someone put arsenic in the bottle of Crown he kept under the seat in the truck. The autopsy said it was arsenic, and arsenic was found in the booze left in the bottle. Only his closest friends could have known about that bottle under the seat."

"Jesus!"

"I've seen even worse. I couldn't sleep one night and was just having a smoke, looking out the window for no reason. It was probably around four in the morning. I heard the sound of a revving engine and caught a glimpse a man tied up, gagged, and being dragged behind a car going about sixty miles an hour right down the main street!"

"Did you call the cops?"

"Nope. See no evil, hear no evil, speak no evil in the Rocks."

"Whew!" I said. "I'll remember that." I never said anything to anyone, taking the advice to heart immediately. I also didn't want to scare my family or staff. These warnings began to settle in my brain, and I wondered, had I, in fact, made a blunder on coming here?

Roy, a thin man, ate his spaghetti and meatballs like it was his last meal, cleaning his plate and asking for seconds on the garlic bread. He ordered the same to go, telling me, "I got a good setup in my apartment. I have a minifridge and a microwave, so I don't need a kitchen." I never saw him again but can clearly remember that visit when things were still happening at a too-slow pace.

I was aware that I'd have to deal with individuals who contributed to the shady reputation the Rocks held, even though I didn't yet know who most of them were. I knew I'd have to turn a blind eye to a lot of things if I were to run a cornerstone business in this town. I had learned a little from my father's Shadyside lounge, Le Mardi Gras. For instance, if a man comes in with a lady, never assume that lady is his wife, even if he is wearing a ring. If you address them as husband and wife, you create an uncomfortable situation for the couple and for yourself. You can't be a prude if you're the proprietor of a restaurant and bar. I also sensed, however, that it was of utmost importance to establish myself as a man of principle if I were to gain the respect needed from this community.

Establishing myself in the Rocks was every bit as important as finding a building and creating a menu. Knowing I'd eventually learn who was good, bad, or in between, I also knew that I *didn't* know and felt that it shouldn't matter. Here again, I was stretching for something bigger and taller when, in fact, I didn't know how to get the elevator to go up in the first place. I planned to take on challenges one at a time, staying true to my principles. I wasn't sure, though, *how* I would do this in a town that was known for bending just about any rule. A friend who had grown up here told me that I'd "have to learn whose palm to grease." I didn't want to grease *anyone's* palm—that would surely be a slippery slope.

I wasn't sure how I would handle things when trouble appeared, but I was pleased with what I learned about myself. I didn't put up with the bullshit that other proprietors might have felt the need to tolerate.

One night, one of the waitresses approached me and said she went to close out one of her tabs, and the twenty-eight dollars that was on the table a minute before was missing. I had a strong suspicion who took the money because a stealthy-looking customer got up to go the restroom around that same time, looked over his shoulder as if to see whether someone was watching, and then quickly disappeared. A busser thought the guy was named Gene. At the time, twenty-eight dollars was a lot of money, so I ran out the door on a mission to recover it.

I went to five local bars and introduced myself to the owners, looking for this guy Gene. My final stop was a seedy but crowded club called the 3D Lounge and Disco. I walked in and spotted the culprit. I was young and naive, so I went right up to Gene and demanded he give the money back.

There just happened to be an off-duty cop named Frank Marciw working at the club that night. Officer Marciw came up to me and asked what the problem was, and I told him I owned The Primadonna down the street, and Gene had taken twenty-eight dollars from a table. He pulled Gene into a back room with me. I introduced the off-duty cop as an officer of the law, and Officer Marciw asked Gene to empty his pockets. I snatched the money from the table, looked Gene in the eye, and told him we were even. This could have ended very badly for me, very badly. But that was the end of it, and I even made a friend and ally in Frank Marciw from that day forward.

There were some customers who also started to think they owned the place, like Jimmy Z. Jimmy was a bad guy with a long rap sheet who used to come in on the nights when there was a DJ. His ex-wife Janet also used to frequent the place. One night around ten, Jimmy pulled me aside, asking me to "shut Janet off," which meant to stop serving her. He said that she was drinking too much and was running her mouth, and he wanted her to stop. I went over to Janet and realized that Jimmy was right; she was clearly blasted. I offered her a cup of coffee, which she accepted, and I thought that would be the end to the story.

Jimmy Z. thought something different. He approached me,

pissed off, and said, "I told you that I wanted her out of here. Get her the fuck out of here."

Angry, I shouted over the music. "Excuse me?" I objected. "You told me to shut her off because she had too much to drink, which I did, but I ain't kicking her out of here. She's a good customer, and she hasn't done anything to warrant me kicking her out of here. You can't tell me what to do in my place. You don't dictate policy here!"

"Well, you do what you got to do, and then I'll do what I'm going to do," Jimmy Z. retorted.

"You do what you gotta do, and then I will do what *I'm* going to do," I followed.

"What the fuck are *you* going to do?" Jimmy demanded. I was actually wondering the same thing myself. What was I going to do? As Jimmy Z. went to the pay phone and started making calls, I realized I could end up in a real Rocks brawl. It was not uncommon for men to teach each other a lesson by gathering a gang and jumping the victim when he least expected it.

I stopped reacting and started thinking fast. Mustering up my diplomatic skills, I pulled Jimmy Z. aside as he walked back into the bar. "Jimmy, I got nothing against you, man. I know you have a reputation throughout the Rocks. You asked me to shut her off and I respected you, but I'm not kicking her out. You can sit down, I will buy you a drink, and everyone's happy. Believe me, you are the last guy on earth I want to fight."

Jimmy Z. sat down and accepted the drink. That was the last problem I ever had with him, even though he returned to the bar many times. Most of the bar owners in town were intimidated by people; I wasn't, and people in the Rocks started to respect me for that.

I got pulled into the worst of what I call The Primadonna's "Bar Era" fights. It was over a woman, of course. The fights were mostly over women, and less often, drugs or bets. The phone rang one night, and a guy asked for me. The caller was a bar customer frantically telling me that a notorious bully, Curt, was on the way to my place to "get Toby." Toby was a relatively harmless man physically; he was a nice guy. His friendly personality had attracted the attention of Curt's girlfriend one night when Curt wasn't around. I have no idea if their chatting at the bar had gone any further.

I told Toby to leave quickly before Curt got there—a good plan in theory. I had led Toby outside and walked with him because it was easier to talk without the music blasting. As soon as we stepped out, we were distracted by the sound of a pickup truck racing toward the Broadway intersection where we were standing. Even though he had a green light, Curt stopped the truck right in the middle of the street, got out, and screamed, "I'm going to kill you, you motherfucker; you're screwing around with my girl."

I told Toby to get back into the restaurant while I tried to take care of this. Toby went back into the building, but Curt came at me like I was Toby. He threw the first punch, and all of the sudden we were rolling around on the main street, fighting. I was able to get him down, and he hurt his shoulder.

The guys at the bar had called the cops, and thankfully, they pulled up to the scene. They handcuffed Curt and took him away.

I walked back into the restaurant with my ripped, blood-stained shirt, and Toby said, "Thanks so much, Joe. I owe you one."

"Owe me one? I could've gotten *killed* out there!"

The police told me afterward that they found a loaded sawed-off shotgun in Curt's truck. I felt like that fight was my initiation; I was no longer a novice in the Rocks.

My friend Donnie told me, "You're beginning to make a name for yourself as a nice guy with strong principles, but a guy that you don't want to be on the wrong side of." He said this during a conversation that, unlike most of the feedback I had from the many doubters, gave me hope that I had what it takes to make this business work in the Rocks.

7

For the first three months that The Primadonna was open, I also worked at the post office. We were only serving about eight to ten dinners a night, and the dozen bar seats were about three-fourths full. When the bar business picked up, it became too much. Although I was making a little profit now, it was less income than what I made at the post office. Donna pointed out that we were eating hot dogs for dinner while The Primadonna customers were eating veal. The difference was that I was doing what I loved, so it didn't feel at all like work. I took a year's leave of absence from the post office so I could return if things didn't work out by that time, although there was no doubt in my mind that they would. I took advantage of this safety net to appease my family, who weren't as convinced as I was.

The bar business was flourishing, but I had a bigger plan. I wanted people to flock to my restaurant from all parts of the city—even from all parts of the country. I was dead serious; that's what I envisioned. Long before the internet as we know it or the Food Network, I somehow wanted my restaurant to be known throughout the states. From Earl Nightingale's *Strangest Secret on Earth* ("We become what we think about") to the words of Winston Churchill ("The positive thinker sees the invisible, feels the intangible, and achieves the impossible"), or any other guru of positive thinking, I totally bought into the mantra of "thinking makes it so." I had already proven myself to myself and others by earning a college basketball scholarship, but most of all, by getting my beautiful wife Donna to marry me. Every twist in a situation was a puzzle to solve; every turn was a challenge to beat.

The twist at that time was to get customers through The Primadonna's door. We tried an upmarket brunch menu for a while, as brunches had become popular in the eighties. The menu included standard items like (huge) pancakes, eggs, sausage, bacon, and toast for $4.00 or Italian French toast with bacon or sausage for $2.75. We also had uncommon offerings, especially for McKees Rocks, like Scotch eggs for $4.25, or a rolled stuffed omelet with cream cheese, spinach, mushrooms, and ham, plus two corned beef hash balls and toast for $4.00. The idea flopped, however, and few came. Rocks people were used to their $1.79 eggs, bacon, toast, and coffee specials at local greasy spoons, and people outside the area who went to brunch rather than breakfast didn't think of heading to the Rocks for fine dining.

I brought in Rocks local Mark Antonich and his excellent jazz trio to play on Saturday nights. Everyone who came in as a restaurant customer got a free order of fried zucchini. I had learned to make the absolute best zucchini from my mother. The trick was to slice it thin (lengthwise), add a little salt and pepper, dust with flour, dip it in the egg wash, and then deep fry it at an extremely high temperature until it turned light golden brown. This is how the zucchini fit into my marketing plan: I would stop at each table, introduced myself, thank the people heartily for coming, and then act as though bringing out the zucchini was an idea born that minute, just for them. Served with lemon slices, Parmesan cheese, and our marinara sauce in a little side bowl, that delectable zucchini was my lure.

Donna wasn't happy with our giving the zucchini away. "Joe, there are two good reasons *not* to give the zucchini away. First, you're taking the edge off the customers' hunger, so they might not order as much. Second, the zucchini is *so* good that people would gladly pay for it. They pay for it everywhere else, where it can't even compare to ours."

"One step at a time, Donna," I reminded. "There's no use debating profits when we don't even have customers. I'm focusing on the quality of the food and the service—*that's* what makes a great restaurant."

Giving product away was something that Donna had a hard time getting used to. She came from a family of eight where money and resources were not wasted. Her parents found creative ways to stretch the dollars they had.

I stood steadfast on the path toward my goal, but I admit now that any criticism chipped away at my confidence (although I hid it well, even to my family). When Donna voiced an opinion that differed from mine, which was often, it caused the most turmoil inside of me. I was never sure whether my wife was the voice of reason that I had better listen to, or another person I had to learn to ignore, no matter how much I loved and respected her. This restaurant was *my* vision.

One of my first and most loyal restaurant customers was a well-known and well-to-do man in town I'll call "Ted." When I told a friend of mine that Ted had become a good customer who brought other people into the restaurant, he seemed surprised.

"I'd watch that one," warned my friend.

"Really? Ted's been great," I replied. Ted was one of my newer acquaintances, but I thought he might be shifting into the "friend" category.

A few weeks later, Ted knocked on the door midafternoon before operating hours. I invited him in and offered him a drink, which he accepted.

"Joe, I have a great idea for you. If you put a few poker machines in this place, you'll quickly increase your revenue."

"Poker machines? That's illegal, Ted."

"On paper, maybe, but this is the Rocks. Most of the other bars have poker machines, Joe. No one cares."

I had previously confided in Ted about my frustration with the lack of customers, so at first, I thought he was just brainstorming for me. It was more than that.

"I can clear the way for you, Joe. You don't have to worry about a thing except how to spend the extra money."

Although money was awfully tight, there were certain things I just didn't want to touch. Poker machines were huge at the time, and in the Rocks, every bar that was any bar had them; however, I *really* didn't want to do this. I didn't want to attract a poker-machine crowd, knowing that if I allowed poker machines, the restaurant would cap out as a local bar. Ted persisted and ended up sending a famous local face on the right side of the law (or so I thought) to have a little heart-to-heart with me.

The prominent figure walked in the next day and basically said, "Hey look, Costanzo, we know you serve after-hours down here, and I am in a position to either help you or hurt you. I would like to see some poker machines in this place."

"No thanks, sir. I'm not trying to be a prude; I just don't think it would be good for my establishment." The prominent citizen and poker-machine pusher walked out the door pissed off, but he wasn't willing to give up yet.

About a week later, the man came back in with a monetary enticement: five thousand dollars cash. He fanned the hundred-dollar bills—fifty of them—and placed them on the table. I was struggling and it was the eighties, so five thousand dollars was a hell of a lot of money when the bar and restaurant were grossing only about five hundred dollars of revenue each weekend night. He said, "Joe, take this money, and we'll split the profit on your poker machines."

During the previous week, I couldn't help thinking about all the things I might be able to do with that kind of money, like get a Beer Meister to keep the kegs cold, a mug froster, and a sink. That's right; I didn't even have enough cash at the time to put in a sink for the bar. The money would allow me to do all that and more. "No, but thanks," I gulped, my heart pounding that I might regret this moment. "I have to pass. My whole idea is to establish an upscale restaurant here."

"Costanzo, if you think that you'll have upscale food in McKees Rocks, you're out of your mind. I've lived here for more than sixty years, and I know that's never going to happen. I'm going to give you one more chance—take this money and buy your wife something nice. I understand she's a good woman who helps you out tremendously here."

It was enticing. "I appreciate what you're doing, and I appreciate the situation, but I still have to decline."

"I thought you were crazy, but now I know it," the man muttered as he took his money from the table and left.

Despite the struggles, I honestly thought that I was destined for greatness. There was no doubt in my mind that it was going to happen.

One night Donna was sleeping soundly. In contrast, I couldn't turn off my mind, and the energy inside me was building. I woke Donna up and proclaimed, "Donna, we are destined for history!"

"What is the matter, Joe?" she asked drowsily.

I repeated, "We are destined for history—me and you."

Donna replied, "Roll over and go back to sleep."

8

Dressed in dark pants and vest with a white shirt open wide at the neck that now reminds me of a more restrained version of Seinfeld's puffy shirt, my picture appeared on the first page of the *Pittsburgh Post-Gazette* on Monday, September 22, 1986. I was standing in front of The Primadonna, looking very Italian with tufts of dark hair on the sides of my head and a large mustache. My smile, however, had a slightly forlorn undertone that matched the article's title: "Stowe renewal: slow 1st year."

The article focused on the Broadway Development Corporation's one-and-a-half-million-dollar redevelopment of the Stowe Township business district, headed by young visionary Bill Vito. Funded by a combination of county, state, and federal funds and grants, Vito founded the effort after a trip to Disney World's Main Street USA. He helped to plan and implement the physical renewal of the neighborhood with quaint lettering on signs and nineteenth century-style street lanterns.

Despite the title about business being slow, that article was the first public record of my positivity and constant focus on marketing:

> A spirited, go-get-'em type, Costanzo sounds like a walking advertisement. "We offer Mount Washington-style food and cocktails, a Shadyside atmosphere, West Park hospitality and reasonable prices . . . Broadway looks like Shadyside, but I didn't need Shadyside-type money to get in. I was therefore

able to set up the only jazz lounge with homemade Italian cuisine in the Sto-Rox area." Sto-Rox has eighty-six bars, Broadway alone has six. "None are like Primadonna," says Bill Vito, whose family owns a pharmacy across the street, "What we need is two or three more Joe Costanzos on Broadway."

Between paragraphs, writer Vince Leonard inserted: "Only the sandwich board was missing."

One of the biggest perks of the restaurant was that I was surrounded by fantastic food. As the proprietor, I had unlimited access to what came out of the kitchen, so you bet I indulged. A couple months after the restaurant opened, however, I had a new concern in addition to the lack of customers. I started to get very thirsty and was constantly reaching for water, or more often, Coke. I was also constantly having to use the restroom. When I began to experience some fleeting episodes of lightheadedness, I went to my doctor, I told her I thought I might have a urinary tract infection (UTI). She said that UTI's are rare with men, and to her it sounded more like high blood sugar and type 2 diabetes.

I was in denial that this diagnosis could be correct. I was young and healthy. At the time I was alarmed and half-obeyed the doctor's advice, drinking far less soda for a while and watching how much I nibbled on throughout the day. The symptoms lessened but never really went away completely. As I felt a little better, I pretty much returned to my old habits.

The Rocks had more bars per square mile than any other type of enterprise. Before I bought the business, I counted eighty-six liquor licenses, but not one decent restaurant in the whole town. After I opened The Primadonna, I quickly realized what people were doing with their money (or lack thereof)—drowning their sorrows. The alcoholics, the partiers, the people with sob stories, the people with too many stories, they are all a part of it. The bar was the setting for a soap opera unfolding daily, and it made a lot of money. What's that saying? "When life hands you lemons, break out the tequila and the lemonade and the *salt*!" Luckily, with the bar as an accessory to my dream restaurant, I was set up to get into this game. For the time being, the restaurant had to be an accessory to the bar.

To bring in a crowd, I did a little snooping around town for DJ suggestions. The name "Dr. McKees Rocks" kept coming up, so I asked one of my best customers, Mark Broda, if he knew of him.

"Joe, if you can get him, this place will be jumpin'! He's the best. He plays great music, and he's entertaining, too."

So I tracked down Dr. McKees Rocks and hired him to spin on Wednesday, Friday, and Saturday nights. This decision to boost the bar business to generate some type of income from The Primadonna proved to be a blessing and a curse, but the blessing part was that Dr. McKees Rocks had a following. This meant instant customers, like making Tang. Provocative yet enormously likable, "The Doctor" made it hip to embrace his passion for oldies, even though the crowd he brought in was mostly in their twenties and thirties. He knew what to say and what to play.

"Hey, y'aaaaalll, this is papa-mama-romper-stomper now . . ." Sir Raggedy Flagg's voice would blare, and when that beat kicked in, Dr. McKees Rocks would urge everyone out onto the small, overcrowded dance floor. "Grab a girl and get up and dance. Or just grab a girl. You *need* to. Tell her it was doctor's orders. Dr. McKees Rocks, that is." Cue the cheers, applause, and bumpin' and grindin'.

"I'm gonna slow things down now so you can refill your drinks, but if you're really diggin' someone, hold them real close while you dance to this next song by Percy Sledge." As the song played, "The

Doctor" would boom into his mic over the opening phrase, "When a maaa-an shags a woman . . ." The crowd would cheer and laugh. He'd play another slow song to give people time at the bar, and then announce, "Let's pick things up again with a song title that, coincidentally, some of you will be saying later tonight—'Hold on, I'm comin'!' by Sam and Dave." There'd be more whoops and hollers and dancing and drinking all night long.

The biggest issue was that most of the cash came in after ten each night, and it was state law to close bars by two. With the staff and other operating costs, four hours of making money wasn't going to cut it. So I "forgot" to watch the clock, keeping the doors open a little later than usual. I had to grab onto whatever would keep me afloat for the time being.

Borrowing from common happy-hour practices, I served homemade pizza, knowing the cost would easily be offset by increased drink sales. Later, I added some late-night menu items like wings and sausage rolls, made with sausage from Ernie Ricci's popular store just a few doors down on Broadway. After a couple of months, The Primadonna bar was the busiest place in the Rocks. When Dr. McKees Rocks played "Shout!" everyone got up and at least bounced before throwing their hands up. When he spun The Drifters "On Broadway," he always said something like, "This is for you, Joe," or "Here's your theme song, Joe," and the crowd went crazy, but for several weeks it went right over my head. Then one night I made the connection—The Primadonna was on the corner of Broadway and Dohrman Streets—we *were* on Broadway (*our* Broadway, not *the* Broadway). I kinda liked that.

Each week the bar was getting more crowded and sales were increasing, but at the time, I hadn't given any thought to the customers having previously been patrons of other establishments in the area. *I* hadn't, but I would learn later that my bar's success was the unexpected glue that bonded the other Rocks bar owners together at the time. That's the curse part.

Donna often helped out during the day, signing for deliveries, cleaning, setting up, etc., but she hadn't been to The Primadonna in the evening for a few weeks. I told her how the bar crowd was picking up since hiring D.J. Dr. McKees Rocks, enough that the business was able to maintain itself without dipping into my USPS income. I suggested she get someone to watch the girls and come see for herself.

A few nights later, Donna decided to take me up on the offer. She dropped the kids off at her mother's house and picked up two of her aunts, both in their eighties, who had been wanting to see the place. During the years since Donna and I were dating, the late-night scene had really loosened up. Led by shock jocks like Howard Stern, people were entertained when DJs boldly used language in public that would have once gotten them arrested. Customers, too, enjoyed "letting it all hang out" verbally. Liquor helped to erase any remaining timidity from the crowd, so F-bombs were dropping everywhere around the unlikely bar guests. You never saw three ladies more out of their element.

The aunts tried in their way to be kind. Aunt Lil commented, "Donna, this place is really nice."

Donna was visibly uncomfortable. "If I were single, The Primadonna would be the last place on earth I would go to hang out. I'm sorry to have brought you into this," she told her aunts.

I felt bad that Donna was embarrassed. I didn't really care what the DJ was playing, nor had I paid much attention—all I cared about was making ends meet. Although she clearly disapproved of what was going on, Donna stood by me and allowed me to keep my dream alive, even when it didn't look anything like what I had first envisioned.

One night a guy came into the place extremely late, sat down at the bar, and had a couple of drinks. Although he had a broad grin, he was an unusually quiet guy, making me suspect that something could possibly be up. I was too busy to start a conversation but made sure that I acknowledged his presence.

"Hey, how you doing? Joe Costanzo."

"Bob—Bob Miller. Pleasure to meet you, Mr. Costanzo."

"What will you be having?"

"Bud Light and a cup of ice."

"Bud Light it is, and the cup of ice is on the house." We both chuckled, but I didn't have time to stay until the joke died out. I was busy. I was greeted by people throwing money at the bar. Like Pacman, I was gobbling it up, and it seemed like I couldn't go fast enough.

Bob seemed nice enough. He was a quiet guy who came and left by himself. This was not unusual in the Rocks or the bar scene in general, for that matter. He came in and looked like everyone else there. He wore McKees Rocks business casual, which essentially meant jeans that weren't ripped, and leave the baseball cap at home. During the night, Bob didn't say one word, but he looked like he was enjoying the atmosphere. I had no idea what brought people to a bar. As a married man with children, these things remained a mystery to me. When the clock struck ten, the people at my house were usually asleep. Here, that was when everyone just started coming out of the woodwork.

In that time and space, you didn't find a professional to talk to about your problems. You found something, mainly of the alcoholic persuasion, to escape those problems—for a while at least. A bartender eventually learned everyone's story. Some wordless stories unfolded before your eyes, like the guy who brought his wife in for dinner and his girlfriend in for late-night drinks. Other stories evolved as you got to know the people, like Chuckie Richards, quietly suffering from Agent Orange, nursing his incurable disease by my side with beer. With no known cure and no friends in sight, I was exactly what the doctor ordered.

I would get lost in my work and in conversation, but thanks to my reliable internal clock, I was scanning the room come one thirty. If I knew everyone in the place, we would lock out the rest of the world, but the party would continue as long as these folks wanted it. The orchestra was in charge, and this conductor was just along for the ride. Tonight there were too many new faces in the crowd, so it was time to call it.

The loud groans and protests of the regulars hinted to the strangers that this was unusual, and comments like "Why so early?" and "It's only two" did not help. As I locked the door that night, I was grateful for a reason to shut down. I was tired. So, so tired. I went out to my car, checked to see if the coast was clear, and then remember thinking that the lack of sleep was making me paranoid.

Since I was not from the Rocks, any new face that graced my business time and again was welcome, and after about five or six times, these new faces became trusted allies. One night just before closing time, I scanned the place and saw no strangers, so I locked the door and let everyone carry on—and so did I.

A couple days later, I got a surprise via certified mail—a citation from the Pennsylvania Liquor Control Board (LCB).

9

It was the dawn of the spring of 1987, one of those days when little kids feel like skipping to school and big kids feel like skipping school. The sun was warming, birds were chirping, and flowers were blooming, but inside I was withering—confused, concerned, exhausted, and scared. I was making it, but barely, and could not afford to lose even one night of business without it having serious implications for my life and my family. I had to keep focused on work because if I let down for even a moment, everything came crashing down in my mind. I kept seeing myself closing and locking the restaurant for good, and I imagined the faces of my wife and my daughters when they learned that both the dream and our way of making a living had come to an end.

On the date stated on the citation, I took off work for the afternoon and drove downtown to the courthouse in my yellow Chevelle, dressed in my best black suit. I checked in and gave my name. The woman behind the counter seemed annoyed, like acknowledging my arrival was an interruption rather than her job. She barely looked up at me after loudly announcing, "Sit down."

"Here?" I asked.

"*Sit down,*" she repeated sternly.

Geez. Was she trained to be that nasty? I took a seat and swallowed my pride. To this woman, I was probably the kind of lowlife that I spent my life warning others about. I felt like I was on the set of the TV sitcom *Night Court*, sheepishly waiting for my hearing amid a motley crew of local drunks, addicts, and gamblers.

The door opened, and I was escorted into a very plain room. The judge was sitting up higher in a desk, just like on television. I was told to put my hand on the Bible and solemnly swore to tell the truth, the whole truth, and nothing but the truth, so help me God. It felt so official. As I surveyed the faces of the people in the room, I saw Bob Miller, spontaneously smiled at him, and immediately felt better. Then a split second later, I wondered, *Why the hell is Bob at my hearing*?

The judge stood up and ordered me to stand. Then "Bob" stepped forward. Bob was, in fact, not Bob. He was a state liquor control board agent. Like it was nothing, he stood up and told the judge all the details of his Bud Light experiences at The Primadonna. He had dates and times of exactly when he was given his beers with ice on the house. He knew exactly when I was open late, and he even recited the times and what I had served him. I was flabbergasted. He had the goods.

This was an awfully hard lesson for me. I'm not sure what hurt more, having one less loyal customer than I thought or the knowledge that there were people out to destroy what I was trying to build. It was over. There was no way that I could talk myself out of this.

The man was an undercover liquor control board worker, still sporting the same grin. I made direct eye contact with him as I was asked if I had served a drink after hours to the man who was sitting in his seat in the courtroom.

"Yes, Your Honor. I did."

"You know that this is against the law?"

"Yes, Your Honor."

"If you knew that, then why did you do it?"

"I was just trying to feed my family. Making a go of the restaurant has been tough. Really tough."

The judge did not know what to say to this. He took a quick recess and came back. I could feel myself sweating despite the comfortable temperature, and my mouth was dry. This was my first run-in with the law.

After several minutes, the judge re-entered the room. "Joseph Costanzo, I find you guilty in violation of serving liquor after hours. You will pay a fine. The details of the decision will be mailed to you in three to five business days."

I was guilty but wouldn't know the price I would pay for three to five business days. Well, shit. I was only able to blurt out, "I understand. Thank you for your time, sir."

"I hope to never see you back here again."

"Yes, sir."

Afterward, Liquor Control Board Bob came up to me in the hallway, still grinning, but the grin somehow looked more sincere now. "Mr. Costanzo, I've prosecuted many people, and they always end up telling me the reason they served after hours is because every other bar owner does it, too. You, Costanzo—you are different. You accepted the responsibility, and I respect that about you. I feel so bad that I had to do this to you. You are a nice guy, but I had to do my job."

We exchanged common courtesies, and I told him that I understood. I knew what doing a job meant. In a way, I was just trying to do my job, too. Although I knew that other bar owners were doing this same thing, I wasn't going to cry about it. *All* the bars in the Rocks were open after hours, which was the only reason I had let it happen. After all, after-hours bars, strip clubs, and Mancini's bread were what the Rocks were known for. But as I thought it through in preparation for the hearing, I thought of how I hated when people pointed to others when they were just as guilty. I also thought of how many times I had heard or said, "Two wrongs don't make a right." I wasn't taking that route; I accepted responsibility and moved on.

Well, maybe "moved on" isn't the right phrase. I had to *try* to move on, constantly suppressing the tumult I felt inside. From somewhere in the back of my mind, most likely from one of the iterations of a dark ride called Noah's Ark in Pittsburgh's Kennywood Park, the same image kept popping up in my mind in OCD-fashion. Even now I not only remember the image, but also remember its unwelcome recurrence. It was a dark figure of Noah trying to push back on a door that kept being blown open by fierce whistling winds. That's an easy one to analyze—I was Noah, and the winds were the constant challenges I faced in trying to get to my vision of what The Primadonna *should* be.

When I got home, Donna ran to the door to meet me.

"How did it go?" she asked anxiously.

"Good. I'll have to pay a fine, though," I said casually.

"How much?"

"I'm not sure yet. They'll let me know."

"That's all? Just a fine, and that's it?"

"Yep," I replied, forcing a smile. Donna hugged me.

"That's wonderful! I'm so relieved that's the only consequence."

I didn't have the heart to tell Donna that I *hoped* this was the only consequence. She had just about had it with the restaurant and all the troubles, and I knew this could be the final straw if the fine were high.

"Did I tell you about that quiet guy with a big grin who started coming in a while back?"

"I remember. You said he just sits alone and has a beer. With ice, right?"

"Yep, that's the one. Well, my new friend Bob wasn't a Bob at all. He was the liquor control board snitch."

"No! *Really*?"

"Yeah, but he half-apologized afterward and called me a nice guy."

Donna laughed, and I knew she felt a sense of relief that I didn't yet have, maybe wouldn't have. Instead of pointing out that this still could be disastrous, I let her enjoy it.

I spent the next five business days starting and ending my day rooting through mail at my PO box in the post office like no one's business. Every day that I had new hope but left with nothing, it was more anxiety that I had to swallow.

One morning I went in and rifled through the mail, finally finding what I had come for. I said a little prayer and sliced the envelope open with a letter opener.

"We, the Pennsylvania Liquor Control Board, have found Mr. Joseph Costanzo, Jr. guilty of serving liquor after hours . . . and the recourse is a $325.00 fine to be paid upon receipt of this notice."

"Sweet Lord Jesus, thank you!" I had never been so excited to learn that I was out three hundred bucks. To me, this was just the cost of doing business, and I was more than happy to pay this price.

10

In 1987, I decided I had to make some physical improvements if we were ever to approach the kind of upscale dining establishment I envisioned. I had no beer system and no sink in the bar, which was technically illegal, but the requirement was somehow overlooked because I bought an established restaurant from Nick Fusco. I installed a sink, along with new carpet throughout the restaurant, a new kitchen floor, a working table and shelves in the kitchen, and an additional ice machine. Coca-Cola installed a fountain machine and soda gun at no charge, for which I always remained grateful.

Somewhere along the line I had developed an affinity for plaques. It started after we were married, and by the time Maria was born, we had quite a few plaques on the walls. How could I not love plaques? They were a permanent commemoration of people, events, and awards that also made the walls look good.

When we were opening the restaurant, the owner of the building said I was free to hang any pictures or plaques on the walls, and that set my wheels turning. For those who visited The Primadonna, the evening would consist of a mixture of charisma and propaganda. Whether they realized it or not, the plaques were part of the propaganda. The first plaque I hung was the *Post-Gazette* article, "Stowe renewal: slow 1st year." After that, there were plaques of the menus, plaques commemorating employees, plaques of our families, plaques with licenses, plaques featuring artwork Maria and Kelly created, and more. They added warmth to the decor and gave people something to look at.

Although it was still a gamble, as the end of the year's leave from the post office approached, I officially resigned. It was a blessing that I at least had some time to get a foothold before permanently giving up my position with the USPS.

I was buying beer from Savatt's, the local beer distributor, but he saw that I needed a tap. Mr. Savatt took a chance on me and made it happen. A man named Bob O'Keefe worked for Savatt, and he installed a Beer Meister at the bar. It held two kegs—Genesee 12 Horse Ale and IC Light.

Bob questioned, "What do you want to do here, Joe?"

I told him, "I want an upscale restaurant with people coming from all over the city."

Bob shook his head doubtfully. "I've been here thirty years, and no one has ever tried selling this kind of food in the Rocks."

"All the more reason to do it," I said with my usual positivity.

As the facilities were being upgraded, the Primadonna "family" was also building. Vic DaVita became another beloved member. With a smaller frame and somewhat of a beer gut, Vic was both offbeat and attractive at once. His uncommon features included a full head of dark, thick, curly hair; eyes so blue that people asked him if he was wearing contacts; and a large gap between his front teeth that was somehow charming. A chain smoker, Vic always dressed in jeans and a T-shirt, some with messages we picked up as bar slogans, like "Sleep Is for the Weak" and "Very Good at Bad Decisions."

One of the regulars at the bar before the restaurant boomed, Vic was a high school basketball referee in the winter and a baseball umpire for school teams and Little League and in the spring and summer. He also worked independent construction and repair jobs and was busier than he wanted to be just from word-of-mouth recommendations. I don't know where he loafed before coming to The Primadonna, but once he stepped through the door, he immediately made the bar his home. I'd get excited when I'd see him come in because I knew he'd liven things up and provide comic relief. Once Vic learned I had played basketball, he often sought me out to tell me something about the night's game, a player to watch on the local scene, etc.

Vic became a living advertisement for The Primadonna. His referee jobs took him all over the Pittsburgh area, and he'd tell other refs, coaches, security guards, and anyone else who would listen to come to The Primadonna. He even asked for a stack of my business cards to give out so people would remember. If Vic refereed somewhere not too far, he might bring in another guy or a small crowd after a game. If he were at the bar and someone came in from one of the schools or leagues where he worked, he'd yell out, "Hey, North Hills!" or "Hey, St. Margaret's!" and then he would always add, "What the hell you doin' at my bar?" One of Vic's recruits who became a semi-regular customer told me that Vic gave him my Primadonna business card and said, "You can find me at the bar any night after ten. If I'm not there, I'm probably dead." Another guy that Vic recruited told me, "He didn't really *invite* me. It was more like The Godfather looking you in the eye and making you feel like you had no choice." Vic had friends everywhere and brought in a lot of new business. I treated him like the king of the Primadonna bar, which he was.

Vic was loud and funny. In the early days, he would shout out over the noise *and* the music, but as the restaurant crowd grew, he knew to adjust his volume to those seated at the bar. His quick wit was sidesplitting, but he also had a half dozen signature sayings that became even funnier as we predicted them, like, "I'm not really funny. I'm just mean, but people think I'm kidding." He would use that one if there were a new face at the bar. If anyone hit on a number or announced anything positive, he would yell out, "Yes, Virginia, there is a Santa Claus!" Every so often, he would matter-of-factly state that he had a "half dick" in normal conversation. He never explained, but those who had heard it before would howl at the looks on people's faces when he'd say it and just move on like it was nothing. On those late nights early on when the bar customers all knew each other, Vic would toast, "To basketball and blow jobs!," his two favorite things.

Vic was responsible for the first fight ever inside The Primadonna. One night a busser frantically called me out of the kitchen. "Fight in the bar! Joe, come quick!"

I rushed out, only to find two females rolling around on the floor, name calling, hair pulling and all; the only thing missing was the mud. Some patrons sprang to their feet around the wrestlers, but no one intervened. Barry jumped out from behind the bar, shouting at the women to get up. I instinctively moved in to break them up, and they separated as they sensed me leaning over them. Every person looked concerned except for Vic. He just sat back and laughed. When I went up to him, he took a drag of his cigarette and started laughing. He said to me, "Joe, I got this big belly and my dick is only two inches long, but these girls are fighting over it. I love the Rocks."

Vic drank a lot, about two-fifths of a bottle of bourbon every night. He liked Benchmark and water, which I had to special order. He was there to drink and socialize, and he hardly ever ordered food.

Vic seemed to have no shortage of girlfriends. Some he brought into The Primadonna; others he just talked about. One night he somehow exceeded his bourbon limit, and by the time anyone noticed, he was very drunk. As I cleaned up, I sat him at a booth in the bar area and served him cheesecake and coffee. When I came back through, Vic was asleep at the table on folded arms, food and drink untouched. I let him sleep for a while and then tried to wake him, but he was still out of it. I wouldn't let him drive home, and he wouldn't let me drive him home. Finally, he called a girlfriend to pick him up.

It was nearly five o'clock in the morning by the time we heard a knock at the door. A young woman in pajamas and a jacket stepped inside. She looked familiar, and then I realized she was one of the women from the bar fight. She looked right past me and said to Vic, "You are a fuckin' jagoff. Don't come near me. I'm driving you to your mother's house."

Vic got up to go, looked her in the eye, and said, "I guess a blow job in the parking lot is out of the question, then?"

Not long after that, one of Vic's girlfriends was at a booth in the bar with some of her friends. I recognized her as the *other* woman from the bar fight. She motioned for me to come over and introduced me to her friends but didn't remind me of her own name. As she took a picture out of her purse, she said, "Mr. Costanzo, I wanted to show you this. Did Vic tell you he has any kids?"

It was still strange hearing people refer to my thirty-something self as a Mr. Costanzo, who in my mind was my dad, but I was starting to get used to it. I answered, "No. He doesn't have kids."

As she held out the picture for me to see, she proclaimed, "He is the father of my little girl."

I looked at the picture of a sweet little girl around five or six years old. She had a big smile just like Vic's, with a large gap between her front teeth. Taken by surprise, I didn't know whether the girlfriend was revealing this to me first or whether this was old news to Vic. I just said, "I thought Vic didn't have any kids," and quickly excused myself.

I acknowledged Vic's contributions to The Primadonna and showed my appreciation. I used to say to him, "Thank you for putting my kids through college," and he would say, "It's my pleasure."

Another unforgettable personality in our bar family was Federico (Fred), whose house was a block away. I thought Federico was an endearing nickname for Fred, but in his obituary, I saw it was the other way around. In his seventies, Fred was the oldest person in the original bar crowd. A rather genteel, quiet widower who was always dressed in a button-down shirt and nice pair of pants, Fred didn't say much unless he thought he had something worth hearing. When the two of us talked, he regretted that his wife couldn't bear children and always asked me about my girls. If my family were there earlier in the evening, little Kelly would run over, climb up on a bar stool next to him and chat. Like pets, children have an inner sense about people.

Once Fred started drinking, though, he couldn't stop. He drank Black Velvet and water. He also would fall asleep at the bar. Once he was so drunk that his head dropped right onto his plate of spaghetti; then he kept sleeping in the spaghetti.

Many nights I would walk Fred home and help him up the steep steps to his house, help him get into the door, then up another set of steep stairs to his bedroom. I would lay him in his bed on his back, take his shoes off, and turn off the light.

Fred was one of the few at the bar who always ordered dinner, and Dorothy was a server in her fifties who usually served food to bar customers. One night when I helped Fred into his bed, I was surprised to hear him say (with a drunken slur), "I want to fuck Dorothy. I want to fuck her so bad."

I chuckled and said, "You are not alone, Federico. You are not alone." Then I walked out of the place.

On the nights when it was late and I was so exhausted that I'd collapse on a bench at the restaurant, Fred would be at the bus stop, bright-eyed, showered, and shaved with fresh-pressed clothes when I headed home before seven the next morning.

11

The way the kitchen staff clicked made me feel like I had found the perfect team for The Primadonna: genuine Italian chefs, including my worn-but-eager mother Helen; Cousin Pino fresh from Italy, eager to realize the American Dream; Anna, who knew how to make killer gnocchi; and Tony, a world-class chef from the Hilton Hotel chain who worked part-time for Fusco before working for me. Experienced waitresses who worked for Fusco before I took over were also willing to be on call. With mouth-watering food and reasonable prices, I had almost everything a restaurateur could want. The only thing I didn't have was dinner customers. On average, we were still serving only eight to ten people a night.

Even with business as sluggish as it was, I tried to make a name for it, putting every penny I made it into advertising. I ran coupons in the *PennySaver*, called in to local radio stations, and even tried to get the surrounding neighborhood buzzing by recognizing a football "Player of the Week" from the local high school, honoring the player and his family a with a free dinner. Confident in The Primadonna's merits, I reached out to Pittsburgh's popular dining critic, Mike Kalina from the *Post-Gazette* (a.k.a. KDKA-TV's Phantom Diner), asking him to come down and review the place. He had a great track record of good and bad reviews that people trusted. He was one of the first food critic celebrities who started the current food crazes—cooking shows, foodie shows, etc. I knew that if he came and I got a good review, this could be a regional restaurant. If I got a bad review, it would be of little consequence because we weren't doing any business to speak of anyway. For more than two years, I wrote letters (probably twenty) and sent my menu. The handwritten letters usually read something like this:

> Dear Mr. Kalina,
> I invite you to dine at The Primadonna on Broadway in McKees Rocks. We have great food at very reasonable prices in a fine-dining atmosphere that we feel sure you will enjoy.
> Your endorsement would mean so much to the restaurant, so I again ask you to visit us soon.
> Sincerely,
> Joe Costanzo
> Enclosed you will find a copy of my menu.

Between the unrequited mailings, I tried calling Kalina many times. Back then, most people didn't even have voice mail; the person either picked up or they didn't. Finally, one day the food critic picked up on the first ring.

"Kalina."

"Mr. Kalina, this is Joe Costanzo from The Primadonna Restaurant. I've written to you many times. I would really appreciate it if you came down to my place."

"Kid, you've got a bar in McKees Rocks. I'm the food critic from the *Post-Gazette*. I have an obligation; I write about places my readers might actually consider going to."

I replied confidently. "I don't just have a bar. I have great food, and this restaurant is a diamond in the rough. I will make you look good if you find a diamond in the rough."

"You know what? I am going to come down just on principle. I'm tired of throwing your invitations in the garbage," he grumbled, hanging up. I wasn't sure whether the snigger I heard before the click of the phone hanging up was a sign of amusement or annoyance, but it didn't matter. Kalina was coming.

Kalina visited restaurants incognito, so we couldn't be sure when he would arrive. In anticipation of his visit, we found someone to take care of the girls in the evenings so Donna could come to the restaurant. Maria and Kelly readily embraced their new sitter, calling her "Nana." She was like having a third grandma who was able to give the girls the TLC they needed, given how busy we had become. The fact that the girls loved her assuaged the parental guilt when we both worked evenings.

I alerted the staff about Kalina's coming, but it wasn't much help because none of us knew what Kalina looked like. His food column in the *Pittsburgh Post-Gazette* carried no image of the columnist. When he appeared on TV as the Phantom Diner, he dressed in dark clothing with a simple mask and high upturned collar, disguising his voice as he broadcast his reviews. People respected his guise, and no one sought to reveal his identity. He could not have pulled it off today with cell phone cameras, the internet, and people who enjoy intentionally disrupting what is sacrosanct.

We surmised that Mike Kalina would be making an entrance quite soon. Normally for financial reasons, we put white cloth tablecloths on the tables on Fridays and Saturdays only, but with the anticipation of Kalina, we started to put the tablecloths on all week.

While we were anxiously anticipating Kalina's visit, another situation popped up with the local police. It was a busy bar night when suddenly two customers, Phil and Kevin, were standing practically nose-to-nose in a screaming match, loud enough to be heard over the music. When I turned toward the shouting, I saw Phil shove Kevin's shoulder tauntingly and saw Kevin reflexively return the gesture. I stepped right in, raising my arm to wedge it in the small space between their bodies to break them up, but each backed away immediately before any physical force was necessary. "Take it outside, my friends," I ordered firmly. "I'm not having any fighting in my bar." Phil went back to the bar, and Kevin left the building, looking angrily at me over his shoulder as he exited.

Shortly after, a cop walked through the door, looking for me. He introduced himself as Officer Patton and said, "I understand someone got stabbed down here tonight?"

"Officer, I don't know what you're talking about. Not here."

"Well, Kevin showed up in the emergency room at Ohio Valley Hospital with a stab wound he said he got from Phil during a fight in this bar. Will you verify this?"

"No, I won't. Nothing like that happened here."

The cop said, "Let's cut through the B.S. Were Phil and Kevin here tonight, and was there an altercation?"

"Yes sir, they were here. There were words between them, but that's all."

Angrily, the officer said, "I'm going to ask you one more time, Costanzo. Now you can either work with me or work against me. I know that there was a stabbing here, and I know that Phil did it. Now all I'm asking you to do is to testify, and justice will be served."

"You are asking me to lie, and I ain't doing that. I broke up the fight. I was right in the middle. There was no blood at all—just some yelling and a little pushing. That's all. Now if you'll excuse me, I have a business to run here." I walked back into the bar.

As Officer Patton left, he said, "We know you're still serving after hours, Costanzo."

About a week later, there was a knock at the door shortly after two o'clock in the morning. I peered out and saw the pizza delivery boy who lived next to the building. "Joe, it's Skip from next door." Flashing a twenty-dollar bill, he said, "I want to buy a six-pack."

I opened the door and let Skip in. He bought the six-pack and was on his way. I relocked the door and he heard another knock, looked through the peephole, and saw Officer Patton. "Costanzo, open up." He stepped into The Primadonna and announced, "Everyone needs to get out of this place. Costanzo, you are coming with me."

The remaining customers filed out the door in silence, and Officer Patton drove me to the police station. He wrote out a citation and said he was going to send it to the liquor control board and to District Judge Mary Anne Cercone.

I pleaded, "Mike, come on, my man. I'm just trying to make a living here."

Patton answered, "Costanzo, shut your mouth, or I'll put you in a cell and not look back." He handed me the citation, and I asked to use the phone. I called my friend Donny to pick me up. When I hung up, Officer Patton said, "Get out of here."

I was scheduled to appear before the local magistrate in addition to a second liquor control board hearing. I knew The Primadonna would not survive without the liquor license.

That night I didn't get a minute's sleep. My brain felt like a gear that was wound too tight. As I tossed and turned, I kept thinking about having the place under foreclosure, imagining my father saying, "See, I told you so."

12

On Friday of the following week, six people walked into the restaurant—three well-dressed couples, differing noticeably from the normal jeans-and-T-shirt Rocks attire. I immediately pulled Donna aside. "Donna, that might be Kalina's party. I want you to wait on them."

"Okay, but I'm nervous."

"Don't be. You're the best, love." The regular servers were fine, but Donna had unusual poise and grace, along with that beauty-pageant smile that won people over.

The hostess seated the group. Donna scurried over with menus, promising to return shortly to take their drink orders. She watched as they perused their menus for a few moments, then took their drink orders. As soon as she served the drinks, she returned with a basket of garlic bread made from Mancini's Italian bread and a plate of fried zucchini with lemon slices and marinara sauce, saying, "Joe sent this zucchini on the house. If this doesn't appeal to you, I can bring roasted red peppers instead." Two of the men said something in unison about the zucchini being fine.

Donna asked the party if they were ready to order. They showered her with questions about the menu: What would she consider the specialty of the house? Which did she like more, the Veal Calabrese, or the Veal Sicilian? With what were the clam appetizers stuffed? Were the gnocchi made with potato or ricotta? I know these details because we relived the scene over and over the next couple of days for anyone interested—staff, family, and our circle of friends.

I waited in the kitchen, and Donna rushed back to me. "I think it *is* Kalina, Joe. They're asking too many questions."

"I think you're right, love, but don't get too nervous. We've got to serve this guy the best meal he's ever had in his life." I gathered the kitchen staff by motioning for them to turn toward me. Then I instructed in a low tone, "Everyone tighten your game; I think Kalina is here."

Donna squeaked, "Joe, I am more nervous than when I had Maria."

"You're the best, love. You're the best in the world. Get back to the table. You have a job to do." I told the busser to step aside while I busied myself at nearby tables where I could get a glimpse of the action.

Donna announced to the table that tonight's soups were French onion, homemade chicken soup with pastina, or Manhattan clam chowder. The vegetable choices were glazed baby carrots or broccoli.

One of the gentlemen ordered first. "I'll have the Mostaccioli all' Arrabiata." This dish was mostaccioli noodles tossed with hot peppers, butter, and brandy, in a tomato sauce. "And the house dressing on the salad."

Remembering his earlier question about the peppers, Donna clarified, "That is a good choice, sir. The peppers are hot?" she asked as she nodded up and down, making sure he had noticed that.

He nodded back as one of the women leaned forward to announce her entrée. "I'd like the Sea Scallops Barsac. Are those breaded?"

"No, ma'am. They are baked in a garlic, lemon, and white wine sauce with fresh mushrooms and parsley, but they are finished with a sprinkling of toasted breadcrumbs."

"Okay. And what kind of soup do you offer today?"

"We always have French onion or homemade chicken soup with pastina, and tonight we also have Manhattan clam chowder," Donna replied sweetly, as though she hadn't mentioned it earlier.

"And what vegetable?"

"Tonight's choices are glazed baby carrots or broccoli."

"I'll have the chicken soup and the carrots."

"A side of spaghetti or a baked potato also comes with that."

"Oh. I'll try the spaghetti."

"Certainly," affirmed Donna, her smile broadening as if to say those were excellent choices.

The second woman ordered Veal al Pino, a dish with fresh veal, breaded and sautéed, topped with a combination of fresh mushrooms, onions, green peppers, and tomato sauce, crowned with a melting of provolone cheese.

The last three guests ordered the homemade manicotti, the Spaghetti all-Amatrigiana, and the Fettuccini Primavera.

I took a familiar walk to the kitchen, passing the cooler filled with my mother's homemade apple pies. When the double doors opened, I gazed around the room and noticed how everything was running at peak efficiency. Everyone was hustling, and everything had its place, from the pepperoncini jars stacked on the shelves to the cove where Anna used her thumbs to print every gnocchi that was made. I remember a few moments in a somewhat surreal state, pleased and calm, yet knowing this moment could be monumental; however, the smell of the pasta all' Arrabiata mixture knocked me back to my senses. I grabbed the hot plate of pasta and helped Donna load it onto her tray.

Donna and her assistants made sure the service that evening was impeccable, continually replenishing the waters, clearing plates, and asking about drink or bread refills. When it came time for dessert, two women ordered the Italian rum cake, and one ordered pineapple sorbet served in a bowl carved from a fresh pineapple. One of the men ordered the chocolate cheesecake, and the other two gentlemen ordered the apple pie. Donna commented, "The apple pie is made from scratch daily by Joe's mother. You'll taste the difference."

The party lingered over dessert as the staff whispered that the guests seemed to be relaxing and enjoying themselves. Before they were done, one of the gentlemen introduced himself to Donna as she poured his second cup of coffee. "Thanks for waiting on us. I'm Mike Kalina from the *Post-Gazette*."

"Oh, my! Now I know what your real voice sounds like," replied Donna cheerfully, alluding to the electronically disguised TV voice of the Phantom Diner. Kalina asked to speak to me.

On her way back to the kitchen, Donna murmured to me, "It's Mike Kalina; he introduced himself. He wants to talk to you."

I wasted no time walking over to the table. "Mr. Kalina, Joe Costanzo. What did you think?"

"Joe, the food was really good; I'm very surprised." He and his party collected their things and got up to leave. "Something will be in the paper about this on Friday. I am really debating about what to give you. I think you deserve four out of five forks, but I have never given a local place like this four forks." Kalina used a five "fork" system instead of stars in his column.

My heart dropping a bit, I replied, "Mr. Kalina, if we deserve four forks, we should get four forks." But I didn't push it.

Kalina walked out the door, and I immediately felt the disappointment. How could he not give us what we deserved? I walked into the kitchen, and they were dancing the bump and singing "Primadonna dreamin' is becoming a reality" to the tune of the Mamas & the Papas' "Creeque Alley." (If you can't remember that song from its title, it's the one with the line "No one's gettin' fat 'cept Mama Cass.")

"Guys, great job tonight. We served Mr. Kalina a fabulous meal, and he loved it." Everyone cheered. "He said we will be in the paper in a couple of days, but he is debating about what to give us. He thinks we deserve four forks, but he may give us three forks."

"What!" Tony exclaimed.

"Why wouldn't he give us what we deserved?" Pino chimed in.

I looked at Anna. "Hey, Anna, you'd better get out your rosaries. We need some prayers."

13

Two days before the *Post-Gazette* review, the phone rang, and I picked up quickly. I rarely answered the phone if any other employee was in the restaurant, but all knew that I would be answering in case it was Mike Kalina, and it was.

"Joe, I need to get some menu prices for my column."

After reading the prices he requested, I said, "Mr. Kalina, I'm so happy you called."

"Don't be too happy; I still haven't decided what I'm going to do with you."

"Mr. Kalina, I've worked so hard. You told me that I deserved four forks, and I think I should get what I deserve."

"Joe, if you get four forks, you will never be able to handle all the business my review will generate."

"All I want you to do is the right thing, and I'll make you look good."

"You know something, Joe? I'm starting to believe some of your bullshit." Kalina hung up.

Friday morning's paper was slated to come out on Thursday night at 2:00 a.m. with the review. I was, of course, busy cleaning up for the night. The phone rang, and it was Danny Cannon, one of the best customers at the restaurant.

"Joe, did you see the paper?"

Hesitating, I replied, "No, Dan."

With excitement Danny yelled, "Joe, he gave you four forks! You couldn't have written the article better yourself."

I held up the phone and screamed, "We got four forks? We got *four* forks? HOLY SHIT, WE GOT FOUR FORKS!"

"He took care of you, Joe."

"I can't fucking believe this! Danny, I'm coming to Sheridan to pick you up."

"Where are we going at two a.m.?"

"We are going to the *Post-Gazette*. We need to buy those papers hot off the press."

"All right, buddy. I'll be ready."

I alerted the bar crowd, and everyone started hooting and hollering. I told them, "I'll be right back," even though it was time for the bar to close and my route to downtown via Sheridan didn't exactly qualify for a "right back." I raced to Sheridan, picked Danny up, and the two of us collected a few dozen papers. When I got back to the restaurant around three, The Primadonna was still filled with my best bar customers and a neighborhood drug dealer. I proudly handed out the papers, and in McKees Rocks style, we all headed out to celebrate at a local "breakfast house" (filled with poker machines). Mark Broda, a regular customer who hung out at the bar nearly every night, took center stage. Standing on the bar, he read the review aloud:

Pittsburgh Post-Gazette, Friday, June 3, 1988
DINING OUT
The Primadonna cooks up 'robust' pasta
By Mike Kalina
Post-Gazette Staff Writer

The Primadonna
801 Broadway, McKees Rocks, PA 15136

Rating: 🍴🍴🍴🍴
Service: Friendly, casual.
Wine list: Woefully inadequate. *Vin very ordinaire.*
Credit cards: Most major.
Hours: Dinner Monday–Saturday from 4 to 11 p.m.
Legend: One fork (poor); Two (fair); Three (good); Four (very good) Five (superb)
The rating is for food and only in relation to quality and price.

Whenever I get the craving for something simple like spaghetti in marinara sauce, or fettuccine fortified with garlic and oil, I'm at a loss where to go. We have more than our share of Italian restaurants, but few can crank out a plate of pasta half as well as a third-rate trattoria in Rome.

The main reason, I think, is that too many Italian restaurateurs here feel pasta's too bourgeois to bother with. So they write menus boasting dishes like veal gussied up with crabmeat, lobster fra diavolo, spots oreganato, chicken cordon bleu or any number of other entrées that are no more Italian than surf and turf is "continental."

If they serve pasta at all, it's usually "angel hair"—a simple breed of trendy tendrils, which no self-respecting pasta-lover would twirl on a fork (unless threatened with loss of limb). In the Italian neighborhood where I grew up (near Scranton), they're proud that angel hair exists there only atop cherubs serenading Christmas trees. I chuckle when considering how vast a culinary non sequitur it would be to dig into a plate of angel hair with chèvre after an afternoon of bocce ball.

My decade on this beat has showed me that the fancier-looking the Italian restaurant, the poorer your chance of getting a good plate of pasta. The more the place looks like the Italian restaurants you see in Grade B movies, the better.

Thus when I got the tip that a restaurant called The Primadonna in McKees Rocks was cranking out a commendable plate of pasta, I took the matter under serious consideration. I figured if there's any place that should twirl robust pasta, it's in McKees Rocks. The name of the restaurant was hokey and blustery enough to make me feel even more confident.

A visit to the appropriately funky-looking establishment proved my intuition correct. The pasta was great. So were the prices. Yes, it even turned out a wonderful rendition of that endangered species—the meatball! No, not the mushy kind larded with leftover breadcrumbs, which has the texture of foie gras but the flavor of Styrofoam. These were firm, spicy spheres of flavor screaming with garlic, which stood up to the tomato sauce like Marvin Hagler to a sandbag.

Oh, what a joy it is to savor a mouthful of al dente spaghetti hugged by a scarlet sauce laced with nubs of spicy sausage, sweet peppers, and onions! Some choose to alternate bites of the pasta with that of the sausage. I like the simultaneous approach. The combination of flavors, spices and textures erupts sensuously on the tongue. (The $6.95 tariff for "spaghetti con sausage," and all pasta dishes, includes salad and garlic bread.)

And let's not forget a macho offering called mostaccioli all-Arrabiata ($6.50). It's actually "stovepipe" pasta—rigatoni on steroids—dressed in a sauce of crushed red pepper, tomatoes, butter, and brandy! A far cry from angel hair, let me tell you!

There's also spaghetti all-Amatrigiana ($6.50), in which the noodles are spun in a bacon sauce; pasta carbonara ($6.50), with the noodles enrobed in a butter-bacon-egg-cream sauce; fettuccine primavera ($6.75), a union of butter, cream, and fresh vegetables; and homemade manicotti ($6.50), Italian crepes plumped with ricotta cheese and herbs. These pillows of flavor were light and delicious, a pleasant contrast to the overbaked tubes of lead I've confronted in the line of duty.

I could go on about other dishes on the menu, like the great, homemade desserts, and the fact that they cut veal from the leg, but a lot of other restaurants do that, too. The Primadonna's cynosure is its pasta. And it's damned near perfect!

14

The next morning—Friday, June 3, 1988—Pino and I went down to the Strip District around nine o'clock and stocked up for the weekend. Even though I didn't get to sleep until the sun came up, I felt energized. To be safe, we tripled or quadrupled our usual orders. First stop was Pennsylvania Macaroni for pasta, and then on to Wholey's for the chicken, sea scallops, flounder, orange roughy, and jumbo Venezuelan pink shrimp. On the way back, we picked up the sixty loaves of Mancini's twist. I keep talking about how lucky we were to be within a few blocks of Mancini's Bakery, a Pittsburgh landmark. The famous Mancini's Twist Italian loaf has a soft but dense and chewy inside with a perfectly golden hard-but-thin crust and an exceptional taste. If you think "bread is bread," you won't understand unless you try it. When we arrived back at the restaurant, Kramer Brothers Produce had already delivered the lettuce and other vegetables. We had recruited and trained extra staff right after Kalina's visit, so I thought we were ready.

Once we were back in the building, the phones went nuts. There were congratulations from friends and family, but most of the calls were for reservations. I'd take a few steps from the phone, and it would ring again. Everyone wanted a reservation at The Primadonna, but I had decided early on that we would not take reservations because it seemed a lot less complicated to seat people as tables came open. For a few hours that afternoon, I thought it was my dream come true. The letters and calls to Mike Kalina over the last two and a half years had finally paid off, even better than I had hoped. Relieved from the tension I felt before the review came out, and buoyed by the number of calls, I felt high.

When the place opened for dinner at four o'clock, there was a line out the door and around the corner. The small foyer only held a dozen or so customers; the rest were standing outside. The staff was only accustomed to serving fifty dinners on the busiest weekend night, and now the demand was running around fifty dinners every hour. As the night went on, Kalina unfortunately proved to be right about one thing: WE WERE NOT READY.

People were waiting for hours to be seated, and then their food wasn't coming out for hours after that. An unspoken but not unfriendly bond formed among the customers; people clapped when anything came out of the kitchen. A guy at the bar yelled, "Hey, I've been waiting for twenty minutes to get a drink in this place. Just sell me a bottle of Stoli, and I'll make my own drinks."

Everything at The Primadonna was made-to-order, so the meals were coming out slowly. I noticed a party of six get their meals one by one with such a delay that by the time the last person was served his Veal Costanzo, the first person had already finished her spaghetti and meatballs. I wanted to fix the situation but felt completely helpless. My role, which I believed to be crucial to the success of the business, had been the relationship builder. I wanted to speak to each table and make the customers feel like I was welcoming them into my home as friends. Instead I was running around behind the scenes, doing what I could to help the staff—throwing zucchini into the fryer, switching tablecloths, thanking and apologizing to those waiting—but we were *way* over our heads.

That wasn't the worst of it. We also ran out of plates and forks, which I didn't realize until it was too late. After the last plate went out, there was an extra lull in things coming out of the kitchen. I was at the front of the house dealing with a few angry, hungry customers who had been waiting for over two hours. After about fifteen minutes went by and I saw workers going into the kitchen but no dinners going out, I went in to investigate.

"What's the problem, Pino?"

"Joe, we are busy. There's nothing I can do," he replied solemnly, making no eye contact while he stirred several pots.

"Get the food out."

"We will, but we are waiting now."

"For what?"

"We are out of dishes and . . ."

"Out of dishes? You're fucking *out* of dishes and no one alerted me?"

"I knew you were busy."

"That is no excuse. How can we run a restaurant without any dishes!"

It was too late. I knew that if I left or sent an employee out to get dishes, we would be one soldier down. We had to wait for tables to finish until we could serve the next. The dishwasher couldn't wash fast enough. The place was so busy that two local bar customers, Betty and Ricky Blatz, spontaneously fled to the kitchen to wash dishes. Another customer I knew did me a favor and drove down the street for twenty more loaves of Mancini's Twist. I took care of them later.

Then I did what every Italian man does when he's in a jam. I called my mother.

"Ma, we are busy down here. Can you do me a favor and bring some dinner plates down? Bring all you have. We ran out. We'll help you when you get down here."

"Okay, Joey. Give me thirty minutes. I'll be down."

"Thanks. And Mom?"

"Yeah?"

"You don't happen to have any pies on hand, do you?"

"Actually, I was just taking a couple out of the oven."

"Can you bring them? Since Kalina mentioned your homemade fare in the article, everyone wants a slice of Mom's apple pie."

"Sure, Joey."

Although the restaurant hours were four to eleven, the last customers were served around midnight. After the situation with the dishes got straightened out, I was able to make the rounds at the tables, introduce myself, thank the guests for coming, and apologize sincerely for the wait. Servers were instructed to do the same as they placated the crowd, and the kitchen staff tried to keep the fried zucchini and roasted red peppers coming quickly at no charge. It was a wild night, yet all but a very few guests were understanding and even good-natured about their long wait. Kalina's review had given the evening an "event" feel, like a grand opening, even though we had already been open for more than two years.

Saturday was much of the same. It was only three forty-five, but when I looked out the front window, there were at least thirty people waiting for the doors to open. Later, the scene became surreal. The street was lined with luxury cars, and the people getting out of them were dressed up for a night on the town. Men in suits and women wearing pearls. These people looked like they came to spend some money, and I was thrilled to accommodate them.

As I peeked out the side window, I saw "T-Bone" sitting outside on the ledge, drinking with five of his friends. Now T-Bone was more feared in the Rocks than anyone; even the police were afraid of him because his behavior was so unstable. One of my employees had pointed T-Bone out to me on the street when we were running errands one day, so I was familiar with his reputation. He could drink openly on the street, and cops would only beg him to go into the alleys. Before The Primadonna was in business, T-Bone was infamous for picking up a garbage can and throwing it through the front window of another establishment on the same block. I always treated him with respect but knew that if he were still there when we opened up, some customers would be too afraid to come in. So as always, I took matters into my own hands.

Walking outside, I approached him quietly. "Hey, T-Bone, how you doin'?"

T-Bone barely looked up to nod.

"I just got this review and could be starting to make a little money after two and a half years. I am not telling you to leave here. I am asking you please could you get up and hang around another corner. If you and your buddies are here, some of these types of customers might feel intimidated. I would really appreciate it. I'm not telling you; I'm just asking you."

T-Bone looked me right in the eye with an expression that was impossible to read, but he didn't say one word. He then picked himself up and started walking away. His friends followed.

Customers filed in, each anticipating an amazing dining experience. I wanted to deliver, and I tried my best. With so many orders coming in at once, though, by four fifteen the kitchen was already backed up. The waitresses had done such a great job selling the specials that by the first round of orders, there was not enough food to make all the specials that were ordered. Nine people had to be told that they couldn't have the Chicken Milano, a pasta with chicken, artichoke hearts, and mushrooms in a white wine-garlic sauce. Each waitress fiercely advocated for herself, explaining why her tables should not be the ones to receive the news. I heard scuffles coming from the kitchen and went in to investigate.

"What's going on in here?"

A fury of accusations erupted about who was at fault regarding the miscommunication of the specials. I wasn't about to hear that petty nonsense. There were people outside who were waiting to be served, and all the servers were inside the kitchen fighting. I quickly made the decision to instruct each of the waitresses to tell two of her customers that the special was already sold out, and I suggested a couple alternatives they should mention.

It was the first time I sensed dissent from the wait staff. The waitresses gave each other looks that conveyed their collective unhappiness with my decision. However, I didn't give two shits about what other people needed at the time. I had a job to do, and people needed to be on board or get off the ship. Once this hurdle was addressed, the rest of the night seemed to go more smoothly.

Between the two nights, more than four hundred dinners were served. The place was rockin', but by the end of the second night, everyone needed a break. The kitchen staff was running on empty. Pino dripped with sweat, and I could see the delirium in his face as he tried to prepare his final family meal of the night for the staff. He could barely keep his eyes open, sitting on a bar stool as he cooked the rest of the meal.

My mother was also exhausted from all the pie making. The pies she brought were not intended for the restaurant, but rather a family gathering, so when she got home the previous night after lending her plates and giving the pies, she had to go to the grocery store and then make more pies. This was a lot to ask someone in her seventies, but she never complained. She always did what she had to do.

The literal overnight increase in business was the answer to our prayers, but the stress of the upcoming liquor control board hearing was looming like a thundercloud over a picnic. Donna, worrier that she is, was sick over it. I was trying to appease her by acting nonchalant and telling her everything would be fine, but I was not so sure myself.

I fought with myself over the one last option I had before the hearing, as I was pretty much defenseless. On Monday I called a local politician, explained the situation, and asked for his sage advice. Asking for advice in that way was the politically safe way to say HELP.

The politician listened sympathetically and said, "Give me a week. I'll see what I can do." I had no idea what he had in mind, but all I could do was wait.

15

Before the week was over, the politician I had called for help got back to me.

"Are you willing to apologize?" he asked. "Officer Patton said you were being difficult."

"I'd do anything to smooth things over."

"Okay. At one a.m., come outside, and you will see a cop car. He and I will be there. Be ready with your apology."

"See you then."

I had to think about this. What was I apologizing for? I had told the truth.

At one I found the cop car parked out front. Just as promised, the politician and Officer Patton were inside. I walked up to the window and asked, "Mind if I get into the car?"

"Sure, Joe," replied the politician. The cop just looked in the other direction.

I got into the car and immediately addressed the cop. "Officer, I appreciate your willingness to talk to me. I know you have a job to do. I'm really sorry if I made you angry. It would be a lot better for me if we could work together."

I put out my hand, and the officer shook it. Then he said, "I know you still have hearings with the magistrate and with the liquor control board. I'll see what I can do about the magistrate, but unfortunately, I can't do anything with the LCB. It's already in."

"I really appreciate that."

It was that easy. A lot had taken place in that short exchange in the bar that was left unspoken. I had probably bruised the officer's ego that night by standing my ground and walking away so brusquely. I also hoped he got the message that I wasn't willing to compromise my integrity, even though I knew by way of the grapevine that Phil was a character who might be better off behind bars for a while. The carefully worded apology didn't address any of this, but it showed respect, which may be all the officer wanted. It was what I wanted, too.

Soon afterward I got a call from Officer Patton and learned that the magistrate hearing was canceled, but the LCB hearing was set for the end of the month. I asked him to come down to the restaurant, and he had dinner on the house. When Donna found out about it, she wasn't happy.

"Joe, how could you give this man dinner on the house? He may cost us our liquor license. What if he frames the free dinner as a bribe instead of an attempt to make amends? I can't believe it!"

"Donna, trust me, I know what I'm doing."

"I've heard that line before, and I believe it just as much now as I did then."

While waiting for the dreaded hearing, my anxiety was exacerbated by the worsening of the same symptoms that had led me to the doctor more than a year earlier. After more extensive testing, I was officially diagnosed with type 2 diabetes. She put me on pills and recommended dietary changes, which didn't work so well. Some people manage this type of diabetes primarily through a radical change in diet, but that was difficult for me. I ate because I enjoyed food, I ate because the food at The Primadonna was practically irresistible, I ate because I was constantly under stress, and I ate because I was already in a habit. Once the cooks began preparing the food, the aromas were like the bell for Pavlov's dog. So just like the first time, I visited the doctor, I was shocked and careful at first, but then I just took the pills and eventually let my guard down again.

The LCB hearing took place about a month later. The judge called me to the stand. "Mr. Costanzo, did you serve people after hours?"

"Sir, I served a gentleman before two a.m., but he left the place after two a.m."

He then called Officer Patton to the stand. "Officer, did this man serve after hours?"

"Your Honor, I think there is some confusion in this situation. I reprimanded him, Mr. Costanzo, for what he did, and he has learned his lesson. Joe Costanzo is good for this community, and I don't think he should pay any further for this."

After a brief recess, the judge looked at me and said, "Mr. Costanzo, I have decided to suspend your liquor license for one day."

Shocked and relieved, I said, "Thank you, Your Honor."

"Didn't you just get that nice review in the *Post-Gazette*?"

"Why yes, Your Honor, I did."

"I thought so; I was looking forward to trying your restaurant."

In the hallway, I personally thanked Officer Patton, and that was the start of a good friendship that lasted for years.

I was able to finagle my suspension to extend the restaurant's one-week July vacation by an additional day, and no one in the community seemed to even know about the violation. I was learning how to play the game in the Rocks.

16

We have all had the experience of wondering what something will be like. Maybe you made the trip in August to look at the rosters on the school doors to see who your teacher would be and whether your friends would be in your homeroom. Maybe you tried to imagine your first day of work because no matter how many questions you asked during the interview, it was just the waiting room outside of the real job experience. As I imagined and planned and designed and built and interviewed and hired, at no time did I come close to comprehending what The Primadonna would become. I had not foreseen that it would be the *people*—not the building or the decor or the menu or anything else that was in my control—that would be the main ingredients.

On that crazy weekend following the review, we all found ourselves starring in unrehearsed roles that demanded more of us than we had imagined, night after night after night. That's when the Primadonna "family" really bonded. Each staff member was an important ingredient to our recipe of success, as were some of our regular customers. Like a great spaghetti sauce, the whole was greater than the sum of its parts.

DONNA

My beautiful wife Donna worked almost every night as my right-hand partner. At times, her practicality clashed heavily with my overly indulgent ways, but at the end of the day, she always found a way to stand by me. She was the quintessential wife from the 1950s revived in the modern world. There's not another woman on earth who could have been so attuned to my needs, nor as self-possessed and capable as Donna. I could trust Donna to interact with anyone who came through the door. From serving celebrities to breaking up a bar fight, she always conducted herself with grace and decorum. With her warm but strict demeanor, Donna was perfect for training and overseeing the employees. She also made our popular chocolate cheesecake. It sounds trite to say, "I couldn't have done it without her," but I couldn't have done it without her.

PINO

My cousin Pino's grandfather and my grandfather were brothers born in Calabria, Italy. Pino came to America in 1984 with intentions of entering into a somewhat more modern version of an arranged marriage and gaining citizenship, which he did. He didn't know the language very well, but he did know authentic Italian cooking. He was able to get a job doing prep work at Guillifty's, a popular restaurant in Whitehall, PA, and worked at Antone's Restaurant in the small village of Pennsbury, but I knew those jobs did not pay well. I reached out to Pino to ask if he wanted to work for me when we opened, and he agreed.

Pino and I were from the same blood, yet we were acquaintances when we started. More quiet and mild-mannered than I was, in his own way Pino was still demanding in the kitchen. He worked fiercely six nights a week, never missing a day of work. I appreciated his traditional ways and the high standards he set for The Primadonna. He hung on tightly when the influx of customers took us all for a wild ride, as we both desperately wanted the restaurant to succeed.

TONY

Tony Mastrandea, also an immigrant from Naples, Italy, was the most influential in terms of getting The Primadonna up to its level of excellence. Since his main job was chef at the Hilton Hotel, he worked part-time for The Primadonna at first. We got so busy that he ended up working full-time for me and for the Hilton. Tony didn't drive, so I would pick him up at the Hilton after his shift there, and someone would take him home late at night. He helped work on the sauce recipe with Donna, my mother, and me. He knew how to cut veal off a leg, deshell shrimp, debone chicken, and make great soups. He never wasted anything, adding scraps from veal and leftover bread to make meatballs. Quiet with an even temperament, Tony was great under pressure and fabulous on the line.

ANNA

A lady whom I barely knew came to my restaurant one afternoon and told me I should hire Anna, who was working at the bakery across the street. She said Anna was a great worker, but she made less than minimum wage and was treated terribly.

One day I went over and bought something at the bakery. On her knees scrubbing the floor was a woman fitting the brief description I had of Anna. When the clerk retreated to the back of the bakery for a moment, I introduced myself to Anna and asked her to stop over at the restaurant. When she came in after her work was finished, I told her I had a part-time job available washing dishes and prepping food. She eagerly agreed to the offer.

A typical Italian nonna who spoke broken English, Anna was already in her fifties when I hired her. Loyal and dedicated, Anna was an exceptionally hard worker who was eager to please. When we got busy, she started making the zucchini and garlic bread. After the four-fork review, I decided she should do full-time prep work. Anna loved being part of the kitchen staff and speaking in Italian with Pino and Tony. After we got to know her, she had a teasing sense of humor that endeared her to the staff.

The three Italians were a dream kitchen team for an Italian restaurant, but after the review we needed more help—pronto!

BETTY

If there had been a Fly-by-the-Seat-of-Your-Pants Award for the night after Mike Kalina's review, Betty Blatz would have been the uncontested winner. Betty and her husband Rick were young, likable bar customers who used to stop in regularly. They'd order bar food—zucchini, wings, and Ricci's sausage rolls—and would drink Budweiser. Betty was actually a housewife until June 3, 1988, the Friday following Kalina's first review. She and Rick were at their usual seats at the bar when pandemonium ensued from the too-large crowd that Mike Kalina tried to warn us about. Waiting customers were standing five-deep at the bar when Betty and Rick left their seats. Rick slipped behind the bar and volunteered to help as directed, and Betty surprised the kitchen staff by popping in and insisting that they let her wash dishes. They worked hard that night and matter-of-factly said they'd be back on Saturday to help again.

From that night on, Betty was with me to the end, missing only one day of work when Rick was knocked unconscious while trying to unplug the freezer in their basement during a flood in the '90s. Responsive and responsible, Betty quickly moved up the ladder from dishwashing to prepping food, then working the fryer and making the zucchini and garlic bread. From there she became a sous chef. She didn't have much experience with Italian cooking, but she had plenty of natural culinary talent, and working at The Primadonna brought out the best in her.

Although barely over age thirty when she started, Betty became the "mother" of the Primadonna family. Everyone loved Donna, but she worked more closely with me in the front of the restaurant among the customers. Betty worked directly with the workers behind the scenes. Quiet, focused, and not easily roused, Betty led by example. She got along with everyone and helped to keep peace in the kitchen.

STICKS

Another bar customer who became part of the family was

"Sticks" (Paul Kirsch), a tall, thin, single guy with a long ponytail who loved to work and make money. He worked at the McKees Rocks Eat 'n Park, a well-known family-owned, family-centric restaurant chain based in the Pittsburgh area. When The Primadonna started to get busy, Sticks asked if he could work part-time for me. We were happy to have him, as he had already endeared himself to everyone from the customer side of the bar. Eventually, he worked at least five out of six days while keeping his job at Eat 'n Park. He caught on quickly because he was a line cook at Eat 'n Park and had to move fast. He learned more from Pino and Tony. He loved the work and never called off.

ANMARIE

After church on that busy weekend, Donna learned from her friend Linda that Anmarie Herman was looking for a job. Linda said that Anmarie was "a nice girl and a hard worker," so Donna set it up for Anmarie to interview with me on Tuesday.

I began, "Anmarie, have you ever been a server before?"

"No, I haven't."

"Do you know anything about Italian food?"

"Not really. I've eaten Italian food."

"Do you know anything about wine?"

The answer was a simple, "No."

I excused myself and called Donna from downstairs. "Donna, what did you do here? This girl has no experience whatsoever. You can't play in the major leagues if you have no experience; you have to work your way up. We need people who know what they are doing."

In her "final answer" voice, Donna asserted, "You just hire her. Linda said she's a nice girl."

"You are out of your mind. We can't be training people. We are too busy."

"I'll train her. Just hire her."

Donna was right; Anmarie quickly turned out to be a great

employee. She was one of the most dedicated and outstanding servers we ever had.

HUFTY

I first met Hufty when he filled in for Dr. McKees Rocks as a DJ in the Bar Era. When we no longer had the need or space for a weekend DJ, Hufty asked me if he could be a busser. Hufty was already seven years older than me, so a busser job didn't seem like something a man his age would want to keep for long. I jumped at the chance to keep him around—his wit, humor, music, and overall intelligence made him one of those people whose presence was always welcome. Donna did not think Hufty would enjoy the work or succeed as a busser, as he had a laid-back demeanor rather the hustle-and-bustle attitude associated with a busy restaurant. He loved to smoke cigarettes, drink, and smoke weed. I knew, though, that Hufty had a history of being underemployed for his talents; he was more about doing what he enjoyed. He used to own a carpet business in the Rocks with an ad that said, "Where prices are always low and the owner is always high." He enjoyed being at The Primadonna, and we all enjoyed him. He turned out to be a terrific busser who pitched in making salads or doing anything else as needed.

LARRY

Larry Gregg was only fourteen when he came to The Primadonna. He knocked on the door one afternoon and said, "Mr. Costanzo, my name is Larry Gregg, and I want to talk to you."

"Sure, come on in. Don't leave your bike out here."

Larry walked his bike into the restaurant and said, "I live down the street, and I need a job." Athletic looking with dark hair and dark eyes, Larry carried himself with a mix of confidence and humility.

"Okay. Well what can you do?"

"I can do anything that you need me to do."

"Okay. Why don't you start by cleaning out my car? It's outside."

"Really?" reaching out his arms to give me a hug. "Thanks so much. I won't let you down." The boy's sincerity was touching.

When Larry finished, I inspected the car. He had done a good job. "Well, it looks like you know how to clean cars pretty well. How are you with dishes?"

"Sir, I can do it."

"Well, come on. Let's put you to work."

"Thanks, sir."

"No problem, Larry. If you take care of me, I will take care of you. That's guaranteed."

Larry was a good dishwasher, but as he grew in age and ability, he also bused tables, worked the fryer, and did prep work. When he was old enough to drive, he would run errands and deliver salad dressing and eventually learned to tend bar. I would let him take my Cadillac because he didn't have access to a car; that's how much I trusted this kid.

MAGOO

Magoo originally worked as a bartender at the Pine Hollow Inn but would come in with friends if his bar closed while I was still open. Like all the late-night bar crowd before Mike Kalina's review, we got to know each other well. Tall and thin with a goatee that made him look like a beatnik and round glasses that resulted in the "Magoo" nickname, he was an easy-going guy. There was a fire at the Pine that forced them to close for several weeks, so Magoo asked if I could use some extra help. I fully expected him to leave again soon, but at the time I did need the help, and he stepped right in like a regular employee. When his original workplace reopened and it came time to leave, he said he would prefer to stay if I still needed him, and I was glad to have him on staff. Quiet but a great bartender, Magoo remembered people and what they drank, and people liked him. He brought in his own little following, so the owners of the Pine Hollow Inn were not happy with me, but it was never my intention to "steal" Magoo.

THEO GEO

I ran an ad for a maître d'. The next day, I answered the phone at the restaurant. On the other end, a polished voice came through. "Good afternoon. This is Theo Giannoutsos. May I please speak with Mr. Costanzo?"

"That's me."

"I am calling in response to your ad in the *Pittsburgh Post-Gazette*. Do you have a moment to speak with me?"

I did a double take in amazement because when the phone rang, it was always informal, and no one cared whether I could spare a moment.

After a pause, I said, "Sure. Tell me a little about yourself."

"Well, I have been the banquet manager at Christopher's Restaurant for five years, and I am looking for an opportunity to grow. I would love to schedule an interview at your earliest convenience."

"Wait, did you say Christopher's as in *the* Christopher's on the mount, overlooking the city? Christopher's that is constantly receiving awards for amazing food and service? Is that the Christopher's you mean?"

"Yes," he replied with a laugh.

"Theo, I'm going home in about an hour. What is your schedule today?"

"I am free and available and could be anywhere you want me to be, Mr. Costanzo."

"Meet me there." I gave him directions to our house. Impressed by the applicant's speech and manners, I felt hopeful as I hurried home.

An hour and a half after his call, Donna and I interviewed Theo in our dining room. In his late twenties with slicked-back black curly hair, Theo was striking in his perfectly pressed dark dress suit, tie, and carefully polished shoes. He came with valuable experience and a wealth of knowledge. We hired him straightaway.

At The Primadonna, Theo always looked the part in a full

tuxedo, a rare sight in the Rocks outside of weddings and prom nights. He ran the front of the house with me and was the yin to my yang. We complemented each other's personalities perfectly; he was a very calm guy, and I was, well, not. He understood his role at The Primadonna and did not step on my feet. Theo knew that I was the main attraction, but that was okay with him. Charming, knowledgeable, and calm—especially under pressure—Theo could make quick decisions on the fly. He was able to appease agitated customers and had the ability to make people feel special. He was exactly what we needed at the time.

Although Donna was pleased with Theo, afterward she said, "We are short of cooks, short of bartenders, and short of servers, but the first thing Joe does is hire someone to do his job."

It still astounds me that these people genuinely became like family. We had our ups and downs, but in the end, we always had each other's backs.

Last but far from least, I will always credit Mike Kalina for The Primadonna magic that began in 1988. In another part of town, we may have been able to flourish on our own merits, but to get people to come to the Rocks, we needed him. We may have built the machine, but Kalina's four-fork review flipped the *on* switch.

I wasn't afraid of most people in the Rocks, but there were a few whose reputations gave me the willies. One such person was Kinzu. He was about thirty-five years old and was well-known in the area for his anger mismanagement issues, which in a town filled with hot-headed Italians spoke volumes. Once during a dispute, he drove his truck through the window of a local business.

Kinzu was not a particularly good-looking guy, yet he was always with good-looking women. What can I say? Some women apparently have a thing for badasses. Kinzu was dating a nice girl named Inez who was older, maybe forty-two at the time. The rumor mill had already pumped out that Kinzu was a jealous man.

One night toward the end of the Dr. McKees Rocks bar era, Inez and I were the only two left in the place around four-thirty in the morning. I was closing up the books, and she was at the bar drinking. I don't know how we ended up being the only people in the bar, but I was always focused on my job, so it didn't seem weird to me. There were many nights that I was there late with others. She asked me if I could drive her home. I knew that Kinzu always had a tough eye on her, so I said, "I'm so sorry, but I can't be doing that, Inez. You've got to walk home." My street smarts told me that Kinzu was not someone to whom I would want to be explaining anything, no matter how innocent the situation might be.

Switch scenes to right after I got the four-fork review. Kinzu must have gotten into an argument at one of the local bars with an older Italian guy, and right before dinner service, I heard screaming outside. "He's got a knife! Run!"

I came out of the restaurant, and right there on Dohrman Street, I saw Kinzu get stabbed twice and fall over dead in the middle of the street. He was alive and well one moment, then totally white and dead the next. It was the first time I actually saw the moment of someone's death and will never forget the look in his still-open eyes. The guy who stabbed him was standing there with the knife, silent.

Someone called 911, and I was out there trying to help with whatever I could to get this situation cleared up in front of my restaurant in broad daylight. There were eight or ten onlookers who waited for the cops and EMT. When they arrived, the perpetrator was just standing there. He admitted he did it, as cool and collected as any uninvolved bystander.

After the surreal incident, the Rocks buzz was that Kinzu's bark was louder than his bite, and that he wasn't a bad guy. I hated to see anyone lose their life, especially like that. Insensitive as it was, the timing of the review and my appearance on the street prompted the joke that, "Joe got four forks and a knife." Damn. Such was running a business in the Rocks.

17

When the business was going strong, I was on my feet at least seventeen hours a day. Going to the Strip District in the morning was not always necessary. The suppliers knew me, and I knew their products, so most things I needed to operate were delivered. In addition to not having the time to shop, the large deliveries that had become customary would have never fit into my vehicle anyway.

I'd pick up my clothes from the cleaners at nine and maybe have another stop, like driving to the Rocks Bottoms for takeout containers. By the time I got to the restaurant and unloaded, it was time for the chef to prep that night's food. The waitresses followed, getting ready for the next crowd by cleaning the place from the night before, memorizing the specials, and mapping out tables. Bus people soon joined them, setting up tables, and before you knew it, the doors were open for business. We served dinner from four to eleven, and then the bar stayed open until two.

When the last patron left, I would lock the door and breathe a sigh of relief. Then I'd get a second wind when I counted the money and closed the register for the night. I have to admit that no matter how tired I was, seeing that amount of money would be like taking a shot of 5-Hour Energy Drink. All that money! Sometimes I went home, but other times I'd have so much trouble unwinding that I'd go to The Snack Shop on Chartiers Avenue, a tiny diner-like place that used to be Barb's Luncheonette when I was a kid. Although known for cheap, tasty breakfasts, there was also a clandestine after-midnight crowd that came by for either the poker machines or the jollity. Most often, though, I came to spending that second-wind energy doing this and that around the restaurant before going home to shower and do it all over again.

After the restaurant became busy, the atmosphere and clientele changed a bit. Diners who chose to wait at the bar interrupted the camaraderie of the usual bar crowd. The removal of both the DJ and jukebox were necessary to transition to the type of establishment I wanted to run, but some of the regulars were not as comfortable. Danny Cannon reverted most often to the Vets, and Vic DaVita's attendance wasn't as steady. If he came in, he didn't show until later in the evening. I always tried to give him some attention, but it wasn't like the early days. Sometimes I invited him to breakfast after the bar closed, and we would catch up. Once I was apologizing for not being able to chat as much as we used to, but he said he was happy that the place was so busy. He said, "Joe Costanzo, you walked up to the piano and said, 'I'm going to play the piano for you.' And everyone started laughing until you started playing, and then they weren't laughing anymore."

By the time the dining business had picked up, Chuckie Richards was comfortable as part of the bar crowd and seemed to have shed his bashfulness. When what I call the "Bar Era" ended, he had no problem transitioning to the upscale atmosphere; it was more like he didn't even notice. He rarely ordered food, but when he did, I picked up the check.

Eventually, Donna had no expectations on an arrival time, since catching a few hours' sleep at the bar happened more and more frequently. Remember, there were no cell phones, but I promised to call before I left if I were going to be anywhere but the restaurant, and she knew she could reach me on the restaurant phone if necessary.

Before this routine, however, the first time I decided to stop at the Snack Shop, I hadn't planned to stay long. Donna had left the restaurant around midnight and was used to my coming in late. I didn't want to call and wake her, so I didn't. That night provided a great opportunity to meet a lot of new local potential customers. One Snack Shop regular treated me like a movie star, announcing my presence to the crowd and telling everybody to go to The Primadonna for the "best damn food in Pittsburgh." Another man affirmed the recommendation, shouting, "Best meal I ever had!"

Then I did what I do well. I went around meeting everyone, shaking hands, learning their names, and urging them to come down to the restaurant. I stayed for quite a while and had a good time.

When I got home, a very worried Donna was looking out the front door, arms crossed and tucked into the sleeves of her robe.

"Joe! Where were you?"

"Donna, honey, I stopped at the Snack Shop."

"The Snack Shop? The *Snack* Shop? You closed the restaurant and went to the *Snack Shop*?" she shouted.

The police pulled up as we were arguing.

"I called the police," Donna said, averting my eyes.

"Called the police? What happened?"

"YOU'RE what happened, Joe! I was so worried."

"Worried about what?"

"Think about it. The Rocks isn't known for safety these days. I didn't know if you were mugged going to your car or beaten and robbed in the place or *what* happened. I pictured some ugly mess with you at a police station. I even thought maybe you had a mistress and fell asleep somewhere. Every possibility went through my mind. Why didn't you call if you were going to come in at dawn?"

"I thought you'd be sleeping and didn't want to disturb you, sweetheart. Besides, I didn't expect to be there that long."

I walked to the squad car and told the police that everything was fine. I didn't want to say where I was, remembering the trouble I had gotten into for staying open late, even though I figured the Snack Shop was on their "allowed" list. Donna joined me, thanked them, and affirmed that we were okay.

A reporter once asked me about my "thought path" behind a decision. Geez. That just wasn't my style. There was no time to think, especially at The Primadonna. I had my principles, and I made decisions quickly based on those principles. When I say I had no time, I mean *no* time. I haven't even mentioned the never-ending interruptions once the business got off the ground. It seemed like if I wasn't running to answer a knock at the door, I was grabbing at the phone:

"I'd like to make a reservation for six tonight..."
"Mr. Costanzo? Sam Morgan calling from All Star Insurance..."
(Silence on the other end)

"Scout Troop 64 would really appreciate a donation..."
"We'd love to hold a bridal shower on a Saturday in May before the restaurant opens..."

"Linens!"
"Is it too late to make a reservation for tonight?"
(Silence on the other end)

"Um, I heard you don't take reservations, but it's my mother's eightieth birthday, and she..."

"Are you open now?
"Hi, Joe. Remember me? Vi from Mother of Sorrows. Could you give us another..."

"Hey, Joe—It's Don from the post office. Me and my wife are comin' down tonight..."
"What time do you open, please?"
(Silence on the other end)

 "Hi, Joe. I came in early today to set up since we cut it too close yesterday..."
"Hello. Do you take reservations?"

 "Sir, I've had no income for eight months. Just a cup of coffee would be..."

 "How you doin', Joe? I have your delivery. Forty pounds of chicken breasts..."
 (Silence on the other end)
"I'd like to make a reservation for next weekend..."

"Joey! Did you have the phone off the hook or what? I called you ten times."

"Sorry, Ma. No, the phone was not off the hook. I told you it rings all day."

"Then just don't answer it."

"Then you wouldn't have gotten me either, right? I have to let people know we're open, even if we don't take reservations."

"Well, I just wanted to tell you that I might be a little late with the pies. The toilet overflowed, so I got a late start. They'll be there by the time anyone orders dessert, though. Don't worry."

"Is the toilet working now?"

"Yeah. I called Frank the plumber. He just left."

"Good, Ma. Do you want me to call Theo and ask him to pick up the pies?"

"Oh, no, no. By the time they're done, Theo will need to be at the restaurant."

"Okay, Ma. Call when you are near, and I'll send someone out to the car to help."

"Ha! If I can get through on the phone."

One afternoon at the restaurant, I got a call. When I picked up, the person was silent. This had been happening about twenty times a day for a while now. I was about to hang up when I heard a voice for the first time.

"Joe Costanzo?"

"Yeah, who's this?"

"It doesn't matter who I am. I want you to know that I know where you live, and I'm going to burn your house down with your kids in it, you piece of shit."

"Oh yeah, is that so?" I replied, trying to sound undaunted.

"Yeah."

18

Saturdays were our most hectic nights. Donna often brought our girls down to the restaurant during the day so she could answer the phone or sign for deliveries while I ran around town replenishing supplies and taking care of any last-minute details before the big night.

On the Saturday afternoon following the call from the mystery stalker, our girls were busy filling salt and pepper shakers in the next room when Donna asked about the hang-up calls.

"You haven't said anything about those pesky hang-up calls for a few days. Did they stop?"

"Yes, they did, honey. They sure did."

"Good. I wonder why."

"I know why."

"Are you going to tell me, or do I have to guess?"

"Remember that I told you Friday was a crazy afternoon? After a number of hang-ups between the usual calls, another call came in. I picked up and said 'Primadonna' like usual, and there was silence on the other end again. I was about to hang up when a gruff voice said some stuff I won't repeat and then called me a piece of shit. I'm pretty sure that was him because there were no calls since."

"So somebody just wanted to tell you off?"

"Uh, not exactly."

"What do you mean by not exactly, Joe? Why didn't you tell me this? Did you say something, or did you just hang up?" Donna sounded worried.

"Yeah, I said something. I said, 'If you are trying to get me or my family, you'd better be packing because I will blow your fucking brains out before you even step on my property.'"

"C'mon, Joe. What did you *really* say?" Donna chuckled.

Donna's response let me know that she supposed I was kidding, because I did not own a gun and had never made such threats, so I thought it best to leave it at that. I hadn't told her because I didn't want to worry her. Why was I telling her now? I was so used to sharing everything that I slipped a bit.

"What did I really say? I used that old line: 'I'd tell you to go fuck yourself, but that would classify as cruel and unusual punishment.'"

"Did you really?"

"Maybe," I answered, with a wink. The wink was what we call a CYA (cover your ass) move, like crossing your fingers behind your back. I didn't want to lie to Donna, but there was no point in alarming her.

"Then what?" She was laughing now.

"Then nothing. I hung up. I didn't even think about it till you brought it up." That was *close* to the truth. It was concerning to me, but like I said, I didn't have time to think.

The staff now included seven cooks, eleven servers, four bussers, two dishwashers, two bartenders, and a maître d' on weekends. I was the captain of the ship. On average we were hitting about thirty thousand dollars in sales per week, even though we were open only for dinners and closed on Sunday in an eighty-three-seat restaurant. I knew the power that Mike Kalina held through his reviews and was always mindful that his nod was key to my success. Mike Kalina's praise was the "secret ingredient" that made food taste better. I have this imaginary vision of an experiment in psychology. You'd have to start with diners who read Kalina's reviews. The participants could eat and rate food that they were told came from a restaurant with a Kalina two-fork review. Then have the same participants taste food from the same source but tell them it was from a restaurant with a Kalina five-fork review. Ask them to rate it. I'd bet a lot of dough that the food would be rated much higher when people thought Kalina loved it. Don't get me wrong—our food was great—but what I call "The Kalina Effect" made it greater.

When business used to be slow, I met with a lot of resistance from family and staff about the no-reservations policy. When anyone called, I always had the same response—"Thank you, but it's first-come, first-served." I had a vision from the start, and it was coming to fruition. The restaurant was full on weeknights and packed on weekends, with a steady line outside. Staff who were with me from the start were amazed that it was all playing out the way I had planned, and newer hires were excited to be working at one of the hottest spots in town. Everyone was making good money, and there was new joy in McKees Rocks.

19

One night as the bar emptied and I was about to close, I was taking liquor inventory to jot down what I'd need to buy the next day. While my back was turned, two people slid into the restaurant. I heard, "Joe, can we get a couple of drinks?"

I turned around to find a regular customer, Frankie, with a girl I had never seen before. "Jesus, Frankie, you scared the hell out of me! I'm on my way out."

Frankie was a good customer who came in every week with his wife and two children for spaghetti and meatballs. His family had a name in the Rocks. Frankie's father owned a local lawn-mower repair shop in the small township of Stowe, which was laughable because few people's yards were bigger than thirty by forty feet, if they even had one, and neighbors shared push mowers. Although Frankie's father Anthony was listed on the sign as proprietor, it was Frankie who could be found stationed behind the small store's counter. A busy bookie who was rumored to have his hand in a lot of other unscrupulous things, everyone knew not to mess with Frankie, and I knew the game. I would send out free appetizers *and* dessert for Frankie's family and donated food to any "business" meeting Frankie ever held.

"Well, hello to you, too, Joe. This is my friend Heather."

Clearly intoxicated, Frankie's "friend" held onto his shoulder for balance. The woman's red stiletto heels and black-and-white checkered mini skirt showed off her toned legs. Her tight, low-cut tank top matched her shoes and nails, exposing enough buoyant cleavage to show off her store-bought boobs. Caked-on eyeliner and false lashes made the whites of her eyes pop, even in the darkness of the night. Brunette roots peeked through her otherwise long, blond hair. She seemed an unlikely date for Frankie, a stout middle-aged guy with a receding hairline and a gut.

"Mr. Costanzo, Frankie tells me that you have quite the place here," cooed Heather.

"Thanks; I try." Walking away, I added, "You two have a good night, okay?"

Frankie followed closely behind, struggling awkwardly to hold up his arm candy. "Listen, Joe, I promise we'll be out in a little while—just a couple drinks."

The young woman stumbled over her spiked heels. Frankie hoisted her over his shoulder, and as he did, she let out a playful scream.

"Frankie, the cops are on my tail here. I have two after-hours citations, and I can't afford a third. I've got a family to feed."

Frankie put Heather down and balanced her against the building. He reached back into his pocket and pulled out a wad of one-hundred-dollar bills. He counted to five and handed the money to me.

"Frankie, I can't accept this," I said, pushing back Frankie's hand in a gentle, soothing manner. "Listen, just come in, but one drink and then you leave. Got it?"

"Thanks, buddy; I owe you."

I opened the door, and the woman tripped over the step, toppling face down into the restaurant, revealing her nearly bare ass, except for a tiny black thong that I couldn't help thinking looked painful. I quickly looked away as to not embarrass her, but she didn't seem fazed. Magoo perked up from behind the bar and ran to help, but the woman was already back on her feet.

"Magoo, get these two a drink on me, okay?"

"Yeah, sure." Magoo looked puzzled.

I went into my office downstairs, and Magoo appeared within seconds.

"Why does Frankie have that girl from Silkies in here?"

"Silkies? She's a stripper? Christ. Just keep an eye on them for me. I hope they'll be on their way soon. I'll be up in a bit."

"Will do."

Like a prize, Frankie blatantly eyed Heather up and fed her drinks. With more alcohol, the girl loosened up and started dancing on the bar. "Turn that radio up," Frankie directed to the bartender. Magoo turned it up just enough to avoid confrontation. Frankie pulled out his wallet and got out his wad of cash. At first it seemed like a joke, but then the stripper started to strip, layer by layer—shoes, stockings, earrings, bracelets—and Frankie handed her a hundred-dollar bill. She teased, pulling her top halfway up, tugging it back down, then pulling it up and over her head, exposing a black, lacy bra—another hundred.

The Primadonna had just turned strip club. According to what Magoo told me later, Frankie erupted in drunken cheers as the young woman swung her leg over her head, leaving almost nothing to be imagined. Meanwhile, I knew if I could hear the commotion from my office downstairs, the cops could probably hear it from outside.

When I got upstairs, I found the barely clad woman and an intoxicated Frankie on top of the bar dancing. Frankie leaned in to try to grab her, but the girl clearly dodged his attempts, flirtatiously at first, but then with suddenly angry looks.

"Frankie, come here a second," I called. "I want to show you something in the kitchen."

"Can't you see I'm a little busy?"

"Just trust me."

Reluctantly, Frankie clumsily climbed down from the bar and followed me back to the kitchen.

"Listen, man, it's after hours here, and I don't want any problems. I already got the cops on my back. Don't piss this chick off."

Frankie looked at me blankly.

"Have one more drink and take her to a motel—I'll go home, and everyone's happy. You understand my predicament?"

Frankie nodded in agreement.

When they returned, Heather was sitting at the bar, clothed again, drinking her scotch on the rocks. Frankie sat down next to her, and the two started talking. He slipped his arm around her. The sooner Frankie sealed the deal, the sooner I could go home. Then Frankie tried to kiss her.

The girl yelled in my direction, "Get him the fuck off of me!"

I shook my head in dismay. This girl could make a scene, and in a blink, my business would be gone. Frankie tried his best to fix the situation with a little sweet talking. "Listen, babes, I didn't mean to upset you."

She crossed her arms and gave him stern look.

I stepped in. "What's the problem?"

"I'm fucking done with him."

"You are done with me? Why?" Frankie asked.

"I ain't talking to you; I'm talking to him," she said, looking at me now. "I'm done with him, and I want him to go."

"Look, you can be done with him, but you've got to leave with him. You came with him."

"I'm *not* leaving with him," she insisted as she stumbled off the bar stool, swaying toward the door.

Magoo came back with some coffee. "Here, drink this. It will make you feel a little better or a little worse, depending on how you look at the situation."

Heather sat back down and sipped the coffee. As she slowly calmed down, out of nowhere, Frankie leaped up and threw on his jacket. "Honey, you don't know what you're missing. Joe, I'll see you later." With that, he stormed out.

"No! Frank! Frankie!" I called out. Frankie had already gone. I ran to the door and looked out, only to see his car pull away. He must've been parked right out front.

What the hell? I tried my best to act quickly. I had to find a plan to get this chick home. "Where do you live?"

"The Rocks."

"Perfect. Magoo will take you home."

There was a reason that Magoo was a bartender. He tasted every drink before he poured. Working on his fourth DUI violation, he'd been banned from driving a vehicle. Since he lived too far to walk, he bought a scooter. Riding it in the streets probably bordered on the illegal, but in the Rocks, what didn't?

Magoo laughed, holding up his cup of coffee, "Joe, you want *me* to take her home? I'm shit-faced, too, man." Magoo gathered his wallet and keys and staggered out the door.

"Okay, looks like it is just me and you, and we've got to go *now*."

"I have to go the bathroom," Heather muttered.

For thirty minutes, I paced between the bathroom door and the front window, convinced the cops would arrive any second. Finally, I knocked on the door. "Everything all right in there?"

No reply.

After a couple minutes, I knocked again. Still nothing. Now I was really worried. What happened? Was she dead?

"Okay, I'm coming in." I entered the women's bathroom and found Heather naked except for the lacy bra, slumped over and fast asleep on the toilet. She hadn't even bothered to close the stall door.

I tapped her on the shoulder, and she woke, startled. "Where's my pants?"

"You didn't come in here with pants."

"Yes, I did."

"No, you didn't. You were wearing a skirt."

Heather seemed to remember. Her clothes were slung over the stall's side wall. She put her clothes on with some assistance but couldn't walk, so I had to pick her up until we got to the booth closest to the front door, where I put her down.

"Look, I'm going outside. I'm going to lock this door. I'll get my car and pull it around front. Then I'll be back in to help you to the car and take you home. Don't move until I come back. Understand?"

She nodded.

I stepped outside and furtively looked around. It was almost four o'clock, and a visibly drunk girl waited in my restaurant. If the cops weren't there, maybe Donna would be. How could I explain my innocence in this mess? What if the girl was sharp enough to change her story? Who would believe me?

I pulled the car around and walked in to get the girl. Then I gave her a little pep talk. "Listen, as soon as I open this door, you have to look sober. My car is the first car out on the road here, but we need to get you into the car. Got it?"

She nodded.

I unlocked the front door and took a deep breath. Rethinking, I said, "Wait here for one second."

Taking a good look around, I didn't see any activity on the silent street. I guided the girl by the elbow, and we walked outside. Then I quickly maneuvered her into the front seat. As I got into the driver's side and locked the door, I looked around. The coast was still clear. I let out a deep sigh of relief.

"How do I get to your house?"

"I don't know how to get to my house from here."

Beyond perturbed, I said, "You have to know how to get to your house."

"I live by Norwood Inn."

I weaved the car up the bricked streets toward McCoy Road, only about a mile away. "Norwood Inn is coming up. Is your place on this side or past it?"

"Hmmm. Past it, I think."

There were only a few homes past the Norwood Inn, then some woods. "Is it one of these?" I asked, slowing the car.

"No."

"Then *where*?" I was growing more anxious as each minute passed.

I maneuvered the car one hundred eighty degrees on the empty road, then drove by the few houses on the other side. "Is it one of these?"

"There," she pointed, looking ahead. "I turn by that yellow church and that playground. It's on McKinley."

"Do you mean McKinney? I don't know a McKinley Street."

"Maybe that's it. I haven't lived here long."

I made a turn into the hilly section of streets called Norwood, or Little Italy of the Rocks. I was familiar with the neighborhood because one of my mother's friends lived there, and so did several of my customers. We also went to Italian festivals and dinners at Mother of Sorrows church and parked at the bottom of this street. I came to the crest of McKinney, where we could turn left or right. "Now which way do I go?"

No answer. I looked at Heather and saw her eyes were closed.

"Hey, wake up! Which way now?"

"I think that way," Heather mumbled as she pointed right. As we headed down the hill, she corrected herself. "No, the other way. I can see downtown from my house. That's not downtown."

"No, it's not," I replied, but I couldn't turn around in the narrow street. I rounded the block and turned the other way. "What's the number?"

Heather slurred what sounded like, "Three or five, maybe."

The street extended only one block each way from the crest of the hill, and the numbers I could see were double digits—no way was there a three or five.

"There's no three or five here. Which is your house?"

"I said thirty-five. It's red brick."

"Most of these are red brick. You don't even know your house?"

"It's hard to tell in the dark."

I drove very slowly, waiting for some recognition.

"There's a garden across the street. I think that's it," Heather said, pointing.

Oh, no. Steep steps. "Are you sure?" I asked, not wanting to make matters worse by going to the wrong house.

"I think so," she answered weakly.

There were no nearby parking spaces, so I double-parked, not expecting any traffic at this hour. Heather stumbled out of the car. She still couldn't walk. I knew I couldn't just leave her. Not only were the houses here physically close with only a walkway between each, but the people were close as well. Any sound would send someone looking out the window. If anyone inquired and Heather mentioned her drinks at The Primadonna, I would be screwed. I quickly jumped out of the car to help her. "Where are your keys?"

"In my purse."

I rooted through the junk in Heather's purse and finally came up with her keys. Then I dragged her up the flight of about a dozen crooked concrete steps to another half dozen wooden steps leading onto the front porch. I wanted to open the door and throw her into the house and be done. It was easier to keep my feet quiet than it was my breath; I was completely winded. She fumbled to open the door and yelled, "Jake, I'm home."

My heart just about stopped. I froze, only to find a cat padding toward her. "Hi, Jakey," she fussed as she picked up the cat.

"Oh my God, you could have warned me. I thought you were calling to your boyfriend. Or your husband. The mind races in these situations."

I turned around to leave, and the woman grabbed my arm. "Stay for a drink."

"No, thank you. I'm out of here."

"C'mon stay. I can get make us a drink. I have to thank you."

"Look, maybe some other time. I have to get going." Heather grabbed my arm, but I quickly pulled away. "I'm double-parked, remember?"

I slid into the car, making the sign of the cross. I drove slowly to the bottom of the street before closing the car door, trying to avoid making any sound. I made the sign of the cross a couple more times, then folded my hands, pointing them upward while mumbling a prayer of gratitude.

Fifteen minutes later, I tip-toed up the stairs of my house and into the bedroom. Donna was sitting up in bed with a book on her lap, waiting. "Where the hell were you, Joseph Costanzo? Why didn't you call if you knew you were going to be late? I got up for a drink of water and couldn't believe what time it was! I called the restaurant, but no one answered. Where were you? Some strip joint or something?"

I couldn't help a weak chuckle. "Well, that's actually pretty close, but not by choice. Donna, I really need to get to sleep. I'm the victim of circumstances. This will all make sense tomorrow. I promise."

Angry, relieved, and exhausted in equal parts, Donna rolled over and scooched to the edge of the bed, signaling her irritation. Although I felt bad that I had stressed Donna again, considering all the ways things could have gone worse, I got off easy.

20

One evening I got a call from a valued customer, Lynn McMahon, who was vice president of public relations for Children's Hospital at the time. Lynn said that she and another loyal customer, Sue Cardillo, were on their way to the airport with someone who was in town for a special event, and she was hoping that I could hold a table for them.

I had to respond with the usual, "I'm sorry, Lynn. There's already a line, and we don't take reservations."

Lynn persisted, "Joe, we're leaving the hospital now, and I can't think of anywhere comparable. I don't know if or when our guest will be back in Pittsburgh and ending our day at The Primadonna would be perfect. Please, can you hold a table for three?"

"That won't be possible. I can't bring someone in while people having been waiting in line."

"It would mean much. We'll be driving through in about twenty-five minutes, and we don't have much time."

"You can check when you get here, Lynn, but I can't promise."

I was curious about the mystery guest, but more importantly, I wanted to accommodate a good customer if I could. Looking around, I thought that if a table opened up in the bar area, people may not notice someone slipping past as they would in the dining room.

Timing was on our side, and a bar table came open. I told the busser to hold off for a few minutes. When Lynn entered, she caught my eye, and I immediately told the busser to proceed with the table.

I walked up to greet them, and Lynn said, "Joe, this is Jamie Lee Curtis."

I couldn't believe that someone of such fame had walked through my door. I wanted to say, "Holy cow, I can't believe one of the biggest stars in Hollywood is here!" but opted for, "Welcome. How you doing?" As I led them through the small bar area and motioned toward the table being cleaned, I explained, "I can put you right here, or you're going to have to wait."

Lynn looked to Jamie, who gave a subtle nod, and replied, "No. We will sit here. It's fine."

I sent out zucchini on the house. Of course the workers were all abuzz among themselves but were trained to respect the privacy of every customer.

Jamie Lee Curtis ordered Linguini Aglio and Oilio, linguini with garlic, olive oil, and fresh vegetables without the anchovies. She was stunning and unmistakably recognizable, so it was amazing that she was sitting right out in the open and no one bothered her. My only theory is that since no one expected a celebrity to be sitting in a restaurant in McKees Rocks (near the bar, no less), no one noticed her. People were wrapped up in their own dining experiences. I was so glad that they were able to have a normal, uninterrupted dining experience, something rare for celebrities of her status.

Afterward, Lynn told us that Ms. Curtis noticed a few people in the waiting area near the bar looking and whispering, so she said, "Time to go." By that time, they were finished with their meals anyway. On their way out, they were met with a few smiles among those they passed, but nothing more.

We also learned from Lynn that when Ms. Curtis was previously filming *A Fish Called Wanda* in Pittsburgh, she befriended a young heart transplant patient at Children's Hospital of Pittsburgh. Sadly, the girl died. In compassionate response, she arranged for VCRs to be installed in every patient room at her expense. On this visit, Ms. Curtis returned to Pittsburgh to make the announcement about the contribution, hoping to raise awareness and garner more support for Children's Hospital, including a specific request for people to donate videotapes for the children.

Having Jamie Lee Curtis come to The Primadonna was an unreal experience, both motivating and affirming. To begin with, there's always something exciting about encountering famous people. In addition, it was gratifying to think that a discriminating customer who had the choice of all the restaurants in Pittsburgh thought enough of The Primadonna to bring Ms. Curtis in. Little did I know that she would be the first of many national celebrities who would grace my restaurant.

While I'm on the subject of celebrities, if you don't know who Tommy Lasorda is, you would have known if you had a TV or radio in the eighties and nineties. Lasorda was a Norristown, Pennsylvania, native who began his legendary baseball career as an MLB pitcher, then coach, and finally manager of the LA Dodgers from 1976–1996. Lasorda's colorful personality made him one of the most sought-after celebrities, but not only in the sports world. He was famous for Rolaids commercials in the eighties and went on to be a SlimFast spokesperson in the nineties. He made appearances in movies and TV shows, from playing himself in shows like *Silver Spoons* and *Everybody Loves Raymond* to playing Coach Cannoli in the Rodney Dangerfield movie *Ladybugs* and doing the voice-over for the dog Lucky Lasorda in *Homeward Bound II*. He was everywhere, and I wanted that "everywhere" to include my restaurant, so I wrote to him.

Not long after the visit from Jamie Lee Curtis, I received a reply from Tommy Lasorda in the mail, along with his photo. He had written on it, "You, the Dodgers, and the Italians are all great. Your Paisano, Tom Lasorda." I hung it right up on the wall. Not long after, I got a call from Mr. Lasorda's secretary saying the Dodgers were playing the Pirates, and Tommy would like to have dinner at The Primadonna.

We were all so excited that Tommy Lasorda was coming! We gave him the royal treatment, of course. (Then again, we tried to give every customer the royal treatment.) I sat down and talked to him for a while, and he told me that he didn't even have a game until the next day; he flew in early to come to the restaurant. That really made me believe in our jingle, coined the night of Mike Kalina's visit by the kitchen staff—"Primadonna dreamin' was becoming a reality!"

21

Once business picked up, every night was like a warm class reunion or a gala event. We never knew who was going to come through that front door—an old classmate, a sports hero, a favorite neighbor, a local broadcaster, a former teacher, a dignitary, a distant cousin, or a movie star. Local news personalities like Fred Honsberger and Ray Tannehill found their way to the restaurant. Not only were they coming to The Primadonna, but we were making them happy with our food and our service. Everyone wants to feel important, and my goal to make each customer feel important was returned to me ten-fold as customers paid back their appreciation in words and dollars. And I was feeling very important, too.

Describing the kitchen as a "flurry of skillets, pans, fast-moving arms and knives spiced with laughter and conversation in both Italian and English," Jim McKay's 1988 piece "Menu for Success" in the *Post-Gazette* captured the atmosphere at the time. He added, "Taped on the door leading to the dining room is a purple 'panic button,' a gag to cut tension."

And tension there was! McKay quoted me at length:

> It seems like a glamour-type job, but it's a lot of hard work. People don't realize there's a ton of stress. You must be constantly concerned about everything that goes on in the place. There's pressure to make a living because there's such

overhead. It costs money for quality food and you have to pay someone to cook it and someone to serve it. Every day you have to be concerned. If I get home by 4:30 (a.m.), that's early. Then I'm up at 10 a.m. to start another day . . . But I'm happier. For one, I have a feeling of self-worth that I've accomplished something in my life, something as far as I'm concerned that a lot of people couldn't do. It gives me a feeling of confidence and security. Success brings disadvantages. You don't spend any time with your children or your wife . . . I have fought with my wife more in the two and a half years that I've been here than the previous twelve that we've been married because of the constant pressure and the struggle of running the business and the strenuous hours.

Looking back, most of those early fights could have been avoided if I would have changed my lens. Donna was *exactly* who I needed to help me get out of my own way when running the restaurant. I loved her, I respected her decisions, and I wanted her by my side. I needed her, but I also didn't like to admit it. After all, the restaurant was *my* idea, and it had taken effort to even get her to buy into it. Maybe that's what made me so defensive when she'd make suggestions, or maybe it was just my personality. In either case, disagreements were inevitable because we operated so differently, and there were decisions to be made on any given day.

There was so much pressure in the restaurant to give impeccable service that it put a lot of strain on everyone. Although I know that mistakes are part of learning, I also believed that if we were going to be the best and were going to make the most money, we *could not* make mistakes. If the servers did something wrong, I wanted them to let me know right away so I could personally make amends with the customer. This didn't always happen. Sometimes the servers would try to cover it up. When I would go to the table and ask if everything was okay, I would find out the truth. A server forgot to put an order in. A server missed a food allergy. A server messed up how the customer wanted their steak cooked.

If it got back to me that a server made a mistake, or if I found out on my own, I would lash out at them. Normally, the servers would be standing hunkered in the kitchen. I would grab the server, and they would regret not telling me the truth. "You fucking messed up this person's birthday and didn't even tell me? I had to find it out by going over there?" Magoo called it my "passionate Italian voice." I would rant, "You need to be focused; people have a choice to go anywhere. What the hell is wrong with you? What do you not get?"

If Donna walked into the kitchen when someone was shrinking in horror as I was completely in their face, she would jump in and rescue the server. One time she even grabbed me and twisted my tie. Rather than telling me to stop or even addressing the person in question, she'd join their cause. "Get out of here," she'd say to me, matter-of-factly. "You are distracting us, and we are all busy here." A couple times Donna sent me downstairs to my office. That didn't happen often because I soon realized that I couldn't afford the timeout.

My quick temper wasn't limited to Primadonna employees. On a busy afternoon as the cooks were preparing for our four o'clock opening, the restaurant stove was broken. An older repairman came in to fix the stove. It was his first time back to the place since Nick Fusco owned it, so I welcomed him, gave him a little tour, and got him something to drink. The man seemed less than pleased and was ready to get on with his work. I escorted him back to the stove, and he went about his business.

I had a way of infusing energy into my employees where everyone had a strong sense of who they were and what they were working for. This bred success, and it was my responsibility to maintain it. I started ranting and raving about something that had happened the previous night and everyone was laughing as I recanted the situation. As I was telling the story to illustrate a point, I overheard someone yell, "Shut up!" It was coming from under the stove, and everyone went silent.

No one ever interrupted me, let alone told me to shut up, especially not on my turf. I walked over to the stove and said, "Excuse me. Are you talking to me?"

"Yeah. Shut up. I'm trying to work here."

"Oh, you are trying to work here?"

"Yeah."

"You look at me when I'm talking to you."

The guy wheeled out from under the stove and looked up at me as he lay on the ground.

I bent down, pointed my finger in the guy's face, and said, "This is my place, and no one tells me what to do. I'm paying you to do a job, so *you* need to shut up."

"I'm leaving," the guy grumbled.

"Do whatever you the fuck you want. Get out of here!"

The guy was so blown away that he ran out of the restaurant leaving his tools behind. He must have learned his lesson because he didn't even return for them. Luckily for us, the stove was working after he left.

Do I regret saying and doing some of those things? Yes. Well, maybe. I felt I had a name to live up to. I needed to be the top guy and would stop anyone in my path, even if their intentions were good.

Despite my shortcomings, most nights laughter and a sense of accomplishment quickly counterbalanced the stressors. It was gratifying to see the staff share the fruits of The Primadonna's success. An ego or a personal conflict may have gotten in the way of a few, but most of the employees benefited in multiple ways, from feeling the joy of a job well done to a great paycheck to bragging rights, working at the city's most trending restaurant before people used the word *trending*.

22

Since I follow sports religiously, one of the biggest rewards of having the restaurant was hosting the sports figures I admired. When St. Joseph's played Duquesne in basketball, I recognized Phil Martelli from the St. Joe's coaching staff as he came in. I introduced myself and asked how he knew about the restaurant. Martelli told me the hotel concierge had recommended it. The next afternoon, I drove to the hotel, found the concierge, and thanked him for the recommendation. I asked if he himself had been to The Primadonna, and he had not. I gave him a $50 gift certificate and invited him to the restaurant. He came for dinner, as did many more hotel guests thanks to his good word. I repeated this strategy to garner other concierge recommendations, and because the restaurant delivered on its promises, everyone was happy.

The cavalcade of sports stars who began to frequent The Primadonna gave me a thrill that never grew old. Tom Barrasso, freshly traded from the Buffalo Sabres to the Pittsburgh Penguins during the '88–'89 season, found a seat at the Primadonna bar. The only goalie to ever play in the NHL directly from high school without some other form of professional hockey first and eventually the first American goalie to record three hundred NHL wins, Barrasso was a quiet guy who drank and ate at the bar, as did his teammate, left wing Kevin Stephens.

Friendly and down-to-earth, Andy Russell, 1971 Steelers MVP, famed member of the Steel Curtain, seven-time Pro Bowl player, author, and business leader, made Pittsburgh his home and visited The Primadonna many times. Teammate Rocky Bleier, who played in the first four Steeler Super Bowl victories and caught the touchdown pass from Terry Bradshaw that gave Pittsburgh the lead during Super Bowl XIII, was another ex-Steeler who settled in Pittsburgh and became a Primadonna customer. Like Russell, Bleier was also a Vietnam Army veteran, author, speaker, and businessman. The Honorable Dwayne D. Woodruff, another all-time Steelers great, is now a judge for the Allegheny County Court of Common Pleas. He sat in a booth in the bar away from the crowd. No fanfare, classy guy. He always made a point of saying hello to me, though. It was a privilege to serve these Renaissance men, some of whom I had admired since my high school days. Younger but of the same lineage, active Steeler Merril Hoge was also a customer. Ron Blackledge, former defensive coordinator, said, "The Steelers travel everywhere, and the best Italian restaurant is right in our backyard."

Bobby Priddy, who played for several MLB teams, was a fan of The Primadonna. He once said to me, "You took a minor league restaurant, and you took it to the major leagues. It is almost impossible to do what you did." Jim Leyland, then manager of the Pittsburgh Pirates, used to dine at the restaurant several times a year.

Former Major League Baseball player and then pitching coach of the LA Dodgers, Ron Perranoski, had come to The Primadonna straight from the stadium after a Pirates-Dodgers game. Most people, celebrities especially, prefer not to be bothered when dining out, but Ron was as interested in us as he was in the food. A big, gregarious, sociable guy, he sat right down at the bar and talked with the bartender and customers.

Every time the Dodgers came to Pittsburgh, Ron would come in by himself or with another coach. He said, "Joe, I've been all over, and this restaurant is the best in the country." Even though he would sometimes be dressed in a three-piece suit, which was different from the normal crowd of bar characters, he was unpretentious. Our bar people knew him, and he became like one of the guys. Because he usually came in late in the evening, I was able to find time to talk with him and get to know him. Strangely, our talks covered just about any topic except work or baseball, the two things you might think we would be most likely to discuss.

Legendary college basketball coach Rollie Massamino was with Villanova when he discovered The Primadonna. He wrote me a letter and said he had been to places all around the world and had never been treated like this. He was a good dude—up there on my list with Perranoski.

Rick Sutcliff, a.k.a. "The Red Baron" who won the Cy Young award for the best pitcher in Major League Baseball, came into the restaurant, sat at the bar, and had dinner. I knew all about him but didn't recognize him. He introduced himself to me at the end of his dinner, and it was such a nice surprise. He also learned about the place through the hotel concierge. When I saw him as a broadcaster on ESPN in later years, I'd always think of that night.

Mike Gottfried, who was the head football coach at University of Pittsburgh, was a steady customer. He sometimes came in with coaches and at other times with family. One day he said, "I mentioned your name to someone the other day. They told me, 'You wouldn't believe that Joe was a really good athlete in high school.'" He was surprised that I had such a strong athletic history, and this opened up high school sports as another topic we would discuss.

On a Thursday night, the Chicago Cubs were playing the Pirates, and someone from Caray's entourage called to say Mr. Caray would like to have dinner at The Primadonna. If you don't follow baseball, maybe you know him as the wild baseball announcer parodied by Will Ferrell on *Saturday Night Live.*

A crew of five or six men arrived in a stretch limo around eight o'clock, and we sat them at the round table in the dining room. Caray introduced himself before I could say who I was, and with a firm handshake, he said, "A birdie told me that this is the best Italian place in the city." I heard that he had opened a restaurant in Chicago, but I didn't know much about it until we talked that night. That first restaurant (there are now several), Harry Caray's Italian Steakhouse, was founded soon after I opened The Primadonna.

Anmarie took complimentary zucchini, roasted red peppers, and fried mozzarella to the table. I went over to check on things, and like Harry was friendly and eager to talk—my kind of guy. The first thing he said to me was, "Joe, these prices are too cheap for this quality of food." Then he asked if I knew who had won the White Sox game. Even though this was the '90s, information was not instantly available on the internet (if you even had a computer), and no one used a phone for information. We talked baseball for a good while, and he seemed concerned about other teams' performances, as the playoffs were nearing. It was fun talking to Harry Caray because his conversation voice was just like his unique announcer voice.

There are markers of success that ordinary people like me think would bring them great pleasure—things like wearing designer clothing, being recognized by strangers, or buying a new Cadillac. The kick that I'd get from such things was short-lived, though; I began to take all of that for granted. But the thrill of hosting celebrities at my restaurant never diminished.

In the way that almost everything about The Primadonna exceeded my highest hopes, so did my relationship with once-elusive food critic Mike Kalina. He began coming to the restaurant a few times a year, sometimes to review the food but other times just to enjoy it. Since his cover was unveiled once he introduced himself after the four-fork review, he liked to chat about food and the restaurant industry when he visited, and a fast friendship ensued based on our common interests. I would sit down and talk with the Kalinas during their meals.

I learned that Mike Kalina's colleagues were restaurateurs rather than fellow newspaper columnists. It made sense; Kalina's livelihood was centered on food, as was the work of the restaurant owners. In 1988, I was invited to his baby's christening with all the big players from the Pittsburgh restaurant scene—the owners of Bravo Franco, Christopher's, Poli's, Piccolo, D'Imperio's, and more. The event was held at the Sheraton at Station Square, and we donated Mostaccoli all' Arrabiata for two hundred people. In a way, it felt like it was my own "christening" into the inner circle of the owners of Pittsburgh's finest restaurateurs.

The Primadonna was featured in Mike Kalina's 1988 Edition of his *Pittsburgh Restaurant & Food Lover's Guide*, in which he wrote, "I wish all Italian restaurants had the soul of this place . . . Prices are reasonable and the food solid, down-home Italian fare like my grandmother used to make." When people asked what kind of food we served at The Primadonna, I would say, "Peasant Italian food—red sauce, meatballs, gnocchi," so Kalina's comparing our food to his grandmother's was a high compliment.

One night Kalina and his wife came to the restaurant for dinner. They were already seated by the time I noticed them. "The Kalinas!" I exclaimed warmly as I stopped at their table. "What brings you in this evening?"

"It's a pleasure trip," responded Kalina.

We were as excited when Kalina came in for no particular reason as we were when he came to review because his presence was in itself a vote of confidence for The Primadonna.

After chatting a while, Kalina said, "Joe, word has been getting back to me from more than one source that you have been telling people that my review really helped you out. I genuinely appreciate it."

"Well, it did. I am very grateful for your endorsement. It changed everything overnight."

"Most people bask in their own glory and forget about the impetus that a good review brought them."

"I don't see how they could forget. That's like the cured lepers not thanking Jesus."

Kalina chuckled. "Well, they do. Not that I'm searching for thanks, but very few restaurateurs acknowledge my role in their success. I appreciate your enthusiasm, Joe. When you said I would find a diamond in the rough with you, I had no idea it was the truth."

In the spring of 1989, Mike Kalina came back as the Phantom Diner and filmed a review for CBS's *Evening Magazine*, a popular local KDKA-TV show that came on after the national news. This time he had a videographer and reporter with him. There were other customers in the restaurant, and a few asked about the camera crew, but I just said that KDKA was doing a little story. We were lucky that nobody seemed to put two and two together and ask if it was the Phantom Diner, as his anonymity was essential to his having an authentic customer experience. He wanted to be just any customer on any given day when he reviewed a restaurant—not a recognizable food critic who would be given the royal treatment.

Opening with "Regional Italian cooking is enjoying a rebirth in this area—thanks to places like The Primadonna" and ending with "Good garlic bread and a hefty house salad are offered with entrées at The Primadonna where a pasta dinner for two will ring in at under twenty dollars. On my scale of 1 to 5, The Primadonna rates a delicious four stars." The trusted food critic kept the customers coming.

As part of the restaurant's image, I started to work on my own image. I had custom suits and even custom shirts made; I bought $150 ties. Everyone at Larrimor's, Pittsburgh's high-end clothier with impeccable service, knew me by name.

On one of my trips to Larrimor's, I also had a personal shopper pick out silk shirts, business suits, designer shoes, and accessories for Donna. Modest and frugal, I knew Donna would never lavish these things on herself, so I decided to surprise her. I drove home with a car full of new clothing for both of us.

As I walked through the front door of our house, I had on my new tie and was carrying bags upon bags from Larrimor's. I put Donna's bags down in front of her and told her to open them one by one. As she did, she was eerily quiet, which wasn't a response I had anticipated.

"Joe Costanzo, why did you do this?" It was hard to read Donna's reaction, but my gut told me she wasn't happy.

"Donna, we've worked so hard, and now it is time for us to see the fruits of our labor."

Although we were able to afford it by then, Donna seemed stunned by my sudden attention to clothing and the accompanying price tags. She stared at me for a long moment.

Trying to break the silence and make light of the situation, I told her, "I want people to think I have more money than I actually have."

Donna's retort was, "Well, you're doing a great job of that."

23

The Primadonna's "house" dressing was an excellent homemade Italian dressing. It was a red wine vinaigrette family recipe replete with all the best Italian spices—garlic, basil, and oregano. It visibly separates into layers and needs to be shaken hard before pouring. I got the idea of trying to bottle and sell it. The idea, seemingly easy in theory, was more problematic than I anticipated. How would we get the dressing into the bottles? Where and how could we mass produce it? How could we move it out of the restaurant and into stores? Where would we get the UPC sticker necessary for selling it? Those were some of the questions we had before we knew how stringent the regulations were on bottling foods.

I had heard about a company in Erie, two hours north of Pittsburgh, North Coast Processing Company, which bottled dressings and sauces. I contacted the owner, who had been to the restaurant before, and he said that they could work something out.

I was initially excited about this possibility, but I should have known nothing comes easy. I gave the company the recipe, but when mixed with the recommended preservatives, the dressing just wasn't the same. They tried and tried to correct it, modifying the ingredients, then the preservatives, then the process, but nothing seemed to work.

I nearly abandoned the salad dressing project because it was time-consuming and frustrating, but we kept at it before and after restaurant hours until we were able to perfect the recipe and the process. Finally, in 1989, the first bottle was made and delivered. The bottle itself was a marketing tool, adorned with PR accolades, the Primadonna name, and my own in big lettering.

Now I had a dressing, but how could I market it? With a degree in marketing, I never went to an outside agency. I knew I had to get it into the grocery stores. Always one to go straight to the top, I went to the headquarters of Giant Eagle, which was the largest supermarket in the tri-state area as well as one of my suppliers.

"Joe, what can we help you with?"

"I just bottled the homemade salad dressing from my restaurant, and I want to put it in your stores."

Chuckling, an executive told me, "I commend you for going out on a limb, but we have to run a business here, and our shelf space is money."

"I realize that, and I guarantee you this stuff will sell."

"Will it sell? Possibly, but how fast it will sell will be the real question. How can you guarantee us that this dressing will move?"

"Well, listen, I just bought an advertising package with KBL, the local station for the Pittsburgh Penguins, Pittsburgh Pirates, and Pitt athletics."

"We'll consider it, Joe. The decision isn't mine alone. I'll get back to you."

I left with the feeling that I'd have to continue to push for this, but some time went by, and then the phone rang. I got the call from Giant Eagle headquarters saying they decided to give the dressing a try. I didn't even have to pay for shelf space, but since it wasn't a warehouse item, part of the agreement was that I had to bring the dressing in and shelf it.

Stocking the Giant Eagle shelves was a big job, and I knew I had no time in my day to do this, so I called on the expertise of my wife. The salad dressing became Donna's baby. She hit the road running, visiting every store she could think of, introducing herself and offering free samples, setting up displays, and promoting the product through customer samples and store coupons. It was no light work.

After only three months, the Primadonna label was in eighty-two Giant Eagles and local supermarkets in the area. The dressing outsold a few national brands quarterly.

The success of the dressing was also a great marketing opportunity. The Primadonna name was on the shelf of almost every major grocery store in the Greater Pittsburgh area. The label itself was a strong advertisement, boasting that the restaurant was voted Best Italian Restaurant in Western PA by the readers of *Pittsburgh Magazine*, *Pittsburgh City Paper*, and the *Pittsburgh Post-Gazette*.

When people left the restaurant, they were usually loaded up with leftovers and other goodies that I gave them. I began giving out eight-ounce bottles indiscriminately as samples, encouraging customers to buy the dressing at their local store. I didn't feel it was necessary to do a formal analysis, as the samples seemed to correlate with an increase in sales.

One time I gave a new face at the bar a bottle of salad dressing to take home. The next day the guy came back and said, "That bottle of wine was so delicious; I drank it all when I got home."

Several reviews mentioned the goodness of the salad dressing, but a letter from a one-time customer from Upstate NY, Ken Clute, is something I'll always cherish. In his letter, Ken wrote:

> . . . Your attention to customer satisfaction is unfortunately all too rare. It is refreshing to meet a restaurateur who makes dining an event. How fortunate for me to see your painted signs on city park benches.
>
> I must say, though, I have a dilemma. Since you gave me the generous gift of a bottle of your homemade Italian salad dressing, I'm addicted! I will not be able to enjoy a salad without it anymore. The thought of not having a bottle on my table at dinner when entertaining friends and family is a frightening thought!

How may I go about purchasing and have shipped, a case of this wonderful dressing? If you could respond to this letter, email, or telephone with your price, I will have a payment shipped to you promptly! You just tell me how much for the dressing and shipping, and I will gladly comply!

One customer, however, took the gift more seriously than his own life. While he was eating his meal, he got massively ill and started to slump over. His wife yelled for assistance, and I quickly called 911. The ambulance came quickly. Paramedics rushed in, and as the man was going out on the stretcher and they were hooking him up to oxygen, he yelled, "STOP!"

Everyone stopped, concerned.

"What's wrong, sir?" asked one of the paramedics.

"I ain't leaving without my salad dressing."

Some great local businesses hesitate to spend money on marketing. With a background in marketing before becoming a restaurateur, I knew well the importance of continually marketing The Primadonna in every way possible. Part of the success of the dressing, though, was being at the right place at the right time. When I began to promote the dressing, the Pittsburgh Penguins were about to win the Stanley Cup, and we were a major sponsor of the cable network.

24

In restaurant lingo, a neighborhood restaurant is just what it sounds like—a place meant to primarily serve local customers. Regional restaurants attract people from outside of the community who travel specifically to dine at those restaurants. Because of Mike Kalina's four-fork review, The Primadonna had quickly become a regional restaurant, but I needed to push myself and my staff out of that comfort zone to make my ultimate dream a reality. I wanted my restaurant to win national acclaim, and I knew the surest way to begin would be to get a five-fork review from Mike Kalina.

For the atmosphere to match the cuisine, we had some remodeling to do. Much-needed upgrades involved both equipment and furnishings. I installed a new linen closet, a six-burner stove and oven, and two doors from the dining room to the kitchen because things got so busy that servers were often bumping into one another, spilling food, and falling, creating hazards of all kinds. I purchased a Panasonic 7000 Point-of-Sale system that cost me twenty-five thousand dollars, making it easier to keep up with the orders and tabs and eliminating mistakes from messy handwriting. I bought more freezers and coolers because of the increased demand for food storage with the volume of meals being served. We put four new booths in the bar and waiting area along with all new cocktail tables, chairs, and barstools.

The plaques covered the windows from the outside and were spreading over every inside wall like poison ivy. I am certain the owner of S and S Trophy (the business that provided me with thousands of dollars' worth of plaques) got down on his knees nightly thanking the Lord above for me and asking only for my health and continued success. The myriad of awards and admired guests who were plaque-worthy thrilled me. Letters and notes of gratitude began to round out the collection.

I asked Pino and the other chefs to come in early every day and stay a little later each night. During this time, we would experiment with pastas. I knew that the key would be to put some upscale seafood and veal pastas on the menu. With tireless trial and error, we perfected our menu of thirty-two different pasta dishes, which was the most for any restaurant in Western PA. Many of the pasta recipes were adopted from things that my friends and family honed for years. The popular Pasta alla 'Bernabo, a hearty dish with penne in a pink vodka sauce topped with fresh prosciutto and Parmesan cheese, was named after my good buddy Donnie.

My girls both had entrées named after them. Maria's was fresh cutlets of veal served in a white wine sauce with capers, onions, olives, and sundried tomatoes with a touch of cream called Veal Maria. After the menus were printed, Maria questioned this choice, pointing out that she didn't even like veal. Too late.

Kelly Pasta featured green pasta in a pesto sauce. I even ran specials with family recipes like my mother's flavorful homemade pasta with tuna fish in a red sauce; Cioppino, seafood soup with lobster, shrimp, scallops, and clams made into a stock with red wine; and swordfish, panfried and baked, to name a few.

After enhancing the pasta and seafood choices, it was all about the wine. I searched carefully to extend the wine menu in both quality and quantity after my otherwise successful four-fork review said the wine list was "woefully inadequate." Wine wasn't my area of expertise. Growing up, we had wine with dinner on special occasions, but it was usually homemade red wine that my grandfather had made or one of his friends had concocted and had given us. I had to turn to the experts on this.

Ed Hart and the staff of the Wine and Spirits store across the street from The Primadonna were helpful in revamping our wine list. They also had some customers who were real wine aficionados who added their suggestions. "Stan the Man," Wine and Spirits' top salesperson, was a knowledgeable salesman who serviced many of the city's upscale restaurants, and he came to the restaurant during off hours for a tasting and information session. We focused on wines from Italy and California, with a few from Argentina. After gathering a nice mix of reds and whites, including a $300 bottle of Dom Perignon, it was time to ask Mike Kalina to return.

As much as Kalina seemed truly pleased with The Primadonna, he had said more than once that he had never given a neighborhood restaurant his five-fork rating. I sensed that was his bottom line on the matter, and that getting a five-fork review was more my idea that I would have to sell to Kalina. I knew that if I were to approach him, I would have to document the changes and additions I had made that would warrant such an honor. This time the pressure was a lot less because we were already so busy. With an already established relationship, I was able to call Mike Kalina to ask him to re-evaluate The Primadonna. Instead of making a new connection, it was more like inviting a friend back to the restaurant.

"Mr. Kalina, a while back you said you'd come down and rereview me." (I still called him Mr. Kalina out of respect.) "I have a brand-new menu and wine list. I was hoping you'd come down and maybe do another review." I knew I was in a great space because I was true to my word in making Kalina look as if he had truly found a diamond in the rough in The Primadonna.

"As I said, I've never given a local restaurant five forks, ever. It's all mainstream restaurants. You have a local restaurant, even though you are busy now."

I persisted. "I really don't. The Primadonna is now a destination because of you." I wasn't sucking up. I believe that giving credit where it is due is a way of spreading the positive energy that everyone needs to be happy and fulfilled in their work.

"I'll think about it, but do you understand, I don't give out five forks lightly. One thing I'd be willing to do is give you a full-page review without any forks."

"Mr. Kalina, I understand that," I acknowledged, "but again, I am striving for excellence here, and excellence is marked by another fork, not another review."

Kalina came back the following week. It was much less stressful this time because *we* knew and *he* knew that things were good. Donna waited on the Kalinas and another couple who had never been to The Primadonna. He ordered black squid pasta with sea scallops and red and green peppers in a garlic olive oil sauce. Others in the party ordered Lobster Pasta Alfredo (succulent morsels of fresh knuckle and claw lobster sautéed with black olives and mushrooms over steaming spaghetti in a creamy sauce), Veal Alla Pino (fresh veal, breaded and sautéed, topped with a zesty combination of mushrooms, onions, green peppers, and tomato sauce, crowned with a melting of provolone cheese), and Portafoglio-Delizia (pocket of fresh veal filled with ham, cheese, artichokes, and fresh mushrooms, simmered in our special brown sauce). I knew that Kalina drank white Chablis, so I brought out a fifty-dollar bottle.

When they finished their meals, Kalina motioned for me to come to his table and said, "It is amazing what you have done here. You are deserving of this. Something will be in the paper next Friday."

"Thank you, Mr. Kalina. I hope you liked it."

"Joe, call me Mike already," was all he said.

At that moment, I just knew we got the extra fork, even though he hadn't really said so. When Kalina left, I walked into the kitchen and announced, "I think this is happening! I think this is happening!" Everyone jumped up and down or gave a cheer, but we didn't have a moment to celebrate.

On Thursday night (technically Friday morning, October 20, 1989), I drove downtown to the offices for the *Post-Gazette* shortly before two o'clock, this time by myself, and waited for the papers to come off the press. As soon as they were put out, I grabbed as many as I could handle and ran back to my car. I leafed through the paper until I found the review, scanning for the fifth fork, which was there! I was ecstatic as I drove back to the restaurant where many of the staff, along with Danny Cannon, Chuckie Richards, Mark Broda, and Vic DaVita were waiting for me. I handed each one a newspaper and didn't say one word. I watched as they each thumbed through the paper and discovered what I already knew. I let them read it for themselves because I knew how much joy it gave me to do the same.

DINING OUT
It's just getting better at The Primadonna
By Mike Kalina
Post-Gazette Dining Critic
The Primadonna
801 Broadway, McKees Rocks (331-1001)
Rating:

Atmosphere: Super casual, comfortable
Service: Friendly, casual.
Wine list: Fair list of mostly Italian vintages.
Credit cards: Most major.
Hours: Dinner Monday–Saturday from 4 to 11 p.m.
Legend: 1 fork (poor); 2 (fair); 3 (good); 4 (very good); 5 (superb)

In the more than 10 years I've been writing this column, I've never seen anything like the success of an inauspicious restaurant in McKees Rocks called The Primadonna.

Many restaurants here are essentially weekend hits only. But no matter what night you walk into the garlic-scented neighborhood restaurant, it's generally packed.

The clientele ranges from locals to diners who've driven all the way from Erie or Youngstown to taste the myriad of Italian dishes in the restaurant's repertoire. And let's not forget luminaries who've dined there in recent months: Tommy Lasorda, Harry Caray (arriving by limousine, no less), Rocky Bleier, Andy Russell, Mac Prine—to name a few.

And just what is the winning formula? First and foremost the price to food-quality ratio is eminently appealing. In fact, in my rating system, price figures into the final analysis. That's why The Primadonna has become the first neighborhood restaurant to achieve my highest rating.

Location also figures into the picture—but not how you'd expect. Ironically, a less-than-appealing location has actually been a bonanza for the restaurant. Driving to raffish McKees Rocks to partake of pasta writhing in macho sauces that you can sop up with bread screaming with garlic is the ultimate in reverse gastronomic chic.

Last—but still very important—is the fact that the people who run the restaurant exude such honest charm it's easy to feel at home and become a regular overnight. I can't tell you how many friends have "adopted" the restaurant, thanking me profusely for the review that initially turned them on to it (June 1988).

I'm proud to report success hasn't spoiled The Primadonna. In fact, the restaurant has improved since I first gushed about it. There's a broader selection of pastas—more than two dozen—and the wine list has improved a bit (it may be the only spot in McKees Rocks where you can buy a bottle of Dom Perignon).

Service is still as friendly as it was when the restaurant

was at the height of its obscurity. Changes include new wallpaper and a new carpet, and glowing reviews are plastered on walls, on menus and in the windows. You can also buy a sleek-looking Primadonna jacket, T-shirt, or mug.

They still spin a lot of the pasta in the kitchen, from the manicotti plumped with ricotta ($7.95) to the surprisingly light, made-on-the-premises (!) gnocchi ($7.95 with meatballs).

The robust pastas are still as daring as ever, including a personal favorite, mostaccioli tossed with red peppers, tomato sauce, and brandy ($7.95); and the perfectly al dente spaghetti with sweet green peppers, onions, and homemade sausage ($7.95).

New pasta dishes include the light, satiny fettuccine Florentine ($8.25), in which the noodles are tossed with butter, cheese, spinach, bacon, and cream; the exciting spaghetti Caruso ($8.25), with chicken livers, fresh mushrooms and onions; seafood spaghetti ($14.95), a delicious mélange of pasta, humongous shrimp, bay scallops and baby clams in a piquant tomato sauce.

Also, spaghetti el Duce ($13.95): scallops, pepperoni, artichoke hearts, fresh mushrooms and onions united with spaghetti in a tomato sauce; spaghetti a la Caplan ($14.95): pasta with shrimp, green peppers, and onions in a tomato sauce; linguine with white or red clam sauce laced with bay scallops sautéed in butter with onions.

The menu still boasts some of the zesty dishes I remembered from my last visit, including fiery hot peppers stuffed with sausage ($3.50), my favorite appetizer. New appetizers include deep-fried ravioli ($3.50) and an eccentric rendition of mozzarella in carozza ($3.50). That's a salami-and-cheese sandwich dipped in a batter, breaded, deep-fried, and baked (traditionally, the sandwich is just sautéed).

Still very much in evidence is the gargantuan antipasto ($5.50, small; $7.75 large); the mouth-watering assortment of dishes made from veal cut from the leg, including veal Marsala, Romano, parmigiana, and piccata (each $11.50); and the seafood offerings. My favorite is a flounder Romano ($11.50), i.e.: simply flounder dipped in a rich egg-and-herb butter and sautéed.

I can go on and on. My suggestion is the next time you're considering peasant Italian cuisine, contemplate having it on the Rocks. McKees Rocks, that is.

After cheering and hugs, we all headed down to the Snack Shop with papers in hand. I went up to people I knew, shared the news, and celebrated by buying everyone breakfast. I got home around six in the morning and yelled to my sleeping wife, "Don! We got the five forks!" She did not mind the rude awakening. At seven, I was still up, calling any employees who weren't there earlier, my family, and my close friends. I wanted to tell everyone I knew.

On that Friday night after our service ended, we popped a bottle of Dom Perignon. Pino raised his glass and said in his thick Italian accent, "Primadonna International!" We all laughed and toasted.

I toasted, "To The Primadonna and five forks!"

We let two bottles of Dom flow that night. It was by far one of the best nights of my life.

25

To top off a great year, I was named Restaurateur of the Year by the *Post-Gazette*, and I celebrated by putting in a downstairs office. This was where I would escape when I needed a little quiet time to work or needed to yell at someone inconspicuously. I also bought my dream car—a brand-new Cadillac Fleetwood. It was the last year this classic car was made. I ordered a vanity license plate: 5 FORKS.

I don't pretend to know any more than the next person about what really happens when we leave this world, but I always felt connected to the people I loved after they were gone from the earth. Whether this is an inborn truth or just a hopeful desire doesn't matter to me. I had photos of all four of my grandparents on the walls of The Primadonna. I would get emotional when I reflected on how far the restaurant had come. I would thank them in a prayerful way. "Thank you because if it wasn't for you and your risks and sacrifices, all of this would have never happened." The opportunity of a lifetime really started with them, not me.

It was important to me to show gratitude, long before the benefits of an "attitude of gratitude" were being promoted as a path to happiness. To show our appreciation to the staff for their outstanding work and dedication, Donna planned a big Christmas party at another establishment for Sunday, December 17, 1989. I rented a bus for all my employees and their significant others or dates so everyone could party hearty if they wanted and not worry about driving.

I'd had to talk Donna into letting single staff bring a guest.

"I can understand spouses, Joe, but these other people will add a lot to the bill."

"Don, when we were dating, if I had to go to an event without you, I couldn't wait for it to be over. That's why I'm including them. I want everyone to have a great time." That explanation ended the debate, although Donna still shook her head in frustration.

Everyone met at The Primadonna that night. We all got on the bus, and Hufty announced, "I'm going to write a poem about the review we got from Kalina." So in the span of about a fifteen-minute ride, he wrote the poem "The Night before Kalina."

After we were settled and had gotten our food, it was time for a toast. Hufty stood up and started to read his poem. Everyone was laughing so hard that he had to pause between stanzas. He was masterfully skilled at coming up with something so clever in about the time that it would have taken someone to read it.

THE NIGHT BEFORE KALINA

'Twas the night before Kalina, and all through the house
Not a creature was eating, not even the mouse.
The menus were placed on the table with care
In hopes that more customers soon would be there.

Donna in her kerchief and Joe in his hat
Had Chef Pino cook fettuccini and this and that,
And what to my wondering eyes should appear
But seventeen people who just wanted beer.

They drank their beer but ate no food.
Joe wasn't busy, Donna wasn't in the mood.
Then out in the front there arose such a clatter—
A *Post-Gazette* car, make up a shrimp and pasta platter!
Then what to my wondering eyes should appear

But Mike Kalina and his *Post-Gazette* gear.

Joe was so happy that this critic came,
He shouted for waitresses and called them by name.
With magical tastebuds like those of a genie,
They started him off with a plate of zucchini.

When he laughed, he shook like a bowl full of jelly.
He ate course after course and filled up his belly.
He spoke not a word, eating pastas and porks.
He knew he had to give The Primadonna FIVE forks!

Then putting his finger upside of his nose,
The Primadonna smelled just like a fresh rose,
And I heard him exclaim as he drove out of sight,
"You'll be in my *Post-Gazette* column tonight!"

I loved the poem so much that I told Hufty, "I'm going to put this in the paper."

"Really? You would do that?" he asked, not sure I meant it.

"Hell yeah, I would." (I did. The poem appeared in the *Post-Gazette* on the following Friday.)

We continued drinking and having a merry time. As the night ended, I said to the owner, "Hey, the party was great, and I want to settle up with you."

"Sure, Joe. That will be twenty-five hundred dollars."

"No, no. That's not right. My wife negotiated with your wife, and the agreed-upon price is two thousand, all-inclusive."

"No, it's twenty-five hundred dollars."

"Bring your wife over here." He called his wife over, and I said, "Hey, you negotiated with my wife. The price was two thousand dollars. She has her notes from the phone call."

His wife said, "I never negotiated with your wife. I don't know what you are talking about."

I went to get Donna. In front of them, I asked her, "How much was this party supposed to cost?"

"Two thousand dollars. That's the price we agreed to on the phone," Donna reminded, looking directly at the owner's wife.

With a straight face, the wife responded, "I didn't say that. We never had that conversation."

Donna and I were fuming at this unexpected scam. I told the owner, "I will give you the twenty-five hundred dollars. I will never promote your business. I will never come back to your place, and I will tell people what you did to me."

That taught me a lesson about trusting people. Without concrete evidence, I couldn't even go to Judge Judy. That guy could have benefited by our return business and my endorsement, but he unscrupulously conned me out of my money instead.

For Donna and me, the night was tarnished because of the swindle, but the party was for our staff and they had a blast, so we accomplished our goal.

NOTE: Many years later, my daughter Kelly was with a date who took her to that same restaurant. She thought the food was good and liked the environment.

Kelly called me that night and said, "Dad, tonight we went to a restaurant that I thought you would like. Apparently, it has been there for a while. Since you took me and Maria to about every restaurant around the city, I can't believe you never took us there."

"Oh, yeah? Where? What's the name?"

When she told me, I said, "I'm well aware of the place. You were just a little girl when they ripped us off. Now I'll tell you the rest of the story . . ."

I have to forgive, but I don't have to forget.

26

After the five-fork review, the business grew even more. We were serving about fifty more dinners a night. Right around this time, I went a little crazy promoting the restaurant. With the money flowing so freely, I didn't feel the need to stay within any type of budget. I had T-shirts printed that said, "I survived the wait at The Primadonna." You couldn't read a local paper without an ad for the restaurant or drive anywhere in Western Pennsylvania without seeing a billboard with Joseph Costanzo, Jr., and The Primadonna on it.

About those billboards . . .

One Sunday Donna and I were driving to visit our parents on the east side of the city, and lo and behold, we were stopped in traffic near a billboard with "*Pittsburgh Post-Gazette*'s Restaurateur of the Year, Joseph Costanzo, Jr., The Primadonna Restaurant" and the address and phone number in huge lettering.

Donna did a double take. "What?" she exclaimed.

I just smiled.

Then Donna said, exasperated, "How much money did you spend on this? You are out of hand!"

It was one of those situations where it was easier to ask for forgiveness than permission. I said, "Donna, I've been hitting nothing but home runs with the business, and customers are lined up at our place. Why are you questioning me?"

I didn't mention that it was just one of *fifteen* such billboards in the area, but I made sure to carefully plan our route when we went anywhere in the following weeks.

With the influx of new customers, even more staff was hired. Like everything else, I was able to step it up a notch to get some cream-of-the-crop people, some of whom had worked at the most exclusive restaurants in the city. I had one consistent message for new staff throughout: "If it ain't broke, don't fix it. I'm not changing anything here."

Some people came in to interview who just didn't find it possible that I could pay them as much money as I said I could. One humble immigrant who was a chef at a little Italian place couldn't believe that I would be able to pay him six hundred dollars a week in 1989. He was the only person who passed up the job because he didn't believe that I could sustain paying him over time.

Great food and great service had become the two cornerstones of the restaurant, so much so that when servers used to come and interview, I would tell them that working here was the best diet ever. Within the first month, everyone lost ten pounds because they ran around so much.

Donna oversaw the training of all new hires. During the interview process, she wouldn't hold back on anything. Part of a server's job was to keep the place clean, and that included the restrooms, wiping down coolers, and emptying coffee machines. Donna would make sure folks were on board with getting their hands dirty before they got any further into the interview.

If people were okay with that, Donna threw out another policy that isn't widely used or accepted in the restaurant industry. To cut back on competition and to entice teamwork, everyone shared tips. At the end of each night, all the servers would pull their tips together and from the top, they would tip out the bus people and the bar workers, splitting the remaining tips equally among themselves. If applicants were going to walk, they would normally walk here, but those who stayed were glad they did. From what they and other restaurateurs told me, on average, they were earning at least double what other servers in the city of Pittsburgh were earning.

When a new hire started, they were never left alone. First, they followed Donna as she outlined all the opening and closing tasks that needed to be done. Then they worked in the buddy system, shadowing a seasoned employee who was already doing an exemplary job. For at least the first week, they would just observe. I wanted it this way because I didn't want to have anyone mess up on my watch. Before anyone could have tables of their own, they had to serve me or Donna, which I'm sure was more stressful than any of the clientele they could have waited on at The Primadonna. We would quiz them on the menu, prices, server protocols, and table numbers.

The staff had grown to around twenty-five. In this small space, each member of the staff was intensely focused on their own work while simultaneously being in a state of flow with everyone else. Like Steve Jobs and friends taking computers to the personal level or the Beatles each having their own talents but being able to combine them to create some of the best music of the modern world, on a local restaurant level, we knew something remarkable was happening. The synergy of The Primadonna resulted in something so extraordinary that I simply refer to it as *magic*. And like a good scientific experiment, it could be repeated over and over with the same results. The gratitude and praise that came from our customers and the food critics validated this.

I would spend Christmas Eve, Valentine's Day, and New Year's mornings and afternoons at the restaurant with Maria. Although we were not open for food or drink, the door was always open for gift certificates. I never advertised this, but everyone seemed to know, and people flocked in. A Primadonna certificate was a highly sought-after gift.

Maria and I had some important conversations about life while waiting to process gift certificates, and we looked forward to these quiet times together. I always kept up with what our girls were doing, but this gave me a chance to learn what Maria was thinking as she grew older. It was one of our too-few one-on-one times together. Most families wouldn't consider conversation that was constantly interrupted "quiet time," but we did. Everything is relative.

Despite the seriousness with which we approached our work, we also had great fun on the job. The sharp wit of a few key staff members made sure we didn't take ourselves too seriously.

Once there was a private party on a Sunday, something we did occasionally in the early years. We had made eight gallons of sauce and then poured it into a large container after it cooled. Somehow Betty slipped and fell into the sauce butt-first, although she didn't knock it over. Hufty spontaneously recited a limerick that we teased her with:

> I fell in a bucket of sauce.
> My dignity was lost.
> I ran out the door,
> They cleaned up the floor.
> I fell in a bucket of sauce.

Rumor has it that that was some of the sweetest sauce we ever served.

27

In 1990, it was time for renovations again, focusing on maximizing our space and expanding as much as the building itself permitted. Eliminating the old bathrooms in the main dining room opened up some table space. We blasted a hole in the wall and turned what was previously a storage area into two large, beautiful restrooms complete with marble floors and granite counters. During these and all renovations over the years, I never closed the restaurant, not even for an hour.

I was so busy that I didn't even have time to go to the bank but about every thirty days. At the time, Mastercard and Visa were not electronic; merchants had to keep a copy and turn in a carbon copy. I remember making a trip to the bank so I could pay the contractor, Paul Cichon, thirty thousand dollars for the restaurant renovations. I first gave the bank the credit card receipts, which totaled somewhere around forty thousand dollars, and asked them to issue a check for Paul. It all felt like Monopoly money to me because it came in and went out so easily. It was like nothing.

We expanded our staff again as well. A relative of Betty Blatz, Mark Kautzman, was interested in working at The Primadonna during his college years. He joined the staff with no restaurant experience whatsoever, but it turned out great because he was a quick learner whom we could train the way we wanted. I would say to him, "I'm not just teaching you about restaurants; I'm teaching you about life here." Loyal as hell when I needed something, Mark was always right there.

Mark could soon jump into any role at the restaurant. If we got into a jam, he would bus, serve, maître d', or deliver salad dressing. Customers loved him, and so did the staff. Like-minded people form quick friendships.

Like Hufty and Sticks, Mark was quick-witted. He knew Danny Cannon's number one hangout was the Vets Club, so when Danny would walk through the door, Mark would sing, "D-D-D-Danny and the Vets" to the tune of "Benny and the Jets."

One night when some of the staff were winding down around the bar after work, Hufty was telling the others that Donna wasn't happy about hiring him as a bus boy. Hufty shared, "When I got hired, I really had to earn my way. Donna didn't think I could do the job. I earned my way."

Mark said flatly, "Donna was right." The bar roared with laughter!

When Mark graduated from Robert Morris College, his girlfriend Tracy told him, "Now that you've graduated, you've got to get a job."

Mark answered, "I have a job—I'm working for Joe Costanzo. I love my job, and I'm making huge money." Mark was a keeper.

Donna and I tried to be thorough and meticulous in our training process; however, sometimes there were things that we just could not anticipate, and this drove me nuts. A new hard worker who started as a busser named Chris was about to spread his server wings and fly. He was the youngest employee, just turned eighteen, which was the legal minimum age in PA to serve alcohol. He completed the vigorous training process. Chris was told that I could be a very intense boss, but as a bus person, he was able to stay under the radar and always thought that people just exaggerated.

Chris passed the training process with flying colors, and on a Thursday night, he got his first table, solo. Ready with his pen and pad, Donna reassured him that he was going to be fine, and if he needed anything, just look back and she'd be right there. Donna stood behind the server station as he paraded to a four-top seated in one of the booths in the bar. This was usually Donna's proudest moment.

"Good evening, everyone. My name is Chris, and I will be your server."

The clients smiled back and then pensively looked through the menu.

"Can I get anyone anything to drink?"

"Sure. Whiskey sours."

"Just water for me."

"Iced tea, please."

"Pin-on-the-wall."

Chris repeated all their orders, "Okay so I have a water, whiskey sours, iced tea, and a what was that again, please?"

"A pin-on-the-wall."

"Okay, got it." Chris ran up to the computer and typed in his drink order. There was one problem—there was no button for pin-on-the wall. He summoned Donna's help. She had never heard of the drink, so she instructed Chris to let the bartender know. The bartender's eyebrows went up as he heard the request. He relied on his handy dandy drink bible to get him through. The bible consisted of over one thousand popular drinks and was the steady fall back (and lifesaver) for the bar.

Chris opened to "P" and scrolled through. He could find nothing. By this time, the clients were clearly looking for their drinks, and Chris had no other choice but to summon me. He knew that with all my bar experience, I had to have heard of the drink. He walked downstairs to the basement and knocked on my office door.

Employees knew to knock before entering.

"Come in," I called. "Hey, Chris, how's your first day of serving going?"

"Well, Joe, funny you ask. I have my first table upstairs and they are requesting a drink that no one has ever heard of."

"Oh, yeah, what's that?"

"A pin-on-the-wall."

"A pin-on-the-wall? What the fuck's a pin-on-the-wall? I've never heard of it, either. Did Magoo look it up?"

"Yes, sir, but it's not in his book."

"Okay, I'm coming up, and I will go to the table and find out."

"Thanks, Joe."

Chris waited patiently behind the server station as he saw me walk over and greet those at the table. I asked how everything was, and they said, "Great! We'd just like our drinks."

I concurred and said the hold-up was the pin-on-the-wall. "What is in this drink?"

The entire table erupted into laughter. "Pin-on-the-wall? I never ordered that; I ordered a Pinot Noir."

"Oh my, I'm so sorry. Your drinks will be out right away."

I heard the table laugh and jeer as I walked away, and I saw that Chris was holding back laughter himself. My first stop was to the bar, telling Magoo to pour this drink right away and get it out to the table. Then I approached Chris, who by this time was doubled over with laughter.

"Get back into the kitchen," I ordered.

Chris knew that he was in deep trouble because I could feel the red-hot look on my own face radiating to the top of my head. When we got back to the kitchen, I slammed the door and erupted. "What the fuck, Chris? I try to give you a chance and you screw it up at the first table? FIRST table! What is your problem?"

"Sorry, Joe." Chris was still trying to quell his laughter.

"You little piece of shit—you think this is funny, don't you? Well, there is a party out there waiting in *my* restaurant, and you're in the back laughing about making an asshole out of me and out of my establishment and getting paid for it. You think this is funny?"

Scared straight now, Chris replied softly, "No, sir."

"Don't you fucking talk to me right now. I'm not done talking to you. Don't you ever, ever, embarrass me in my place like this again! I don't need to have stories spreading about the incompetence of my staff. I will fucking fire you right on the spot next time. Do you understand me?"

"I'm sorry, sir."

"I'm not asking for an apology; I'm asking if you understand me."

"Yes, sir."

Donna came into the kitchen, grabbed my tie hard and said, "Come with me." Her look left no doubt that she didn't approve of the way I had handled the situation. She led me as far as the door to the downstairs and commanded, "Go and cool down."

With that, I stomped downstairs, and Chris went back to his duties, having learned a little about how seriously I took this business.

28

By 1990, great reviews, testimonies, and awards bestowed on The Primadonna provided top-notch PR that I didn't have to generate myself. I must also give credit to great customers and friends or customers-turned-friends, like Terri and Drew D'Allesandro.

Terri was an administrator with the YMCA, and Drew worked for purveyors of heavy contracting equipment. Terri and Drew were a striking couple, impossible to forget once you saw them. Drew was about six foot five with a head full of dark hair. Handsome and in great shape, he dressed like a GQ ad. Terry was his female counterpart with an enviable figure, blond hair, impeccable taste in clothing, and a beautiful smile. She reminded me of the actress Joey Heatherton. Their fun-loving, dynamic personalities, however, surpassed their head-turning appearances.

After reading newspaper reviews, Terri and Drew drove from Bethel Park, a much more well-to-do suburb of Pittsburgh, to test the cuisine. They came on two consecutive Saturdays, gave their names to the maître d', and waited at the bar. The wait was so long that on both occasions they drank too much and went home. The third time was the charm for them. When they introduced themselves to me on that visit, they said, "It's our third time here but our first time eating."

The D'Allesandros would come in once or twice a week, often bringing friends and family from outside of the Rocks. They would have a drink or two at the bar while they were waiting, have dinner, and then go back out to the bar for more drinks. Terri would usually order Chicken Marsala with a side of pasta, and Drew loved the hot banana peppers for an appetizer and the homemade ravioli for his entrée. Not scared off by the Rocks's clientele, they seemed to fit into both worlds—the upscale restaurant customers and the rowdy bar crowd as well.

Terri was hammered one night, stumbling into the bar from the dining room and calling for everyone's attention. The guys at the bar gladly complied. She announced, "I want to make a toast to love, sex, and Christmas." On another night, they brought her father in for dinner. He was a WWII German veteran. He looked at the menu and said, "The only thing on the menu is Dago stuff." He ordered the pork chops.

Just as Terri and Drew expanded our customer family, Erv Panik came on board, adding to the employee family. A big guy with a big heart, Erv was a social worker who worked at the Whale's Tail, a teen shelter and outreach. As everyone knows, such work doesn't pay much, and Erv had two kids and their mom to support. Although he had a college education, he was happy to wash dishes several times a week to help make ends meet.

Once when one of Erv's friends expressed surprise at his washing dishes, he told him, "Joe Costanzo treats us with so much respect. We all have a job to do here, and I have a good feeling about myself just washing dishes. It's great to be here and be part of something big."

When a good review was published, we'd always notice a spike in attendance. One such review by *Pittsburgh Press* food critic Betsy Kline described the state of the restaurant at that time in "Primadonna boasts a delicious taste of Italy." She noted, "... A good peasant sauce and a dollop of ambiance have launched many a happy venture, but few have done it as well as Joseph Costanzo, Jr . . . . Pace yourself because dinners are served in table-groaning portions . . ."

Mid-Atlantic Travel & Leisure featured one of our waitresses on the cover, hoisting a steaming trayful of entrées. The out-of-town writer described his experience as he waited in the line outside of the restaurant:

> "Are you sure this is the place . . . ?" A fifty-ish gent in a Hawaiian shirt assures us this is the place. "They say Robert Goulet was in last night," he says happily. "You know, a year ago, nobody knew this place was here. Now, some nights, you gotta stand outside for two hours. *Two hours.*"

Mike Kalina gave us another booster shot of publicity with a September 1990 article, "The Primadonna Phenomenon":

> When I wrote about The Primadonna Restaurant in McKees Rocks about a year ago, I noted that the restaurant was a phenomenon. It still is—and then some . . . When I first visited the place, a twenty-dinner night was considered a score. My subsequent rave may have helped bring people into the place, but it took owner Joe Costanzo a tremendous amount of promotional effort to keep 'em coming back. He has since built up a clientele that would bring a glow to the cheek of any restaurateur. There's a lesson to be learned in this. Rather than being a hindrance, the restaurant's location is a plus. There's something roguish about venturing into the Rocks for some down-home Italian food. But let's not forget the most important thing: the food, which resulted in the restaurant's being the first neighborhood Italian spot to earn my highest rating . . .

In another part of the city, someone else's curiosity was piqued as he began to read the great reviews we were getting . . .

Once in a while you notice someone who, without doing anything out of the ordinary, exudes class. Such a man was David Rigo.

David came in one day to explore the possibility of working at The Primadonna. He had read about the restaurant but was a little apprehensive because it was in the Rocks. I learned later that he had come to the restaurant to see things for himself one evening before approaching me. David had been working at Piccolo Mondo, a fine restaurant in the Greentree area of Pittsburgh. I thought, *Wow! This is exactly what any restaurant owner hopes for—a seasoned, well-mannered, well-spoken server to come in voluntarily.*

We sat down, and I showed David the numbers that we had been serving. Sensing that he would be a real asset, I told him he could help me, and I could help him. He went home to think about it and then called the next day and said, "I'm in." We put him on the schedule for Wednesday through Saturday nights.

David trained quickly because he was experienced. When he first started, it was strictly business and a bit of small talk. As he became accustomed to the restaurant, we became friends. During the day, David worked on art restoration projects, including church icons. We would discuss world events, philosophy, films—anything. Knowledgeable and well-rounded, he was a true Renaissance man, one of the most intelligent people I've ever met. If we ever needed something settled, David Rigo was our Google before Google existed.

David could serve, bartend, or step in as maître d'. He had a soft-spoken manner, very refined, but he was also quite personable. He quickly became the most requested server as well as a bona fide member of the Primadonna family. Hufty nicknamed him "El Magnifico."

A regular customer and his wife were arguing at home, and

she left to go shopping. The customer retreated to the Forest Inn across the street from the restaurant with his buddies, drinking. A few hours went by and the customer's wife made her way back to Kennedy through McKees Rocks. This all happened right around 3:45 pm, which was about the time that The Primadonna opened on that Saturday night.

Crowds lined Broadway waiting to get into the restaurant. The people were dressed up in suits, dresses, and other attire that would have been saved for funerals and weddings in the Rocks. The customer was nicely feeling his buzz, so when his wife, whom he lovingly referred to as "Duck," made the left-hand turn from Broadway onto Dohrman Street. He yelled, "Duck! Duck! Duck!"

The wife kept on driving, either ignoring him or not paying attention, but what *did* happen was that the entire line of people waiting for dinner hour fell to the ground, ducking! The customer and his buddies were laughing hysterically. Jeers were heard from the Forest Inn, "You just roxed those rich people!"

The customer could see the look of dread on the clientele, some of whom may have been on the streets of the Rocks for the first. Feeling bad, he shouted to the people in line, "No, don't worry. Nothing is going to happen to you. Duck is just my pet name for my wife."

Hearing the commotion, I ran out to see what the problem was. I was pissed. Apologizing and swearing under my breath, I opened my doors early, and the zucchini flowed to everyone.

Later that night after dinner hour, the customer came in for a late-night drink, and I joked, "Look, can you find a new pet name for your wife? We can't afford to lose any customers down here due to your lovers' quarrels." We all laughed our asses off.

29

As incredible as our employees were, not everyone who came looking for work at The Primadonna could "cut the mustard," as they say. The record for the shortest term of employment goes to an older guy I hired for the kitchen, who lasted about an hour. He was cutting bread and deboning chicken breasts when he said he had to go to his car but never returned. Another young lady shadowed for a few days, seemed like she'd be terrific, but pulled out because she said she couldn't see herself ever learning the entire menu or being able to memorize the specials.

There was a customer in her fifties who really needed a job and convinced me that she would be a hard worker, but in retrospect, was not a great choice. I realized early on that she couldn't work at a fast pace under pressure. She couldn't handle as many dinners as the other servers. At first, I thought it was just a learning curve, but when the other servers came and complained, I saw this was not improving over time. She was splitting tips but serving about half the number of meals as the other servers. I felt bad for her, as she was obviously trying, but I knew I couldn't keep her unless I wanted to handle a mutiny.

I should have fired her, but I was so concerned about her well-being that I came up with another idea. There was another restaurateur who came in for dinner who owned a smaller, much slower-paced restaurant. One day after his meal, I talked to him privately and truthfully told him the situation and asked if he could use her, and he hired her. I thought all was good until I heard that she couldn't do the job there, either. Then I felt bad for both of them.

There were workers I had to fire—a kid who was seen putting a bottle of liquor in his backpack, someone shorting the register, things like that. One server was having an affair, and her lover frequently hung out at the restaurant all night, dragging his meals out for hours. The other servers knew the situation, so eventually I did, too. When I talked to her, she said that she wanted out of the relationship, but he made it difficult. When she tried more firmly to cut all ties, he not only threatened her, but continued to come in and give her the evil eye while she worked. The guy looked sleazy, and I did a little digging and learned he had done some jail time for domestic abuse. We mutually agreed on her leaving for her safety and ours.

I was starting to understand that although I was the proprietor, I was also outside of the culture of the worker bees in the restaurant industry. Time and again, I had learned there were things the employees kept among themselves.

As I walked downstairs to go to the office one night around closing time, I saw a cloud of smoke and a cluster of employees huddled in the corner. I ignored it and took care of what I went downstairs to do. Afterward, I asked Hufty what that was all about.

"Mandatory drug testing. I told everyone to bring in their drugs and I'd test them."

"Very funny, Huf."

"Joe, that's what we call the Medicine Shop. It's where we relieve all the stresses of working in this crazy place."

"Well, that's good to know," I said, hiding my genuine concern well. "Please wait until after work and do that somewhere else, though. It's a risk I can't afford to take, if you get my drift."

Magoo reminded me that there were two wait staff interviews scheduled for the following afternoon. I suggested, "I think my new interview process should go something like this:

Do you drink?

Do you smoke?

Do you use drugs?

Do you steal?

Do you gamble?

Have you ever cheated on your husband/wife/ boyfriend/girlfriend?

If you answered yes to most of these questions, you are hired. You are going to fit in here great."

We doubled over laughing.

30

Frank Sinatra made his first Pittsburgh appearance in 1941 with Tommy Dorsey and his orchestra. On May 16, 1991, he was appearing at the Civic Arena on his Diamond Jubilee World Tour with Steve Lawrence and Eydie Gorme. Frank Sinatra Jr. was conducting the orchestra.

Around seven o'clock, someone from Sinatra's entourage called. "Mr. Sinatra wants to eat at your place, but he needs to order the food to go because we're flying out right after the concert." He seemed to know what was on the menu and ordered linguini in a white clam sauce with *giardiniera*, an Italian vegetable relish. The caller said he'd be there around ten thirty to pick it up.

We had everything ready and waiting—the linguini as well as zucchini, salad, garlic bread, and a complimentary piece of my mom's apple pie. The man who picked it up looked like he could have been one of the Jersey Boys—early forties, full suit, black slicked-back hair, and a New York accent. The credit card he used had his name on it, not Frank's. We made small talk as I cashed him out. He told me that Frank wanted to know the best Italian restaurant in the city, and the concierge recommended The Primadonna. We shook hands, and the man said that Frank said thanks a lot, too. We never heard from anyone afterward, but the event really boosted my energy and is a piece of Pittsburgh and Primadonna history.

Just days after Sinatra's takeout, I was delighted to learn of a feature in the Sunday edition of the *New York Daily News*, a widely circulated newspaper, where Mike Kalina wrote about some of the great Italian feasts of his childhood having taken place after funerals in the Italian neighborhood where he grew up outside of Scranton, PA. In a piece titled "Beloved: Pasta and Bacon," Kalina wrote

> When I get hungry for the lusty, post-funeral cuisine I enjoyed as a youth, I head for The Primadonna Restaurant in McKees Rocks, just outside Pittsburgh, PA. Chef Pino Costanzo, a native of Italy, makes food that's, well, to die for. Chef Pino and cousin Joe Costanzo, who works the front of the house, are proud of the fact that their food has been well received, simply because it's the kind of food they grew up on. Chef Costanzo shared some of his simpler pasta recipes with me.

Acknowledging that Pino used his own secret recipe sauce for this recipe, Kalina suggested that a good store-bought variety can be substituted. He shared our recipe for Pasta with Bacon:

Pino's Pasta with Bacon
Serves 4
Takes 15-20 minutes to prepare

- 16 slices bacon, coarsely chopped
- Vegetable oil
- 1 medium onion, coarsely chopped (about 1/4 cup)
- 1/4 cup white wine
- 3 cups spaghetti sauce (your favorite)
- 1 pound spaghetti, cooked al dente, drained
- Freshly grated Parmesan cheese

Sauté bacon in a little vegetable oil in a large skillet until it is nearly cooked through. Drain off most of fat, but leave enough to cook the onions in. Add onions and cook until they're tender and bacon is completely cooked.

Raise heat to high and add wine; cook for a few minutes. Lower heat to medium and stir in spaghetti sauce. Heat until it is cooked through. Toss with the spaghetti, toss with a little Parmesan cheese, and serve.

Included with the article was this Tip of the Week: "When cooking bacon, don't heat the skillet first. Cooking it in a cold skillet over low heat will draw out more of the fat."

That recipe was also featured in 1991 in Kalina's winsome *Mike Kalina's Pittsburgh Cookbook*, along with Mostaccioli Primadonna and critics' favorite, Spaghetti Caruso. Mike featured these recipes along with a picture of Donna, Pino, and me gathered around a plate of pasta outside the restaurant, plaques visible in the window behind us. The caption read, "Primadonna owners Donna and Joe Costanzo with Chef Pino Costanzo outside what may well be the most popular neighborhood restaurant in Western Pennsylvania." More than a cookbook, this volume was evidence of Kalina's genuine affection for and knowledge of not only food, but also the history of food in Pittsburgh, people in the food business, the history of Pittsburgh, and Pittsburgh itself. Peppered with trivia, tips, old menus, pictures, and anecdotes, this book was a Pittsburgh treasure, sold exclusively at Kaufmann's Department Store.

While I'm mentioning Spaghetti Caruso, that dish was featured in several reviews. While it's a hard-to-find entrée that would make some people say, "Eww," critics loved it. *Pittsburgh Press* food critic Betsy Kline's comments were gratifying: "The Spaghetti Caruso set this chicken liver lover's heart singing. The livers, perfectly cooked and pink in the middles, were generously heaped atop a sizable bowl of spaghetti laced with a bracing tomato sauce with a slow, peppery burn. Delicious."

Favorable reviews continued to bring in new business as well as validate the loyalty of regular customers. The Primadonna was voted #1 Italian Restaurant by readers of the *Pittsburgh Post-Gazette* and Pittsburgh's *City Paper* and Best Italian Cuisine by *Pittsburgh Magazine*. Most reviews were similar, mentioning the crowds and describing the most popular entrées. Reviewers Renaldo and Mirella gave the salad dressing sales a boost in an *In Pittsburgh* "Munchtime" review: "Very high praise for the house salad, especially the marvelous Italian dressing. You may think that's foolish: how creative can one be with vinegar and oil, right? But trust us, it's something special." They also warned, ". . . seconds on the bread won't be enough."

Mike Kalina wrote one more piece in October '91 for the *Pittsburgh Post-Gazette* weekend edition: "I'll be honest. I thought this might be the year that the bubble would burst for The Primadonna Restaurant. But in my year's hiatus from the McKees Rocks establishment, I was surprised to see it's still attracting SRO (standing room only) crowds . . ."

I called Mike to thank him, and we shared our usual good-natured conversation. Never would I have guessed that our next conversation would not be so happy.

31

I was at the restaurant one weekday afternoon when two men around my age dressed in suits knocked at the door.

"How can I help you?" I asked.

They showed their badges and handed me a subpoena. Then one said tersely, "There is a federal grand jury investigation for Mike Kalina, and you must testify."

Aggravated at the very sound of it, I questioned, "For what?"

One of the men said, "You paid to get into his cookbook."

"No, I didn't," I said firmly.

The other man said, "We are investigating the matter, and yes, you did."

I don't like when someone tells me I did something that I know I didn't do. I repeated, "No, I didn't. If he would have asked me for the money, I would have given it to him, but he asked me for nothing, and I gave him nothing."

"We know that people paid to be in the cookbook."

"Mike Kalina didn't ask for money, and I didn't pay. There's nothing illegal about that, anyway. It happens all the time—people come to me to ask if I want to be in books, and they give me a price and I pay it. It's a form of advertising. That is how it works."

The men left me with the subpoena in my hand. What I had said didn't matter.

A grand jury investigation is one that is meant to determine whether there is enough evidence to indict someone for a crime.

A grand jury does not decide whether there was wrongdoing; they gather evidence and listen to witnesses to decide whether there is enough for a case. The rules are much more flexible for grand juries; there are often twenty-three jurors, their time could be spread out over many months (but not every day) while they gather more information, and decisions are made according to specific majority guidelines. I wanted to be called in because I knew my testimony would help Mike Kalina.

Another restaurateur called me on the phone and asked me if I had gotten a subpoena. He told me he had paid fifteen hundred dollars to get in the book, and others did too. I told him I didn't pay.

I called Mike.

"Mike, what's up? I got a subpoena here."

Mike said, "This is all bullshit."

"What's the deal?" I asked.

Mike explained, "They're investigating me for people paying to get into the cookbook."

I already knew there was some truth to this because of the call with the other restaurant owner.

Confused, I questioned, "Why didn't you ask me to pay? He said, "Joe, you've been so good to me. I didn't ask you."

A week or two later, Mike came to the restaurant alone on a Thursday night, and at a glance, I knew even before he spoke that he was distraught. For one thing, he was visibly sweaty, but it was January. I sat down and joined him.

Kalina asked, "Joe, if I get fired, could you help me open a little pizza shop somewhere?"

I chuckled but quickly saw he wasn't kidding.

I told him, "Mike, it's going to blow over. Don't worry about it. If you lose your job or anything, I will help you. Don't worry about nothin'."

32

On the following Monday morning around nine, I was at the restaurant and turned on 99.7 WISH Radio. I heard the newscaster announce, "Food critic Mike Kalina has died in an apparent suicide." I just shook my head. I can't really say I was shocked because I had just seen how disturbed he was, but I was deeply saddened. Obviously, my reassurance hadn't been enough.

Right after, I got a call from Biki Cochhar, another Pittsburgh restaurant operator. Biki asked, "Did you hear the news?"

I told him I had just heard it on the radio. We talked about how talented and matchlessly knowledgeable Mike was, especially when it came to food. It was a such a heart-breaking ending to a great man's life. The rest of the afternoon was consumed talking about the tragedy. I called Donna and some family members and close friends, and then reporters started calling me.

The afternoon edition of *The Pittsburgh Press* added an article to the morning's front page, "Food critic Kalina's death termed suicide." I was the only restaurateur quoted in the article. The next morning, Tuesday, January 29, 1992, the headline of the *Pittsburgh Post-Gazette* read, "Food critic Kalina found dead: P-G writer, TV personality a suicide, grand jury probing his dealings." Just a few paragraphs into the article, I was quoted:

> [Joseph Costanzo Jr.] said Kalina was at his restaurant Thursday after many of the subpoenas had been served on restaurant owners. The critic "was so nervous it was not

even funny," Costanzo said. "He told me the advertising fee was... legal but not ethical. He said, 'Joe, I didn't do anything wrong. I'm a victim of circumstances.' He thought he was going to lose his job at the *Post-Gazette*. I told him not to worry, that I was going to go to the grand jury to tell them the truth: that he never asked me for anything.

The *pull quote*, or excerpt that had been pulled from the article and used as a highlight in large text was, "'He never asked me for one cent, and he gave me a lot of reviews.'—Restaurateur Joseph Costanzo, Jr."

To illustrate how far-reaching Mike Kalina's impact was, a large spread (excerpted here) in the following week's *New York Times* detailed the tragedy:

Pittsburgh Food Critic's Suicide Leaves a Trail of Suspicions

By Michael Decourcy Hinds
Feb. 8, 1992

Mike Kalina, a 49-year-old restaurant critic and travel writer for the *Pittsburgh Post-Gazette*, was well on his way to becoming a national television celebrity when his health and career began crumbling in the last two months. He committed suicide a week ago, leaving behind no explanation, only a trail of suspicions that he was involved in unethical and possibly criminal business dealings. Friends and colleagues said this week that they found incomprehensible the accusations that are nonetheless the subject of a federal investigation.

Mr. Kalina, who has appeared as a food critic on local television for a dozen years, became known nationally as the amiable host of a television program called "Travelin' Gourmet" and the author of a cookbook by the same name.

The television series had 13 programs about dining in Europe, and it was broadcast on 30 commercial stations in 1988 and on 230 public stations in 1989. Mr. Kalina wrote two other cookbooks and two syndicated columns. The most popular column, also entitled "Travelin' Gourmet," was carried once a week by 15 newspapers. He had a 28-year-old daughter by his first wife and a 16-month-old daughter by his third wife, Doris Kalina.

On Jan. 27, Pittsburgh police officers found him dead in his car, which was parked in a lot in downtown Pittsburgh. One end of a garden hose, which Mr. Kalina had bought two days before, was taped to the car's exhaust pipe, and the other end was snaked through a rear window of the car. The coroner ruled the death a suicide by carbon monoxide poisoning. A memorial service on Saturday drew about 175 people, including family members, Mayor Sophie Masloff of Pittsburgh, restaurateurs and reporters.

Barry Paris, a Pittsburgh writer and Mr. Kalina's best friend, spoke of him as a creative neurotic genius, an amateur photographer, pianist and comedian who wrote songs, plays, and scripts.

"Nothing will tarnish him in my mind," Mr. Paris said. "The fact that a set of vicious and unproven allegations might have put him over the edge does not mean they are true."

Mrs. Kalina told the police that her husband had been depressed since before Christmas when he found out that a throat cancer might have returned after three bouts with it 20 years ago. He had been told then that more throat surgery would leave him permanently disfigured. But what friends say might have undone Mr. Kalina was finding out in late January that the Postal Service and the United

States Attorney in Pittsburgh were investigating his financial dealings with restaurants. These were restaurants that he had written about in a new cookbook and that he had reviewed over the years for the newspaper and for KDKA-TV, a Pittsburgh television station owned by the Westinghouse Electric Corporation.

Mr. Kalina's apparent suicide is a reflection of the terrible stigma that comes with being named in an investigation. "I wouldn't want to second-guess the prosecutor's judgment without knowing what evidence he had, but you have to wonder if he jumped in with both feet before testing the waters," said Gerard E. Lynch, a professor of law at Columbia University and a former chief of the Criminal Division in the United States Attorney's office in Manhattan. Or, put another way, John G. Craig Jr., editor of the *Pittsburgh Post-Gazette*, said in an interview: "I don't know why the United States Attorney is mucking around in the integrity of our dining reviews. It seems like an ethical question, not a criminal question."

The prosecutors have filed no charges and, apart from serving subpoenas on 40 restaurateurs to testify before a grand jury this week, they have refused to talk about their investigation or even to say why they are continuing to pursue the case after Mr. Kalina's death ...

Although the wake and the funeral were well-attended, there were only a few restaurateurs. Many were afraid that their very presence would bring more government scrutiny. I attended both and held my head high, as I had nothing to hide.

I felt like I had to do something for this man who had done so much for me. I thought about how many letters I had sent and phone calls I had made to get Mike to come to the Rocks to give me that first review, the opposite of what people thought. I only knew Mike Kalina as an upstanding and honest critic. I put together a little tribute and ran it in the *Post-Gazette*:

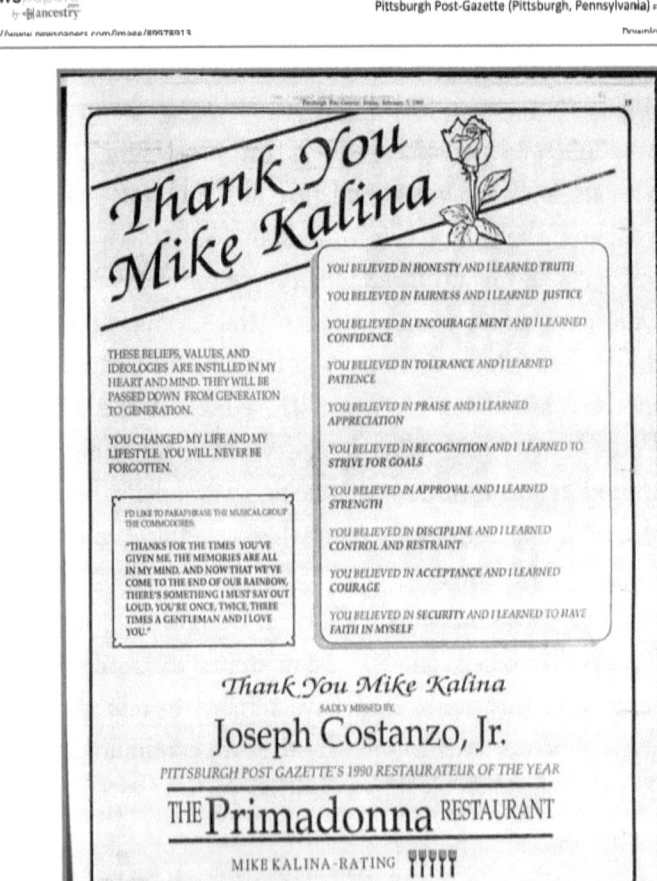

Local media coverage was heavy, but much of it focused on the investigation rather than the heartbreak of Mike's suicide. To his credit, *Post-Gazette* Editor John G. Craig wrote a piece titled "A sad, sad story: The tragic death of Mike Kalina saddens all of us who knew him," in which he applauded Mike's talents and virtues while articulating a few of the many "Why would he . . .?" questions we all had, never to be answered by the only man who knew for sure.

33

Even after Mike Kalina's death, agents were still investigating payments for the cookbook and for reviews. While we dealt with our personal grief and loss of an exceptional friend, I couldn't help feeling that the government was transferring the heat onto me.

A good customer who was an attorney had talked to a colleague who was involved with the case. The attorney-customer called me.

"Joe, I'm calling you as a courtesy, trusting you won't say you heard this from me."

"Sure. Of course," I replied. "Heard what, though?"

"The government may be coming after you. They want to get someone, and now that Mike Kalina is dead, I advise you to lie really low right now." The nervousness of the attorney's voice surprised me.

"Thanks, but that ain't my style, and I have nothing to hide."

A couple days later, a *Post-Gazette* reporter came to the restaurant to interview me before business hours. He was a crime reporter.

The reporter said, "Mr. Costanzo, people are saying there is no possible way that you could do all you did without underworld help."

I said, "I work eighteen hours a day, and I bust my ass."

He went on, "Rumor has it you are laundering money for the mob."

My patience was already fading. "You have connections on the street. You ask your connections if I do any business with these people or have any dealings with them."

As though he were holding an ace up his sleeve, the reporter claimed, "You have done business with them. These people have been seen here."

"I'm not saying these people didn't come here to eat. I'm saying I have nothing to do with them. Maybe they like Italian food, like everybody else."

The guy tried to press on, but I'd had enough. I told him off. "Talk to your friends on the street, and they will tell you how it is. Someone died here. Shouldn't you focus your news on the wrongful death instead of these fucking monopoly stories?"

The reporter left. He had wasted his time.

My good friend Danny McIntyre, an attorney, explained to me, "Whatever you say in the grand jury can be held against you. If you go for immunity, you bring an attorney in and you get off."

I asserted, "Thanks, Danny, but I didn't do anything wrong."

When prosecutors offer immunity, they're trying to catch the "biggest fish." If they offer immunity to the little fish in that crime pond, the little fish provides testimony in exchange for immunity from prosecution for their lesser crime. I had no reason to want immunity.

The grand jury proceedings began. As they say on TV courts, "to the best of my recollection," the questioning went something like this:

"Mr. Costanzo, You are one of only sixteen restaurants that got a five-fork review. Did you pay for that review?"

I answered, "NO. Anyone who has been down here knows I deserved the review, and I got what I had deserved."

"Did you give Mr. Kalina free food?"

I said, "Yes, I gave him food. It's my food. I give customers free food. If you come down, I'll give you free food, too. This ain't no crime. Do Broadway critics pay to see the plays they are going to review? Do NYC food critics pay for their food? The answer is no."

"Did you pay to get in the cookbook?"

"No, he never asked me. If he would have asked me, I would have done it."

They were pissed. I walked away without a care in the world.

A second grand jury investigation was opened, this time with the underworld figures with whom they thought Mike Kalina was involved, and I was invited once more. How about that shit?

Since I had gotten another subpoena, there was nothing I could do but show up again. Trying to be helpful, an attorney took me into a side office and sat me down.

The attorney cautioned, "Joe, you could be looking at ten years in jail. If you paid for a review, that's five years because it went through the mail, which constitutes mail fraud, and another five for lying to a grand jury."

I said, "I didn't pay for any reviews, and I didn't lie to the grand jury."

The attorney said, "At least two people said they saw you pay Mike Kalina for a review."

What! I couldn't wait to go into the grand jury and tell them it was all B.S.

I demanded, "Bring these people down here right now. They are either former disgruntled employees or people who have some grudge against me. Where did they say they saw me pay Mike Kalina?"

"Behind the dumpster at The Primadonna."

"That's really interesting. So, just so you are clear, I know where he lives, he knows where I live. My restaurant doesn't open until four o'clock, and employees don't even get there until one. You are telling me that I did this outside in open air at a time when all my employees were down there watching me? Does this make any sense to you?"

"Go home, Costanzo."

"What?"

"Leave now. You are free to go."

I said, "I don't want to go home. I want to go in there. I want to tell the grand jury what a joke this is."

The attorney repeated, "Go home."

I left. No charges were filed against me.

In the long run, it was never proven that Mike Kalina had done anything wrong. Not one person came forward to say that Mike pressured them for money. It really would have blown over, and Mike essentially died for nothing.

34

Danny Aiello was filming *The Cemetery Club* in Pittsburgh, which I knew nothing about until I got a call one day from someone on his staff. A woman on the other end of the phone said, "Hey, Danny Aiello wants to have dinner at your restaurant tonight."

"Okay, then, bring him on down," I replied. Danny Aiello's name was familiar, but I couldn't picture him. Again, life was different before Google. I called my buddy Jimmy Carr to refresh my memory. I wanted to be sure to recognize my guest when he walked through the door.

Jimmy helped. "Did you see *Moonstruck*?"

"Yeah."

"He played Johnny Cammareri, the guy Cher was supposed to marry until she met Nicholas Cage."

"Oh, yeah. I know who you mean."

"He had a small part in *The Godfather II*. He said, 'Michael Corleone says hello.'"

"You have a good memory, Jim."

"Not really. I saw him on a talk show not long ago, and he said people always say that to him when he signs autographs."

Instantly recognizable, I walked toward Danny when he came in that evening, and he greeted me with a strong handshake and a broad smile. He was a bigger guy with a NY accent, but I immediately thought about how well he fit right into the Rocks. He was totally casual and easy to talk with from the first interaction.

He was with two other people to whom he introduced me, but I was so starstruck that I can't remember who they were. Donna seated the party at the first table in the dining room. After the server had taken care of their drinks, I took the fried zucchini over to his table myself. If the word *gregarious* were in a picture dictionary, Danny Aiello's smiling face would be next to it. The opposite of everything I thought I knew about celebrities, he seemed eager to chat and said he was impressed that I was the owner and was there working the crowd.

Danny ordered veal Parmesan. When I came by again to check on him, wiping his mouth with a napkin, he asked, "Can you sit with us for a few minutes?" That was something I had never done before on a busy night, but I happily obliged and sat down in the fourth seat at the table.

I asked the basic questions—how long he would be in town, where he was staying and the like, but talk somehow turned quickly to where we grew up and our traditional Italian families. At one point, Danny complimented, "I love that this veal is panfried and not deep-fried."

"It's better that way. We bake it after we pan fry to maximize the tenderness," I explained.

"It's perfect. Everything is delicious, Joe. This meal rivals the best restaurants in New York City."

Taking my cue, I attempted to excuse myself. "Thanks so much. I'll leave you alone to enjoy your meal."

"No, Joe. I mean unless you need to tend to something."

It didn't take much to convince me to stay at the table. We continued our conversation and found that we had so much in common, growing up in traditional Italian families, even though Aiello was from Manhattan.

He asked how long I had been in the restaurant business, and I told him, "I was a mail carrier until a few years ago. I even kept that day job when we first opened here."

He matched me with, "Get out! I was a bus driver. I didn't get into films until I was almost forty." We were kindred spirits working in different industries.

Before he left, Danny said, "Joe, give me your card. I'll send you an autographed photo."

"I'll be back in a minute," I said.

Along with a business card, I gave him a Primadonna Five Forks T-shirt, which he loved.

Not long afterward, Danny sent me his autographed picture, and I hung it on the wall.

I was saddened when I heard on the TV news that he had died. Of all the major celebrities who came to my restaurant, he was by far the friendliest.

35

Being busy can be a *blessing* or a curse, depending on how you look at it. I've thought it to be both, but it was surely a blessing after the death of Mike Kalina. Mike's passing sat like a pall over my heart; keeping busy was the only thing that helped me get my mind off the irreversible tragedy. And busy we were!

Chuckie Richards was still a regular at the Primadonna bar. As much as I knew he liked coming there and we enjoyed having him, his loyalty was also contributing to my income, so I liked to show my appreciation whenever I could. I had learned that his mother loved two things—pork chops and scratch-off lottery tickets. I occasionally sent him home with a pork chop dinner in to-go containers for his mother without his asking. Then I got the idea to surprise him with lottery tickets for her as well. I would buy fifty dollars' worth of different Pennsylvania Lottery scratch-offs. When I gave him the tickets, Chuckie was astounded. You would have thought I had given him a car.

"No, Joe, no. I can't, really. This is too much. You can't do this."

"I already did, and I'll do it again. Just take them to your mom and tell her I said, 'Good luck.'" I knew it made her happy, so that's why I kept doing it.

Late one night, Chuckie was describing to me how he was just two employment quarters short of getting his full Social Security. It seemed to me a shame that six months of work would make a difference in the amount, especially since he was a man who had given so much for this country.

The next time I saw him, I made a proposal. "Chuck, what if I put you on the payroll for two quarters? Just hold off a while on the Social Security, and then you'll be able to collect a full pension."

"No, Joe, I can't impose on you in that way."

"It's no big deal," I kept insisting, and finally Chuckie relented. I told him I'd gather the paperwork he needed the following day.

The next day, Chuckie showed up before we opened, which turned out to be a good time for him to fill out the necessary forms for payroll and taxes. He was dressed better than usual, wearing a button-down shirt, tie, and dress pants.

When he finished the paperwork, he said, "Okay. Now what do you want me to do?"

"To be honest, Chuck, I haven't had a second to think about it since yesterday. Nothing at the moment."

"Really, Joe, there must be something I can do now."

"You don't have to do anything right now."

"Oh, yes, I do," he insisted.

I told him, "I'll tell you when I have something for you to do. I promise. And you don't have to dress up."

Chuck stopped me once again midevening and asked if there were something he could do.

"Yeah," I said, giving him a friendly pat on the back. "Get back to your place at the bar."

For a couple more days, Chuckie came in about half an hour before we opened, asking again to be put to work.

"I told you I'd let you know when I have something for you to do. We're like a well-oiled machine here. Relax. I'll let you know when I need something." Again, Chuckie returned to his place at the bar.

This went on for a few days, until Chuckie received a modest paycheck.

"I can't take advantage of you like this, Joe. I really can't. You have to put me to work."

"Chuck, it would be harder for me to stop and train you on

anything right now than it is to give you that paycheck. I'll let you know when I need something."

"I'm always here for you if you need something, Joe. You don't need to put me on the payroll for that."

"I put you on the payroll to help you out," I responded.

Chuckie had his uncashed payroll check in his hand. "I can't accept this, Joe. I'm never cashing it."

I could tell he wasn't going to budge. "Okay, okay. How about this? Just sign that check and give it back to me. I'll deposit it back into my account, and I'll pay the Social Security. Look at it as a retainer if I need you sometimes. When you start working more hours, then you can keep the checks."

Chuckie reluctantly agreed to that arrangement. I sent him to Mancini's for bread on occasion and assigned him a few other local errands from time to time. To tell the truth, when I made the offer, I really thought I could have used him somewhere. There were some jobs he could've done at the restaurant, but space was tight, and it would've seemed like he was pushing out someone else. In my mind, I tried out various arrangements, but there was really nothing for him to do that someone else wasn't already doing.

Chuckie got his full Social Security, and he never forgot this gesture.

36

Mario Lemieux led the Pittsburgh Penguins to back-to-back Stanley Cup Championships in 1991 and 1992, and the mayhem that surrounded the games was an electric binder for the city. Just as with the Steelers, people had their own hockey game-time rituals. Superstitions abounded, compelling people to not only wear a favorite jersey, but also sit in a lucky chair, eat certain snacks, or perform countless varieties of quirky rites to bring good luck to the team. People swear by these traditions, and they're still part of America's die-hard sports culture to this day.

The Penguins fan frenzy provided a perfect marketing opportunity upon which I could capitalize; I had to get The Primadonna onto the Penguins bandwagon. I knew that if I could get my restaurant's commercial on during one of these games, it would yield large returns.

The playoff games were slated to begin in a week. I called the local KDKA news station to inquire about a thirty-second ad, and they transferred me to Advertising.

"This is Joe Costanzo, owner of The Primadonna Restaurant. I'm interested in running a thirty-second ad during a Penguins playoff game."

"Sure. The rate for these games is per second, Mr. Costanzo. The current rate is one hundred dollars."

"So that would be three thousand dollars?" I confirmed.

"Yes, sir."

"That's a little steeper than last time I called."

The salesman explained, "We expect a large audience, so prices are up a bit."

"Let me call you back."

"Sure, Mr. Costanzo, but slots are filling up quickly. You'll have to call back soon."

Then I said, "What the hell? Let's do it!" I imagined Donna cringing at the cost.

"What kind of ad did you have in mind?"

We discussed my idea for the commercial. Donna's brother Russ was a professional videographer, so he would do the filming. Time being at a premium, the ad would just feature me at the restaurant, calling attention to our menu and awards, and inviting people in a sincere way. No gimmicks.

I gave the excited salesman my payment information, and he confirmed the transaction. "Okay, Joe. That is one thirty-second ad during a playoff game for a total of three thousand dollars."

As had become the norm, my days went all too fast. Being open and packed six nights a week, it was common for any of us to wonder momentarily what day it was. I was thinking about how to break the news of the pricy ad to Donna because we normally consulted on big expenses, but time flew by. On that night of the playoffs, I was only reminded that the game was happening by the sea of Penguin shirts at the bar. I got a little rush, realizing this was the night that my ad would debut.

I walked into the kitchen and had the wind taken out of my sails. It was Donna, suiting up for waitress duty. Donna didn't work every day, but with the recent crowds, I found her at the restaurant more than usual, which was, until tonight, a *good* thing.

"Hey, Don, I didn't know you were coming down tonight."

"I figured with the game and the recent review, you'd need an extra hand, so I'm here to help the wait staff."

We needed the help, but I also knew that the chances of Donna seeing this ad would be much greater here at the restaurant than at home, so I tried to give her the night off.

"Love, you've been working so hard. We should be okay down here. Why don't you go home and get some rest?"

"Joe, I'm fine. I dropped off the kids early at your mom's, and I took a nap. I feel great, and I'm ready to work."

With that, I knew that there was nothing more I could say. I talked myself off the ledge. I took a deep breath and hoped that for the thirty seconds that my ad appeared, Donna would not happen to be in the bar. Donna was not the person who hung by the bar. She only went in when she needed to pick up drink orders, and thirty seconds was a short window of time. Odds were heavily in my favor that she would not see my TV commercial.

The ruckus began in the bar the moment Magoo turned the TV channel to the hockey game. Already staunch hockey fans, the gang was on fire because they had personally gotten to know Penguins Tom Barasso, Kevin Stephens, and other players at that very bar. With voices deep and loud, they cheered on the team. Things got pretty rowdy.

Two couples were dining at a booth in the bar, and it was obvious that they could no longer carry on a conversation. As I watched them, I noticed that when one of them would lean in to talk, the bar crowd would roar, and they'd just sit back and smile. This happened several times. I checked on the dining room seating and then went over to the booth and said, "It's getting loud in here. Let me move you to the dining room. We're cleaning a table now."

"No, we're good," insisted one of the gentlemen. "We don't follow hockey, but we're having a good time watching everybody else." The ladies nodded in agreement, so I left, but later I offered them free desserts, which seemed to delight them.

Donna was in and out of the bar, as were all the servers, but I had begun to relax. Distracted by my responsibilities and the game itself, I had all but forgotten about the commercial.

Then my ad came on. Donna and I were both in the kitchen at the time. When the bar crowd saw my face on the screen and heard, "Hi, I'm Joseph Costanzo, Jr., owner of The Primadonna Restaurant . . ." they doubled their boisterous cheers, and Magoo ran out from behind the bar to get me.

"Joe! Joe!" he shouted, motioning for me to follow. Naturally, Donna followed, too.

With Donna close behind me, I watched the last seconds of the commercial as the bar crowd high-fived and patted me on the back. When I turned toward Donna, she averted my eyes and left abruptly.

A few minutes later, Donna and I were both in proximity to the door to my downstairs office. She opened the door, and with a pointed finger and a swiping motion, signaled for me to join her. At this point, we had a packed house, and every moment away for both me and Donna was a precious moment that was getting us backed up. In the restaurant industry, everything works like a set of dominoes. If someone is too slow busing a table, too slow seating a new party, too slow putting in an order, each of these things affects the already impatient guests who are anxiously awaiting their dinner. I was helping the maître d' assess which tables were about to come open, but I knew I'd better follow.

"Joe, what was that all about? You ran a commercial today on TV and I had no idea about it?!"

"Don, I was going to tell you when . . ." I hesitated slightly, and she interrupted.

"When *what*, Joe? When you needed to because I either saw it myself or saw the money leave our account?"

"No," but I knew that was pretty accurate.

"How much did that cost?"

I figured the approach of the advertiser would be best here. "It was one hundred dollars per second."

"A hundred dollars per second! Are you kidding me?"

I wished I were. "No."

Donna probed further. "How long was that commercial?"

"Thirty seconds."

"So you're telling me that we spent three thousand dollars on a thirty-second ad? Three thousand dollars?"

"Yes, but there's a large audience tonight."

"What happened to sticking to a budget? That is not in our budget for advertising."

"Look, Don, I knew there would be a lot of people watching. I'm making all the decisions that are helping keep us as busy as we are, so what's the big deal?"

"If you know what's best for the restaurant and the business, then why do you need me? I quit!"

"Don, you can't quit."

"Why can't I?"

"Because we're too busy."

"Watch me."

With that, Donna untied her apron, flung it at my chest, and stormed up the stairs. I ran behind her, but she proceeded full speed ahead right toward the door.

David saw tears in her eyes, and in passing immediately asked, "Donna, what's wrong?"

She looked right at him and said, "I just quit."

As Donna stormed toward the door, waitstaff slowed their comings and goings, and nearby customers watched. Waiting customers in the entranceway had their eyes glued to the scene. The slam of the door punctuated the drama that had just ensued.

The next several days at home were rough. I tried to explain. "At first, I thought it was a lot cheaper, and then when I said I'd call back, the guy said slots were filling up fast. It was a spur-of-the-moment decision."

Donna was not ready to talk. I learned that Donna deals with things by silence and process, which is totally opposite of me. I gave her the space that she needed and constantly apologized anytime she would let me. After three days, she finally decided that she would rethink and come back to the restaurant. The staff was constantly asking me, and I told them she would likely return soon.

On the afternoon of Donna's return, the waitstaff made a huge *WELCOME BACK, DONNA* banner and hung it in the dining room. She felt the love, and all was right again.

37

With all the effort needed to keep things running at the restaurant, a new house had been the farthest thing from our minds. Coming from a poor immigrant family, you landed where you landed and made it your home. When we were finally able to start saving money, we were thinking about the girls' educations and maybe a new car. The concept of having a starter home was foreign. We had no plans to leave our home, but sometimes life chooses for you.

I was about to leave the house through the garage one day when I looked over to our mudroom and noticed a cut in the screen door. The slice in the door was definitely not something that could have been done by the wind or a stray cat. Upon closer investigation, there were other signs of attempted forced entry. The most disturbing piece of evidence was that one of my tennis shoes that I kept right outside the garage was missing. As I walked around the outside of the house, I found my shoe in the back of the house directly under one of the windows. It appeared that when the perpetrator(s) could not access the house through the mudroom, they looked for another way to break in. Luckily, when we put in new windows, we also put glass-block windows throughout the ground level because of this very possibility.

My street sense seemed to have paid off, as the criminals apparently fled before it became an issue, but what if they hadn't? I was working nights, as was well-known. Had we, in fact, become the low-hanging fruit in this neighborhood? I wasn't going to stick around to find out. Ingram had provided so much joy and fellowship for our young family, but things had changed. On our street, about six blocks away, a housewife had been raped in her own home during the day when gang members broke in. In worst-nightmare fashion, her kids watched in horror as all this went down. I just couldn't leave things to chance, so we started talking about moving.

Ingram, where we lived, was part of the Montour School District, which had an unusual geographic configuration. Ingram had a Pittsburgh address and was a typical older Pittsburgh borough. We had our own elementary school, but the middle and high schools were about five miles away, as the crow flies. Those schools were in Kennedy and Robinson townships—the "up-the-hill" suburbs to which social climbers born in the Rocks had fled. It made sense that moving to one of those townships would be the least disruptive move—still in the same district for the girls, still close to The Primadonna.

I asked Paul Cichon, who had done our bathroom renovation at The Primadonna, where to look.

"Joe, have you heard of Cobblestone Commons?"

"No, where's that?"

"It's a new plan in Robinson, right off the main road. Used to be farmland. It's close to your girls' schools and would be a straight shot down the hill to The Primadonna. It'd be perfect. It's not a cookie-cutter housing plan. Really nice houses, each one different."

A few days later, Paul picked Donna and me up around noon, and we drove around the new neighborhood. He showed me the slice of land that he thought had my name all over it. It was the middle plot on top of the first hill as we made a right into the development.

"Imagine. You pull into Cobblestone Commons and look right at your big mansion set on top of this hill like a lighthouse, a welcome center. It will be the first thing people see, and it will be a sight to see—like a design right off the cover of *House Beautiful*."

I loved the sound of that.

Paul continued, "The biggest thing would be that you would

not have to worry about your family when you work late. Anyone living here would be a professional. No lowlifes sneaking around. Everything's visible."

Donna loved the sound of that.

I was thinking *Where do I sign?* but said, "We just started talking about moving. I hate to rush into anything, Paul." This housing plan really was a cut above anything I had seen on this side of Pittsburgh, though, and the lot that Paul pointed out was the prime spot.

Although we started our housing search with nothing much in mind except for the general location, it didn't take long for my wheels to start turning. Why not go big like I did with everything else? We bought the lot within a month of that meeting. It was thirty-five thousand dollars in 1991, and building was in progress until 1993. Paul himself was the builder, and we worked closely together on the details.

Our new six-thousand-square-foot home had a living room, solid oak study room, family room, five bedrooms, three-and-a-half bathrooms, and a fully finished basement complete with a man cave with a solid marble bar and a wine closet. The master suite with vaulted ceilings was the ultimate nighttime retreat, and each of the five bedrooms had a spacious closet. The dining room had ample space for large family gatherings. In addition to an expansive enclosed porch, there was a two-car garage, an indoor storage unit, and several offices throughout. It was the most beautiful home I had ever been in, and it belonged to Donna and me.

I remember those days when we were building. Instead of collapsing in a bar booth at the end of a hard day, I'd be on my way up to see my new house. As each additional piece materialized, the excitement was renewed. As the house started to take shape, I offered a few of my best customers an after-dinner house tour to complement their meal.

Meanwhile, David Rigo and his restoration partner, Bob, began to work on a beautification project at the restaurant, too—a hand-painted mural depicting an Italian villa—spanning the entire width of the wall in the back dining room. The exquisite one-of-a-kind scene added another layer of beauty and class to the restaurant.

38

The year 1993 brought hot new crazes for both Hollywood and The Primadonna. America's newest love story, *Sleepless in Seattle,* had recently come out, and the strangest thing happened after it did. We kept on having to answer the newest popular question from our customers: "Do you have tiramisu?"

On the phone, in the restaurant, on the street, no matter where it was, people were in search of the dessert that Sam asked his buddy Jay about during the bit in the movie about what Sam, a new widower, needed to be prepared for as he started to date again. For all the years I spent sampling and eating Italian food, tiramisu had never been in the mix. Not only that, but the funny thing is also that I had never heard of it before people started schooling me on it. Once people started asking, I knew that I would need to deliver.

The first step was to try to figure this out. My parents came from immigrant Italian families where desserts were luxuries, not staples. I tried to snoop around and ask my customers who traveled from more affluent areas to come dine at my place. Keep in mind this was well before the days of Google and the internet. I would poke around trying to figure out the secret sauce to ingredients that were in the mix. I even went as far as watching the movie just for that scene.

Luckily, my cousin Pino was not as in the dark about this one as I was. He had grown up in Italy and at least had an idea of the good makings of a tiramisu. Three staples were mascarpone cheese, lady fingers, and Kahlua. We tested and did trial-and-error runs.

From our cursory "ask a friend" research, one thing was for sure—the only thing consistent about people's tiramisu recipes was the inconsistencies. Some people served it as a round cake, others in a bowl like pudding, some like a casserole. We developed ours for the ease of serving at a restaurant; exactly one lady finger doused in Kahlua long-ways was the ticket, topped with a healthy dose of mascarpone cheese mousse, topped with a dash of cocoa.

Sounds so simple, but it did take about eight to ten trials before we perfected it. Pino had an idea of how he wanted it to look and taste, but hopes and reality were sometimes far from each other. Pino would come in early, whip something up, and then we would taste and rate it. It reminded me of the modern-day kitchen TV shows you would find on the Food Network. We would give feedback on taste, appearance, and texture, and then it was back to the drawing board to do it all over again. It was a labor of love, and you could feel it in the final light, fluffy recipe that so many longed for.

When we finally got the recipe down, the tiramisu would be gone before six o'clock every night. Between customers being in the *Sleepless in Seattle* craze and my giving customers an extra slice for free, hoping to hook them like a crack dealer for next time, I knew that we didn't have the capacity to keep on making this with the staff we had. I phoned a friend.

Theresa Vasselo owned Theresa's Italian Bakery a couple of doors away, and her famous cookies were starting to take off in the area. Like me, however, Theresa was from an immigrant family, and fine Italian food really wasn't part of her repertoire. When I asked her about making tiramisu for me, her response was, "Tir-a-ma *what*?" I realized it was time for me to walk a slice down to her. Theresa tasted it and fell in love, so she and Pino worked together to come up with a way to home-make yet mass produce this delicacy specifically for The Primadonna. She couldn't make it fast enough, and anticipating the additional $5.50 a slice per person, I couldn't wait to pick it up every day. With the addition of this dessert to the longtime trio of Primadonna favorites--Mom's Apple Pie, Donna's Chocolate Cheesecake, and Homemade Rum Cake--there was something for everybody's taste.

My father passed away two days after Christmas 1993 from lung cancer complications. I walked into the hospital room after a long night at The Primadonna to find my mother by his side as he lay lifeless. We called for a nurse who confirmed the inevitable—my father was gone.

This was a big loss in an Italian family, so we were going to have to do some reconfiguring for the next big family event. Hence, we started a new tradition of going to The Primadonna on holidays to spend the day with my mother, her sisters, and their families. The Primadonna was closed on Sundays and holidays, so this worked out well. Together we took over almost every one of the eighty-three seats in the restaurant.

My family would go earlier than everyone else to open up for our special event kitchen staff. Everyone got all dressed up for these occasions. My mother took over Pino's role as head chef, and her sisters assumed the other kitchen roles. They always had everything figured out. Aunt Yolanda dressed and cooked the turkey, Aunt Mamie made the wedding soup, Aunt Josephine made the candied yams, Aunt Esther's specialty was pineapple pudding cake, Aunt Rosie made pumpkin pies, and my mother made everything else—sauce, pasta, ravioli, and apple pies.

My girls have their own version of these holidays that they tell with loving humor. It starts by imitating the adults being in awe of how big they were getting or how pretty they were. Then they describe what they loved about our holidays—from making concoctions with the soda gun to playing on the computer or dancing on the bar—things the adults were too busy to notice while they were catching up with each other. We were so blessed to have a place to make this all happen.

39

With the bar business staying steady, some of my customers got a little too comfortable. When one guy named Don got way too drunk and screamed at me, I was not going to take it. I 86'd him, which in bar terms means that I shut him off. I told him where the door could hit him on the way out.

In the midst of rage and disbelief, Don said, "I'm leaving, but I'll be back with my friend T-Bone, and then we'll see how tough you are."

I had already met T-Bone. Six-foot-four and around three hundred pounds, T-Bone had been in and out of jail. I needed a plan because things could become ugly very quickly. I was sweating, but I couldn't let the other customers know how scared I felt.

After about fifteen minutes, true to his word, Don returned with T-Bone. I relied on intuition alone, approaching the pair without delay.

"T-Bone, I don't really know you, but I've seen you around, and I've heard you are a decent man. This man, your friend Don, disrespected me. I'm just trying to run a business here and feed my family. The last thing on earth I want to do is to have a problem with you. I do, however, have a problem with your friend. I am asking you not to start anything here. If you would like to come in and have a drink on me, that's fine, but Don cannot stay." I held my breath, thinking that it may be my last.

T-Bone paused for about a minute, and I could feel everyone's eyes were on us, even those who were out of earshot. T-Bone turned to

Don and said, "You heard what the man said; get the hell out of here."

T-Bone came in, took a bar stool, and I let out a huge sigh of relief, "What would you like to drink?"

"Dewar's on the rocks," he said.

"It's on me." All I could think as I poured was, *That was a close call.*

Throughout the years, I kept in touch with T-Bone. He was down and out, living in his car. He usually had no money, and when he did, I'm not sure where it came from. Whenever T-Bone got desperate, he would come by and hit me up for a twenty-dollar bill and a bowl of spaghetti.

It was a Saturday night, and there was a two-hour wait down the block. People had flocked from all over to dine at the city's latest hot spot. T-Bone walked in. The room went quiet, and everyone was staring at him.

The maître d' quickly ran back to the kitchen to find me.

"Joe, T-Bone is here."

"Where?"

"He is in the front."

"Outside?"

"No, he is in the waiting area with all the people."

"Geez." I dropped everything and ran out.

"T-Bone, come outside, my man."

"Joe, I need a twenty, and I need some spaghetti."

"No problem, my man, but you can't come into the restaurant like that during business hours."

"Why not, Joe?"

"Because you'll scare my customers. They've never seen a homeless man up close and personal."

T-Bone started laughing so hard he was cackling. "Joe, I'm sorry."

"No problem. Nothing to be sorry about. Meet me at the side door next time, my friend."

I gave T-Bone the goods, and as he walked away, I had such conflicted feelings. I was relieved that T-Bone laughed about the situation but ashamed of myself at the same time. Here was a man who had only shown his gentle side to me, but I was asking him to leave because of the unfounded, unfavorable judgment the customers were likely to display at his appearance. I did what I thought was best in the moment, but I also felt hypocritical—and I hate hypocrites.

T-Bone could have perceived my actions as a real snub, even though I gave him food and money. I couldn't tell whether he overlooked it, was used to it, or even might have thought it cool that he could scare customers away, but it didn't deter him from coming around periodically.

About to leave one afternoon with his free spaghetti, he stalled a bit, and I could tell he wanted to talk.

"Joe."

"What's that, T-Bone?"

"Has anyone ever did you wrong?"

"Of course."

"Joe, let me take care of it for you," he said genuinely, implying that his taking care of things was much different from how I would take care of a situation.

"Nah, don't worry about it, T-Bone."

"Joe, you have been so good to me. Better than anyone else in my life. Let me hurt someone for you. People listen real good that way."

"Thanks, T-Bone, but I'm okay."

"Does anyone owe you money?"

"Yes."

"Joe, let me get it for you."

"No, T-Bone, but I appreciate the gesture."

"I gotta do something for you. You been good to me."

"I don't do this stuff because I'm obligated, I do this because I care. I just want you to take care of yourself."

As T-Bone walked away, he brushed a tear from his eye. There are many versions of humanity, and this was one.

40

With my incessant focus on marketing, opportunities continued to spiral bigger and bigger for The Primadonna. As always, marketing plus excellent food plus excellent service were the three ingredients in the recipe for success.

At one point I bought a list of area residents who matched my target audience in age and income, and we established a birthday card mailing program, enclosing a ten-dollar gift certificate in each card. Quite a few people came in with those certificates, and many became regular customers.

Another strategy I implemented was a Primadonna Dining Club card. For a nominal one-time charge, the cardholder would be entitled to a fifteen-dollar discount on two meals.

Underwriters are people who voluntarily contribute cash to finance the production of a program partially or fully for a radio or TV station. I thought about underwriting a radio show centering around the restaurant industry. People love to hear and talk about food, so I envisioned doing interviews with other restaurateurs about food.

I contacted WJAS 1320, a popular talk station in Pittsburgh. At first the station was hesitant. They asked me how or why I would want a show that would promote our competition. I knew that by talking with different restaurateurs each week, I would not only be promoting them, but also myself. I knew that very few restaurant goers go to the same place every night out, so by sharing customers, everyone wins.

On August 6, 1993, *Fine Dining in Pittsburgh and around the World*, aired on WJAS 1320 for thirty minutes weekly every Saturday morning from seven thirty to eight o'clock and held steadily in the middle of the morning show ratings. Dom Piazza, also a disc jockey for sister station WISH 99.7, was the producer. In August 1993, "Sun Shines for Everyone" was the title of an article in *The Server*, the respected newspaper of the Pennsylvania food industry. The article began, "You seldom hear of a restaurateur initiating a project that promotes other restaurateurs, but that is exactly what Joseph Costanzo, Jr., owner of The Primadonna Restaurant in McKees Rocks, is doing."

Although the show had a local angle, mostly interviewing local restaurateurs about their businesses, I also talked about industry-wide trends, which helped to hone my own expertise. Just as I expected others to patronize my place, I was a big supporter of other restaurateurs, and this became part of my marketing plan. I figured if I knew what the competition was doing, it could help me in my own business.

In November of that same year, *The Server* featured me in another article, "The Marketing Maverick of Pittsburgh." The article opens with a quote from me. Here it is, along with some excerpts:

> "You can have the best-tasting food in the world and a terrific chef in the kitchen. Your service can be truly wonderful. But, if no one knows you're there, your business goes broke. That's a fact." Joseph Costanzo, Jr., owner of The Primadonna in McKees Rocks, ought to know. He took one of the worst locations in a depressed area to open a risky business eight years ago and has turned it into a premier Italian restaurant in Western Pennsylvania.

The article goes on to describe the radio show:

> Discussion is on what's new or notable, menu changes, staff changes, new facilities or parties' arrangements, offering positive aspects of the business and its operations. The target audience is 35 to 60, someone who is looking to eat out at an upscale operation, is sophisticated, and is interested in and informed about the business. Guests on the show have been articulate, knowledgeable, and prepared. Costanzo said he would like to expand the format in the future, possibly offering recipes or a call-in segment. Overall he spends several hours a week on the show's preparation, lining up guests, researching what has been written about the operation, and then the actual taping.

An editor's note followed:

> In putting this article together and after listening to several shows, I want to congratulate Mr. Costanzo on his effort to promote our livelihood. He's an engaging interview and a lively force focused on the industry's behalf. I urge all of our readers to tune in on Saturday mornings, and then to contact Mr. Costanzo . . . with your thoughts and ideas.

After funding the show myself for six months, *PA Food Service News* publisher Mike Romanus contacted me. He wanted to help underwrite the show due to its popularity. He talked to Ron Rome from the *Entertainment* book, a popular book of coupons for local attractions that organizations could sell as a fundraiser, who came on board to help fund the show.

Romanus was a great help at the time. He started to promote the radio show, taking photos of me with my guests, headphones on, and putting me on the cover of *The Server* three or four times.

He helped me pick people who would be good to interview. Other than Mike Kalina, Mike Romanus was the most influential person in promoting my business.

People were listening, and people were interested in learning about food and service with a restaurateur. I began each show saying, "This is Joseph Costanzo, Jr. Let's talk food. Let's talk service. Let's talk restaurants."

I used to talk to the guests beforehand, telling them I was going to ask about their restaurant and their menu. I would also say, "Give me some questions you would like me to ask you on the air. Then you are going to be more comfortable with what I'm asking." Guests were usually surprised that I would do that. I'd tell them I would be promoting us both. It didn't cost guests anything, and they got great publicity. Pittsburgh's most successful restaurateurs were guests on the show.

By this time, my skin had grown thicker when having to deal with a Gloomy Gus or Negative Nelly. One weekday, a listener from the previous Saturday's show called me at the restaurant, ready to argue. I had a guest on the show who had opened his restaurant with money from lots of investors. The caller started right in attacking me as if he were my boss.

"Why would you have him on your show? He's a crook. I invested and lost money."

I fired right back. "It's none of your business what I do and who I have on my radio show, so why are you calling me? When you underwrite this show, you can have a say-so, but until then, you got nothin'."

The guy didn't stop there. "The only reason your restaurant is so busy is your marketing machine that you run."

I sniggered back, "Sir, to me that is a high compliment. This place is the busiest in the city. Making money is the name of the game, my man. Have a nice day, asshole."

Froggy Morris was a big restaurant celebrity in the eighties.

His three-floor iconic bar and restaurant in downtown Pittsburgh, Froggy's, had a long run—1979 to 2003. It's the bar that was replicated on the set of *This Is Us*, the place where Rebecca and Jack most probably would have hung out in that era in Pittsburgh. Froggy also opened Bimbo's in the South Hills, The Raspberry Rhino in Shadyside, and Zelda's Greenhouse in Oakland.

Although I didn't realize it at the time, the similarities between Froggy and me were many. The biggest difference was that my goal was for customers to have an unsurpassed fine-dining experience, and Froggy wanted his patrons to have fun. A friend who was a regular at my restaurant for dinner and at Froggy's for drinks and socialization told me, "You and Froggy are alike in this way: your greatest marketing tool is your personality."

When my father shut me down rather than supporting me when I opened the restaurant, I told him, "Once I get into this restaurant business, I will be more famous than Froggy Morris." My father laughed at that statement, but now Froggy was calling me and asking if he could be a guest on my show.

Knocking off marketing avenues one by one, the only place I hadn't yet capitalized on was the newspaper. On one hand the number of great reviews in a variety of publications exceeded my expectations, but I wanted to use the newspaper more frequently in a way that was under my control. I approached the paper with the idea of writing a column called "Restaurant Talk." The deal was that I would pay for the advertising, but to the layman, it looked like I was a regular staff writer. It was all about illusion and innovation.

41

On a beautiful Sunday afternoon when we were deciding where to go to eat, Donna bemoaned, "I'm sick and tired of going places and being recognized. Tired of people asking you for gift certificates and donations. Then you pick up their checks. I just want to be anonymous again."

"I know a place where ain't no one going to even know who we are." I got the idea of taking a road trip out of town for a pleasant drive as well as some privacy. I had heard good things about Lock 6 Landing, a restaurant housed in a shell of what was part of a historic lock-and-dam complex on the Ohio River in Midland, Pennsylvania, about thirty miles from home. In good weather, Lock 6 served lunch outside on Saturdays and Sundays on a lovely patio overlooking the river. Seated at an umbrella table, we were pleasantly surprised at how close we were to the river traffic, which provided an unusual and interesting setting as we watched water skiers, pontoon boats, and tugboats pass by.

Donna was pleased. "This is so nice. I'm glad you thought of this place."

I agreed. "Something different, no? Sunlight, peace, and fresh air." So used to being inside, it felt like we had just emerged from a cave.

We had just ordered our meals when a boat pulled right up to dock, and I heard someone calling my name. What were the odds?

"Joe! Joe! I can't believe you're here! I was going to call you." Barry

Woznichak, known for his dedication to the Kennedy Township Little League, bounced right over to our table while another dozen people were still climbing out of the boat. "Hey, can you sponsor the Little League outfits for a team? The Primadonna name will be printed on the shirts, of course."

I agreed to buy the shirts *and* give a gift certificate, and the rowdy gang found a nearby table.

If this were a one-off event, Donna would probably have shrugged it off, but it was an ongoing issue between us. When she would nudge me about giving away too much, I'd always say things like, "Don't worry about it. We are just a little business in the Rocks; ain't no big thing," or, "I don't have time to penny-pinch." With a share-the-wealth attitude, I thought nothing of giving organizations a couple hundred dollars or comping someone's one-hundred-dollar meal.

Donna just shook her head and said, "I've somehow lost my appetite."

In the way that a person's tragic flaw can be a virtue, long before The Primadonna existed, I looked for opportunities to support others. When I was still a postal worker, I once bought jackets for the entire St. Rosalia basketball team. My mother-in-law was going downtown on the bus, and an acquaintance said to her, "That was really nice of your son-in-law to buy jackets for these kids."

When my mother-in-law mentioned it, Donna's comment was, "Why does he want to feed the world? Why can't he just feed his family?"

In his book *Restaurant Man*, Joe Bastianich wrote, "Anything you give away for free is bad." That wasn't me. Giving things away was part of my marketing plan and my personality. These opportunities were the greatest benefits of my job. I got so much satisfaction seeing the ways in which a little kindness could affect people. Donna had a generous heart, too, but she knew I could go overboard. I was finally making enough money, however, that I *could* go overboard and still make a good profit. It was wonderful to be able to show my appreciation for people in a tangible way.

My generosity did not stop at money or tangible items. Even though I was reputed to be a difficult person to work for because of my high standards, I was also lavish with my praise when it was warranted. I made certain to thank people profusely when they helped me, and despite the long work hours, I sent plenty of congratulatory and thank-you notes. I loved to put pictures and news clippings on plaques and give them as gifts. I gave credit where it was due.

I looked for ways that I could repay my customers and the community, so I went to the Sto-Ken-Rox Meals on Wheels and offered to subsidize a day's meal for the two hundred twenty people on their list. They estimated the cost would be approximately twenty-five hundred dollars for one day's meals. One morning soon afterward, the Meals on Wheels crew came to The Primadonna kitchen to prepare a special lunch. We all had a good time as Pino and the crew prepared the food and the rest of us packaged and organized the meals for delivery. It made for a long day, but we happily did it a second time.

Ruthie Dines, one of our first customers—who happened to have grown up on the street where The Primadonna was located—turned out to be Maria's English teacher in seventh grade and again in high school. Her husband A. J. was the girls' history teacher and Kelly's track and cross-country coach when Kelly broke school records in the two-mile run and four-by-eight relay. They came in regularly, usually with their three young sons, and loved the food. We would chat about the girls' accomplishments and school district news, and I would comp their meals.

Ruthie maintained, "Joe, we love it here, but we don't feel comfortable coming back unless you let us pay."

I'd say, "Okay, okay. Next time. Let me pick this one up. I appreciate all you two do for our girls." Then the next time I'd do the same thing.

Anmarie was waiting on the Dines family on a Saturday night. As soon as they were seated, the Dineses told her that they insisted on paying, and no matter what I said, they wanted her to bring them the check at the end of the meal. Ruthie even explained that there were things she wanted to try and was willing to splurge, but she held back from hiking up the bill too much because I always picked up the tab. It was naive of them to think that a convincing argument could cause a server to go against my wishes, but they tried. They thought that Anmarie was complying with their request when she presented the bill, but I headed them off at the pass. They gave her their charge card, but she returned it and even refused a tip; I had already taken care of everything.

After repeating this routine many times, the teachers were telling our mutual friend Mitch Galiyas how going to The Primadonna was the highlight of their weekends, but they did not want to take advantage of my generosity. Mitch advised, "If you really mean it, just go somewhere else to eat."

"Where else would we want to go instead?" replied Ruthie. "I'm not going to cut off my own happiness!"

42

In a 1993 "Spotlight" interview in the *Robinson Community Magazine*, when asked to complete the phrase "Someday I would like to . . ." I said, "Get involved in politics and run for a state office." In 1995, I ran for Allegheny County commissioner. A county commissioner not only had jurisdiction over the Rocks, but also over Pittsburgh proper, the east side of town where I grew up, and all the surrounding towns. The county had nearly one and a half million people at the time, a larger population than some states. Allegheny County was a great place to live, but it still had untapped potential. There was a lot of exciting work that could be done.

Through the restaurant, I had made friends all over town; my name was recognizable throughout the area and had become synonymous with The Primadonna. I hoped that voters would think I could "make things nice" in every way. I certainly thought I could. I believed if I applied the same care to running the county that I did to running the restaurant, I could do a lot of good for a lot of people. It didn't matter if I didn't have a political background per se; I had learned plenty about politics while growing The Primadonna.

Donna didn't want to hear it. "*Why*, Joe? *Why*?"

"I just feel called to do it, honey. I really do."

"You don't get any rest as it is; running The Primadonna is more than enough for anyone."

"It runs itself now for the most part, Donna. I'm there because I enjoy it. The staff can keep things going without my being there all the time."

"There were plenty of times when you were needed immediately, Joe."

"I'll still be there for the most part, and when I'm not, I'll wear a beeper."

"Do you know how much money a political campaign takes? I'm not willing to dig into our hard-earned savings, Joe." Donna's usually soft and lovely face hardened with that rare look that let me know she meant business.

"Money is not a prerequisite. I have a lot of friends. I'll raise the campaign funds."

"You'll use your own money, Joe. I know you will."

"No, I won't. I'll do a lot of free or cheap strategic PR. I have friends all over town and a lot of friends in the press now, too. I'll keep fundraising."

"Joe, we have a miracle here. A *miracle*. We're happy. We're comfortable. Why would you even *think* of risking what we have?"

"There's no risk, love. Think about the influence a county commissioner can have and all the good they can do."

"We do plenty of good right here, Joe. We make people happy. We're happy. Let's just count our blessings, for God's sake."

Donna's reaction was worse than I expected. I had even deluded myself that she might be excited about the idea, too. Damn.

That uneasy feeling crept back—was Donna my voice of reason not to be ignored, or was her practicality another obstacle that I'd have to work around? It had been a while since we disagreed, but when we did, I'd so often find myself teetering exactly on the fifty-fifty point, which at the least interfered with my momentum. This was big, though; it wasn't like disagreeing on whether to comp the zucchini appetizer.

Soon afterward we were with Jimmy Carr, my longtime friend and best man at our wedding. Jimmy asserted, "Politicians don't use any of their own money in their campaigns."

Donna corrected him, insisting, "I know my husband, and I know he will."

Jimmy said, "It will never happen."

Donna was sick of hearing about it. Against her better judgment, she relented. "Just so we don't use any of our own money." Was that an *okay*? I wasn't completely sure, but what else could it mean?

I proceeded to take the preliminary steps that would allow me to run for county commissioner. It's not that I lied about it or did it behind Donna's back; let's just say that I didn't say much at home during the process. I was always out and about for the restaurant and rarely gave an account, so it was easy to take care of the paperwork. When everything was in place, it was time to tell Donna.

We were home alone one morning, and I took her hands in mine. "Sweetheart, please listen. I feel compelled to run for county commissioner. I'm going to announce my candidacy."

I think Donna understood on a certain level, but she wriggled her hands from my grasp and walked away before I could even see the expression on her face.

When I announced that I was going to run, I quickly got great press. The *Pittsburgh Post-Gazette* and *Tribune-Review* both ran big stories. I was interviewed on KDKA-TV and was on the radio a few times. The response was highly encouraging, and I was riding a new wave of euphoria.

Very soon afterward, however, I learned from a reliable and empathetic source that John Craig, editor of the *Post-Gazette*, had put a halt to it all. He associated me with Mike Kalina, and with no time to explore the facts of the Kalina investigation, labeled me a political hot potato. I'd have to run without the aid of Pittsburgh's most influential newspaper.

Something had to give in my nearly impossible schedule, and the only thing that could be eliminated was the radio show. My mistake was not telling Mike Romanus first. He heard it through the grapevine and called me. I meant to tell him first and wish I would have. There were no cell phones, so he beat me to calling. I still regret to this day that I didn't stop at a pay phone somewhere to talk to him about the radio show before talking to anyone else.

Mike, who had been so instrumental in the success of the show, was angry with me. He got right to the point. "I did you good, and you are quitting on me here."

"Mike, I'm so sorry. I'm running for Allegheny County commissioner, and I can't do both."

When that show came to an end, many people called to express their appreciation, and most said they noted a spike in business after their show, so I had done what I had set out to do. Having other restaurateurs on the show made me look good while making them look good.

The campaign itself was exciting. My childhood friend, Jimmy Carr, put up signs everywhere. Dan McIntyre, another longtime friend, was the treasurer. Bob Hemmerick was my campaign manager. We weren't really organized because we were novices; however, we portrayed an image of confidence while being serious about what we were doing.

One of the first moves in my political campaign was to have a gigantic sign made. If you're driving the Parkway east toward downtown, there's a house in the hills on the right that everyone can see from both sides of the road. Jimmy Carr was with me, and we found our way to that house. I knocked on the door, introduced myself, and asked the owner if we could put a sign in his yard. He was so receptive, as if we were doing *him* the favor.

"Sure!" the homeowner consented. "I've heard a ton about you." I gladly paid the one hundred dollars he requested and gave him a one-hundred-dollar gift card as well. He came to the restaurant afterward.

My first fundraiser was held at the Sheraton Station Square, an exquisite and popular place on the riverfront directly across from downtown Pittsburgh, at one hundred dollars a ticket. Gene Connelly, the manager, was my friend, and he generously covered the space and hors d'oeuvres in support of my campaign. There was to be a cash bar, where guests pay for everything they drink and tip the bartenders themselves.

There were few indoor venues as stunning as the Sheraton Station Square, its vast tiered lobby adorned with fountains, rich colors, and live piano music. Windows spanning several stories framed the up-close view of the river and the city's venerable skyline. As much as I loved my restaurant, when I walked through the revolving doors, I got the exhilarating feeling that I was looking at my new world—physically and metaphorically.

I had driven down to Station Square myself that morning to help set everything up. Within the hour, a voice speaking softly into my ear was asking, "What do you need me to do?" My heart dropped at the sight of Donna. She was always so beautiful, so gracious, and in my case, so supportive. I was ever aware that Donna's class and charm made me look better. She was the quintessential candidate's wife that day, and I knew she would be an asset to the campaign in the same way she was to the restaurant. Not for a blink did I intend to use her in that way, but I have to acknowledge the truth of it.

As guests began to arrive, I felt so grateful for their support that at the last minute, I decided to pick up the tab for the liquor. The afternoon consisted of mingling, eating, and drinking, and there was a lively, hopeful vibe in the room. At one point, I gave a brief speech thanking everyone and promising to give my best.

As it turned out, the fundraiser looked and felt like a great success, but the liquor bill headed toward nine thousand dollars, much higher than I had anticipated. It put a little nick in my confidence that the campaign could be subsidized by supporters. The fundraiser came close to being a fund-lowerer.

43

Everyone from my parish priest to my old high school teacher urged me in their own manner to drop out of the race. A well-known national political figure called me on behalf of one of the other candidates and asked me to drop out. He said, "Joe, if—gets in, you could be board president."

I said, "I don't want that job. That's like being a bus boy at The Primadonna."

I went for the party endorsement but was told brusquely by party officials that they wanted the opposite—me out of the race completely. Even though I didn't win the endorsement, which would have made things easier financially, I knew that their wanting me out of the picture meant that I was a viable candidate.

In the election, as in the restaurant, I learned quickly that you must ignore the inevitable negativity of others. If you let the naysayers bother you, it will drain your energy. The places where the negativity would pop up, however, were sometimes surprising.

One of my high school teachers was a WWII veteran and an intimidating tough guy. I heard somewhere that he had eventually ended up homeless, which was unimaginable to me.

I was on the campaign trail when we went to the Gandy Dancer in Station Square to have lunch after church one Sunday. We sat down, and I looked across the room and saw my old teacher. Although unkempt and unshaven, he was still recognizable.

I asked the server, "What's that guy eating?"

She answered, "Nothing. Just drinking coffee."

I told her, "Go over and tell him, 'An old student wants to buy you breakfast.'"

She came right back and reported that he said he didn't want anything.

I left my seat to go over and say hello. "I don't know if you'll remember me, but I'm Joe Costanzo. I was in your homeroom."

He grumbled, "I know who you are. I read in the paper that you are running for county commissioner. I thought it was a joke. You actually think you're going to beat Forrester?"

I said, "I'm going to try. Can I get you anything?"

"No, I'm good." As I walked away, he yelled, "Costanzo!" I turned around. With a familiar scowl, he said, "I never thought you were going to make anything of yourself."

My mother-in-law ("Nanny" as we called her) knew a committee man from Greenfield. They had grown up together. Worried about my taking votes away from the traditional candidates, he said, "You are wasting your vote by voting for Joe Costanzo."

Nanny said, "He's my son-in-law. I have to vote for him."

He replied, "You are wasting your vote, Rita."

None of that bothered me. From my Primadonna experience, I had come to look at the uninvited comments of cynics as an inevitable part of doing something daring—something most people would not attempt.

What *was* bothering me, though, was that I quickly learned that Donna was right about one thing. I had started to dip into our own money to fund the campaign, especially in the final weeks when I spent lavishly on TV commercials. With the restaurant booming and no reason to think the money would stop flowing, however, I made a mental note to begin putting it back into the savings as soon as the campaign ended—all $250,000 of it.

That night after the polls closed, Donna and I watched for election updates on the television at The Primadonna while my entire family gathered at my mother's house. At either place, we ate pasta while we watched the election results. The news crews flashed from poll to poll, interviewing voters and showing clips of the candidates out campaigning. We all had a big laugh because in every scene they showed of me, I was somewhere different. Even during one clip where they were interviewing a voter, I was in the background. The news crew called me Mr. Ubiquitous because when there was a camera, I was on it. One newscaster commented that he couldn't believe how hard one person could work in one day.

We waited patiently for the election results to post. The preliminary numbers came up. I had 35 percent of the votes, five percentage points above any of the other candidates. As soon as the numbers came up, everyone started to cheer. The phone rang and rang at The Primadonna as well as at my mother's house. Relatives. Neighbors. Friends. I had psyched myself out so much for this day, and it was finally here. I had a feeling in my gut that this was going to work. Just like The Primadonna, this was going to be another dream come true.

I was so excited, I could barely sit still. I continued to listen to the news but only really cared about the numbers. When they came up again, to my dismay, I had dropped down to 25 percent, which was second place. My heart skipped; this was not the way it was supposed to go.

Phones rang again, but this time people were calling to tell me or my family to keep our heads up, and in the end, people would do the right thing. For a short while I believed everyone's rationalizations, but when the numbers flashed again, Forrester and Flaherty were barely in the lead, followed by Dawida and then me. I was slipping, and there was nothing I could do about it except witness the loss with the people I loved the most.

The worst part of this all was the expression on my wife's face.

From the beginning of this political ordeal, I told her that politicians didn't spend their own money, and then I started spending more and more of our own dollars. I looked at Donna and realized all the things she was to me: sweetheart, wife, mother of our children, helpmate at home and workmate in the restaurant, and I knew just how much this was going to disappoint her. How would I make this up to her?

In the final election, I garnered twenty-five thousand votes, but the incumbents got fifty thousand. Still, the *Tribune-Review* reported that getting twenty-five thousand votes out of the gate was in itself a miracle.

At a party a couple years later, I spotted the guys from my opponent's campaign. One of the big names took me aside and said, "Joe, we like you. If you want to run again, come and see us. We'll help you out, and you'll win. Do you know why I know you'll win?"

"Why?" I asked with a defensive posture.

"We know how to cheat," said the politician.

The other gentleman burst into laughter.

After a confused silence on my part and a hearty laugh on his, the man added, "You'd be a great candidate, Joe. We could help you out next time."

"I'll contact you if I ever change my mind," I muttered as I walked away.

44

I got into a big jam with the campaign. I had cleaned out our retirement savings, over $117,000, without mentioning it to Donna, and she had found out. I was sleeping in a booth at the restaurant when she opened the door around five o'clock in the morning. I was scared out of my mind.

Donna charged, "You took all the money; we are done."

"Donna, I am so sorry. We have twenty-five years together and two kids. Please don't talk like that."

"No, we are done."

"I had good intentions. I was going to put it back, but I couldn't. I will. Just give me a little time."

She repeated, "Done!"

Donna's startling appearance while I was in a deep sleep made it all seem surreal. I babbled, "Most guys my age want a twenty-two-year-old girl. I don't want no twenty-two-year-old-girl. I want you, and I want to be governor."

She didn't think it was funny. She left.

I went home but knew I would not be welcome in our bed, so I headed downstairs. I was sleeping on the green sectional sofa when the light came on and Donna stormed down the stairs. It was the second rude awakening of the morning.

Donna started screaming, "Why did you do this? You ruined everything!"

I pleaded again, "Please, love. I'm sorry. So sorry. I'll make it up to you."

Donna saw red. She straddled my back and pounded on it for several minutes straight, with force, like a punching bag workout. I protected my head and just took it like a man.

Don't underestimate a woman's intuition. A couple of weeks earlier, she'd had a dream that the money in our savings was gone. The dream crossed her mind once or twice, but a few weeks after that, Donna was having trouble falling asleep. Her hunch was strong enough that she got out of bed and checked, and the money really *was* gone. That's when she got dressed and stormed right down to the restaurant.

Donna called my mother afterward, crying. She admitted to her that she lost all control and pummeled me. I was expecting my mother to be on my side, but I expected wrong. I overheard my mother saying, "Don't cry, Donna. He deserved every one of those punches. If he comes over here, I'll hit him, too."

We were going to drive Donna's parents, Nanny and Pappy, to the airport in the morning, so they just happened to be staying with us the night Donna found out I had taken money to cover the campaign.

Nanny said, "I worked for an Italian, and I understand how these dagos do things."

Donna corrected her. "My husband is a great PR person and marketer, but he has an F in bookkeeping."

"Where else did all that money go?"

"Nowhere else, Mom. The campaign was that big."

Donna was about as angry with me as a woman can be. She said to Pappy, "Dad, I want you to yell at Joe when he comes in today. I want you to yell loud. Tell him what you are really thinking."

When I got home, Pappy didn't say a word to me.

Donna fumed, "That was the first time in my entire life that my dad disappointed me."

I answered, "He knew I had good intentions." She didn't like that.

Donna and I went to counseling sessions over my spending our savings on the campaign without her knowing. She was not easily able to forgive me. She told the counselor that she was going to get her education and then decide what she wanted to do after that, not really knowing if she would stay or go.

Donna went through various stages of grief that naturally followed what she perceived as a betrayal, but over time the wound showed signs of healing. After finding out about the money, Donna no longer devoted herself to the restaurant. She had taken a big step back. She was there off and on as a hostess, but she was out of the day-to-day operations. Donna returned to college, preparing to go back to an industry she loved—the airlines—and eventually took a job with AirTran.

I was on thin ice for many years over that money. I had gotten caught up in the moment and made a bad decision that would affect me for the rest of my life. Looking back, I was 100 percent wrong. I had "borrowed" over a hundred thousand dollars from my wife without asking, and it was gone.

One of the things I learned from other people in a marriage situation is that if you cheat on your wife, she *might* forgive you. But I'm telling you, if you take her money, good luck! It is one of the top regrets of my entire life.

45

While everything was going on with the county commissioner campaign and election, it was business as usual at The Primadonna. Although I was deflated by the politics and worried about the time and money that now seemed wasted, the positive feedback from restaurant patrons and food critics provided the steady fuel I needed to work at such a frenzied pace.

One of my steady customers, Leo, was dating a cute girl from the Rocks. He told me, "This is the best place on earth. We come here, we have a nice dinner and a few drinks, and then we have some great sex. Joe, she ain't going for anything unless we have dinner here first. You are amazing, buddy. Your food is like female Viagra."

I made a point of serving Leo and his girlfriend myself the next time they came in, announcing, "This sauce is like Love Potion Number Nine," as I served their pastas. After that, I'd sing or hum the lyrics when I saw them. I don't know whether Leo's girlfriend knew he had confided in me, but if she did, it didn't bother her because she'd giggle like crazy.

46

The Pittsburgh Pirates were a strong team in the nineties, and baseball fever was spreading again. The vice president of public relations for the Pirates, Rick Cerrone, came to The Primadonna a few times during this era. Rick had previously worked for the Yankees, and I always took it as a compliment to have a New Yorker as a returning customer, since New York City is famous for terrific food.

Possibly inspired by all the pictures and plaques on the Primadonna walls, one night Rick gave me a five-by-seven autographed picture of Roberto Clemente, which I proudly hung behind the bar.

One night on a jam-packed weekend, a guy was waiting at the bar to talk to me. He asked if he could take a closer look at the Clemente picture. I took it down from the wall and gave it to him.

He exclaimed, "This is unbelievable! It's not stamped, it's signed in ink. This is unbelievable!"

"Yeah, it is. He signed fifty of them before he died. They were not made out to anyone."

The guy said, "I'll give you one hundred dollars for this."

"Not for sale."

I went into the kitchen and asked Sticks, who would know about this kind of thing. "Hey, Sticks! How much do you think that signed photo of Roberto Clemente is worth?"

He thought for a moment and guessed, "An original signed photo of Roberto Clemente? I'd say about a thousand."

On my way back into the dining room, the man tapped me on

the shoulder and said,

"I'll give you two hundred dollars."

"Sorry. Like I said, not for sale."

"Three hundred?"

I just shook my head—no.

"Four hundred?"

I kept shaking my head—no.

"I'll give you five hundred in cash, right now."

"Sorry, buddy."

"Six hundred? Seven hundred? Eight hundred?"

I just kept shaking my head—no.

At first, I felt annoyed at this stranger asking for something that was precious to me. Then suddenly my mind was conversing with itself, arguing whether it was just a picture or a rare treasure.

The man pressed on. "One thousand dollars cash."

Now my mouth was salivating because I had just finished my run for county commissioner, and I was really hurting for money. I was no better a bookkeeper with the campaign than I had been at the restaurant, and there were a few bills left to pay. I'd have to rob Peter to pay Paul on my taxes. A thousand in cash would be amazing at the moment, but I held my poker face.

"No offense, sir, but why should I sell it to you?"

"I can't tell you how much this would mean to me. I would cherish it."

I held on. "I'm sorry."

He continued, "I'll give you eleven hundred dollars for this photo. Cash. Right now. Take a look."

I looked down and saw the crisp one-hundred-dollar bills, eleven of them. I could smell the green. I paused for a long moment and then handed over the photo and put the money in my pocket.

Word spread fast. The next time I entered the kitchen, I walked into boos and jeers. Sticks bemoaned, "Joe, this is sacrilegious. You sold the Roberto Clemente picture? You sold out."

Immediately I felt really bad. I walked back out to the bar and found the guy.

I said, "Hey, my man! I hear you have a signed Roberto Clemente picture?"

He smiled. "Yeah, right here. It's an original, signed not stamped." He held it up proudly.

"I'll give you fifteen hundred dollars for it."

He replied, "Not for sale."

47

In 1996, my cousin Pino had grown restless and allowed his own thoughts to lure him out of the great setup he had. He was in a sweet spot at The Primadonna, but he couldn't seem to realize it. Pino was very well compensated without the hassle of proprietorship. In my public relations I touted him often, so he had made a name for himself (or I had made a name for him) and had garnered some awards of his own. Just as I said so many times about the restaurant, it doesn't matter how good you are unless your marketing gets the word out. Pino didn't realize how my "word" had promoted him. He announced that he would be opening his own place, House of Pino. In fact, he came out of the kitchen in the weeks before he left and announced it to my customers, saying it would be the same food at lower prices. That really hurt me.

I ran into Froggy one day. He said, "Hey, I didn't see you at Pino's grand opening!"

I was straightforward. "I wasn't invited. I'm going to tell you something. My cousin left me after ten years. He walked out and didn't even thank me." I told him how much Pino was making at The Primadonna. He was making minimum wage before he started working for me.

Froggy said, "There is no one in the restaurant business making that kind of money with no ownership. He is out of his mind. He will never see that kind of money again."

Froggy was right. In less than three years, Pino's place went belly-up. I didn't offer to hire Pino back when he closed, and he didn't ask for a job either.

The kitchen staff was strong enough that the restaurant was not affected by Pino's departure. It was unfortunate for him that he was gone by the time we received the most prestigious award a chef could ever add to their résumé.

Maria chose to attend Syracuse University to study public relations, so in the fall of 1999, we drove there and moved her in. Like other families, we were experiencing the heartache that parents go through when their firstborn goes off to college, especially when the school is far from home.

The ten-hour round-trip drive and the move were physically and emotionally exhausting, so I slept in a bit on Saturday morning. My legs and feet were swollen, so the hot tub seemed like a good way to start the day.

Donna came into the room and saw the steam coming off the water and exclaimed, "Joe! How hot is that water?"

When I got out, I saw that the skin on my left leg was bubbled and puffed-up like bubble gum. Donna and I were both alarmed, but it was time to go to work. I wrapped some gauze around my leg, got dressed, and went to the restaurant, hoping it would improve once it cooled down. I remember showing Betty Blatz the condition of my skin on my shin. She urged me to go straight to the hospital, but I didn't.

It was nearly five Sunday morning when I got home from that busy Saturday night, so I slept, but when I woke and Donna saw the condition of my skin, she immediately drove me to the emergency room at Sewickley Hospital.

The hospital staff measured my sugar, and it was off the chart. The bubbling skin was a burn, not a weird reaction to something. The neuropathy in my leg had progressed to where I couldn't even feel the temperature of the water. The burns were so bad that I needed a skin graft, but to do that and have a chance at healing, my blood sugar had to be at a healthy level.

Before this, I had totally resisted the idea of using insulin, but the doctor had a straightforward talk with me. They couldn't help me without using insulin to get my blood sugar to a manageable level, so I had little choice. In addition to the hospital staff treating the spike in blood sugar, I was given a kit and supplies along with the education necessary to monitor my sugar finger-prick style once I was released.

I had never taken time off from The Primadonna before, so staff knew that something serious was happening. Everyone stepped up, and I knew the restaurant was in good hands.

Donna had to close the restaurant each night during my absence. Part of the closing and getting ready for the next day routine included Hufty's trip to pick up bread. Mancini's was open twenty-four hours a day, and we'd put in an order each night that Hufty would pick up after two o'clock and bring back to the restaurant for the following day. On one of the nights, he picked up fifty loaves of bread at Mancini's and returned as usual. The door was locked. He knocked and knocked, but finally gave up and drove home with the bread. Donna had forgotten about the bread run and had gone home. Other than that, everyone did fine without me.

When I left the hospital, I had graduated from pills to insulin, but I still didn't take it seriously enough. I didn't check my blood sugar levels as often as advised, and like the other times, I could not break the eating habits that aggravated the condition. The would'ves, could'ves, and should'ves can really come back to haunt you.

48

April 4, 2001, was a memorable day in my life. I received a letter that The Primadonna had been chosen as a recipient for the most coveted restaurant award in America, the DiRōNA Award from the Distinguished Restaurants of North America. In the restaurant business, that's like receiving an Oscar, or maybe more like a Lifetime Achievement Award.

The mail came to the restaurant. Having no idea we had won this award, when I read the letter, I was jumping up and down like a game show contestant. The DiRōNA Award was the epitome of all my hard work. I will forever appreciate Mike Kalina's reviews, but this was my icing on the cake.

The staff didn't know too much about the award, but when I started talking about it, they became excited with me and for me. Hufty hollered out, "DiRōNA in da Rocks!"

I floated through the day in a euphoric state and was so keyed up that after closing the restaurant, I was still nowhere near sleep. I had a Cuban cigar that someone gave me, so I took it out to celebrate. I smoked that sucker the entire night. They say there is something in the soil of a good Cuban cigar that makes the difference. I was high from the award, but I felt high from smoking that cigar, too. I stayed right in the restaurant at the bar until the sun came up, feeling nothing but elation, doin' fine on cloud nine.

Here is the DiRōNA Award news release:

DiRöNA Award

Named one of North
America's Finest
Restaurants

NEWS RELEASE

MONTEREY, California—If you think it's hard getting into a top college, just try getting a DiRöNA Award. The Primadonna Restaurant of McKees Rocks recently achieved that rare distinction, making it one of only 723 restaurants in more than 300 North American cities to do so.

Based in Monterey, California, The DiRöNA Award was established in 1990 to promote distinguished dining throughout the United States, Canada and Mexico. Its influence and stature and the prestige of its award program reflect a growing trend among consumers to seek restaurants that combine superlative experiences with excellent value.

The Primadonna Restaurant will be honored in Montreal, Canada, at the Grand Awards Gala ceremony September 26, 2001, and will receive the prestigious DiRöNA Award. Presented by Distinguished Restaurants of North America.

While the rewards are delicious, winning such an honor is no piece of cake. According to Chef John Folse, Chairman of DiRöNA, "At the Oscars, a single performance may win the gold, but to merit a DiRöNA Award, everyone and everything in your restaurant has to be superb every day. That's a tall order, and only the very best can attain that.

Clearly in that league, The Primadonna Restaurant first had to pass the rigorous 75-point criteria evaluation program conducted anonymously by one of DiRöNA's forty independent inspectors. The DiRöNA Award is, in fact, the only program of its kind in North America, scrutinizing every aspect of the dining experience from reservations to dessert.

Kevin Joyce, proprietor of the Carlton, had been to the DiRōNA Awards previously, so he prepped me. He said the ceremony was a black-tie event with great attention to detail. *Unbelievable* was the word he used, which got me pumped up months ahead of the event. Donna and I got our plane tickets and made hotel reservations right away. Unfortunately, the terrorist attacks on September 11, 2001, took place, and someone from the DiRōNA organization called to tell me the event would be postponed under the circumstances. People were afraid to travel or congregate at that time.

Later that year, in November, it was announced that the restaurant would be included in the DirōNA Guide.

2002 DiRōNA Guide

The new DiRōNA 2002 Guide to Distinguished Restaurants of North America has a full page, with color photos, directions and other details, on restaurants in each city that have received the DiRōNA award. From the Pittsburgh area, there are three: the Carlton, Downtown; Hyeholde, Moon; and Primadonna, McKees Rocks.

I was in the most excellent company, being grouped with the Hyeholde and the Carlton. The Hyeholde is a castle-like building on a beautiful, wooded site not far from the Pittsburgh International Airport, a high-class place to wine and dine corporate customers. The Carlton, originally housed in the Carlton Hotel near the courthouse in the center of downtown Pittsburgh, had built its reputation decades before moving to BNY Mellon Center in the eighties after the Carlton Hotel was razed. Another favorite among wealthy and corporate clients, even I couldn't believe that The Primadonna, located on a corner in McKees Rocks, had tapped into this league. I bought pins for all of my staff that they wore with honor, as we were all in this together. I began to publicize this ultimate honor by putting the DiRōNA Award and its logo on my business cards and ads.

Instead of holding the traditional awards ceremony later that year, the DiRōNA Awards were presented at the Chicago Restaurant Association convention for restaurateurs in 2002, several months after the originally scheduled awards. This was a huge event but of a different nature from the traditional DiRōNA Awards event, so the ceremony itself was anticlimactic.

49

One night Michael McGinley, minority owner of the Steelers, came in with his wife. They ordered a one-hundred-dollar bottle of wine.

Hufty was busing, and I wanted to make sure the couple was well taken care of. I said to Hufty, "Go over there and refill their water."

Hufty did as I asked, but he bumped the bottle of wine and it spilled onto Mrs. McGinley's dress. As Hufty scrambled for more napkins, I rushed over and apologized to the couple. I told them that I'd take care of the cleaning bill and brought another bottle of the expensive wine. (At the end of the evening, I comped the entire meal, but the McGinleys never returned.)

Inside the kitchen, Hufty said, "I am so, so sorry."

Agitated by the incident, I blurted out, "Don't be sorry at all. I'm mad at myself. I should have known better. I should have never asked you. I should have known you were going to screw it up. I'm pissed off at myself."

Hufty restated, "I'm so sorry, Joe." He took off his DiRōNA pin and handed it to me. "I don't deserve it." I took the pin.

Harsh. I know. Staff was used to my knee-jerk reactions. I wasn't proud of them, but they happened. It was over that night. The next day it was business as usual, but I kept the pin for the time being. When the time was right, I gave Hufty the pin back. I wanted to.

"Here's your pin back, Huf. You deserve to have this. You really do." Hufty knew that was my way of apologizing.

He said, "Thank you, Joe. This means a lot to me."

It was impossible to stay cross with Hufty for long. I would never want to lose him; he was too important to our collective mental well-being with his loyalty, versatility, humility, and quick humor. Back when Maria had first been considering going to the University of Syracuse, I had asked him, "Hey, Huf—how far is Syracuse from here?"

"Two joints up and two joints back," he answered matter-of-factly.

One night around the bar, Vic DaVita was describing an extremely well-dressed couple who had come in earlier, looking like they were about to step onto the red carpet. Vic said, "She was definitely a ten; you could tell she wasn't a Rocks girl."

Hufty shot right back. "Hey! What do you mean by that? The Rocks has a plethora of girls who are tens."

"Yeah? Who's a ten in the Rocks?" Vic challenged.

"A regular four with a six-pack." That's how Hufty kept us entertained.

We joked about the Rocks, but there was nowhere we'd rather be. Rocks people were unpretentious. Upwardly mobile people had already left town; those who were left were salt-of-the-earth people with grit and a sense of humor. They worked hard and had each other's backs. Once people in the Rocks trusted you, diversity and community meshed in a manner unlike anywhere else. The diversity was not only racial, but also encompassed age, education level, ethnicity, political affiliation, sexual orientation, religion (or lack thereof), and income level, yet the sense of community was fierce. Remember the guy I was warned about when we first opened—Clem Smarra, the one who was reputed to have fought twelve guys in one night? He became a good customer, and yes, he was known for fighting and was proud of it. He gave me a photo of himself with Muhammed Ali. He was bigger than Ali and looked a lot tougher.

I had plenty of opportunities to move elsewhere once the restaurant was a success, but I had found too much good here to leave.

50

Sometime before noon on Tuesday, May 29, 2002, I was going about my usual late-morning preparations at the restaurant when Maria, home from her sophomore year of college called.

"Dad, listen, two guys from the US Treasury Department are here looking for you." She was practically whispering, so I blocked my open ear with my finger to better hear her.

"The US Treasury Department? No big thing—just send them down to the restaurant. I'll be here."

"Okay. Dad?"

"Yeah?"

"Call me as soon as they leave. They seem serious. I'm scared."

Within minutes the men were knocking on the restaurant door. My bartender, Larry, was off that night but had come in to set things up for the evening, so I asked him to answer the phone for a while.

I opened the door, told the men to come in, and then led them to Table Ten, which was one of the best tables in the restaurant, set in a corner. We had privacy there.

One of the men took something out of a folder. "This is about the Information Act," he explained as he handed me some papers. "You are going to have to look through this and respond."

Baffled, I asked, "What's this for?"

"Tax evasion."

"Tax evasion? For me? Why?" I asked in rapid succession.

"Because of how you live. Your lifestyle is one indication."

"How I live? My *lifestyle*? What do you mean? I drive a twelve-year-old Cadillac, work seventeen hours a day, and haven't been to a family wedding in fifteen years."

They looked at me blankly and continued questioning. "What's your interest in Casa di Pino?"

"I have no interest in this."

"It's under your name—Costanzo."

"My cousin Pino has the same last name. It's *his* place."

"Are you involved with that restaurant?"

"No."

"What about the salad dressing?"

"Yes, that's mine."

"What is your wife's involvement?"

"I am the sole proprietor here. My wife has nothing to do with any of this stuff."

The rest of the questions were all over the map and only confused me further. They also indicated that another person under investigation had implicated me in something. Because of the Kalina investigation years earlier, at first I thought these men were barking up the wrong tree again. It was obvious that they were still suspecting some kind of underworld connections, but some of the questions were directly about my own taxes, which scared me. When they left, I immediately called my attorney, Stanley Lehman, and made an appointment for the following Monday.

When I walked back into the bar area, Larry pulled me aside.

"Joe, your daughter Maria called three times and needs you to call her back. She asked me not to tell anyone but you. Is everything all right?"

"Yeah, Larry, thanks. She's been going through some things with her boyfriend," I lied. "I'll call her now."

I called our home. "Dad! What's going on?" Maria asked frantically.

"Maria, meet me at Georgie's. I can't talk here."

By that time, two other employees had come in early. I thanked Larry and told them all I'd be back in a little while. I was always running errands, so they thought nothing of it.

Georgie's was a diner on Route 51 that we had been going to for years. It was a good thing I had been there a million times; I was able to get there on autopilot.

Anxiety had made its home in my chest. I didn't see Maria's car, so I parked and was deep in thought when Maria knocked on the window. Caught by surprise, I jolted and then unlocked the door.

"Are you jumping into the car, or are we going into Georgie's?"

"I'm getting into the car." Maria opened the door and jumped in, wasting no time. "Now tell me what this is all about."

"Listen, Maria, those men were there for *me*. I had no idea why they had come and why they were questioning me. At one point, I even asked if they had the right Joe Costanzo."

"Uh-huh."

"There was a federal grand jury investigation, and the person being prosecuted was offered a plea bargain to mention someone else that they had 'suspected' was also not acting in accordance with the law."

"Okay. So?"

"In turn, they would get the 'get out of jail free card.'"

"Mmm-hmm."

"This someone took the plea bargain and decided to mention my name."

"What! How could they do that? Who could do such a thing? Who is this person?"

"Listen, I tried to find out as much as I could, but the two guys wouldn't tell me anything. I have no idea who this could be."

"Okay. So what did they want?"

"According to the federal law, since my name was mentioned in this investigation, they are obligated to investigate it further."

"What does that mean?"

"Well, it means that they need to look at me, the business, and our family, and they will see what they can find. Don't worry too much about this. I need to talk with my lawyer, and we'll go from there."

"Dad, is this going to be okay?"

"Listen Maria, I think it is going to be fine, but I need to figure this out a little more. Whatever you do, don't tell anyone about this yet. Not your mother, not Kelly, not Aunt Diane, not Grandma. I need you to keep this between us for now. Can you do this for me?"

Maria nodded in agreement but then burst into tears. She tried to continue talking but had to put up her index finger, gesturing "Wait a minute" until she collected herself. My heart broke as I watched her crying so hard that she was gasping for air. Tears welled in my own eyes, but I fought them back. I *had* to be strong to make her believe things were not so bad.

Maria was still sobbing. I gave her a big hug and waited until her tears slowed down. We never went into Georgie's; Maria got into her car and headed home.

51

Even with this heavy secret weighing on me, life couldn't afford to slow down. As I liked to say, the place was rockin'. It was a little before five o'clock, and there was already a line out the door. I knew most of the staff was feeling the incomparable high that we all experienced when everything came together on a busy night, but my mood was punctured repeatedly throughout the evening by disturbing thoughts of my afternoon visitors. Various questions they had asked floated back into my mind as I tried to connect the dots. I knew I had done a good acting job that night, though. I kept the smiles, handshakes, and zucchini flowing as usual.

Maria had come in late for her waitress shift. I walked downstairs to bring up some wine, and she followed. She was wearing more makeup than usual, and I could see through her glasses that her eyes were still a bit puffy, but probably not noticeable if you weren't looking for it.

"Dad, what's happening? Did you call anyone else about— (Maria paused, as if the walls had ears)—the situation?"

"Listen, not here, Maria. I'm very busy."

"Busy, yes, but can't you give me a quick update on what's going on?"

"No, not now. I have a business to run."

"You always have a business to run, Dad. That's part of the problem!"

Maria stomped back upstairs. I was angry at the dig when she knew I had enough tension, and Maria seemed angry with me, but I realized I needed to put it aside for the moment. The place was packed, and by this time there was a two-and-a-half-hour wait. I tried to block out everything else and focus on helping out, knowing that there was no other place I would rather be while I dealt with the stress.

The night proceeded as usual, and although I felt the looming threat, I was kept busy enough to keep from dwelling on it. I got home around four the next morning, taking my time despite the strain and exhaustion of the day. As I had hoped, Donna was sound asleep. I still couldn't turn off my brain enough to be able to sleep. I remember noticing that it was turning light outside. I must've slept for a short while at some point after that because I caught a fragment of a dream. Then I lay there for another long while, finally giving up and going downstairs around seven.

I made a pot of coffee and attempted to read the paper to get my mind off the situation, but I could barely concentrate. Maria was first to join me, and with Donna and Kelly asleep, I knew it was okay to talk softly. We would hear them coming if they woke.

"So, did you get a hold of the lawyer?"

"Yes."

"And?"

In a whisper softer than I knew I was capable of, I confided in Maria. "It's not good. This thing is bigger than I had thought. It looks like it's going to be a criminal investigation."

Shocked, Maria continued, "*What*? What do you mean?"

"The stakes are higher in a criminal case, and if I'm convicted, I might have to do some jail time."

"Are you *serious*?" she asked in disbelief. "For *what*, Dad?"

"I don't know, Maria. Stuff I didn't think much about at the time. Robbing Peter to pay Paul on the taxes after the campaign, paying the servers in cash sometimes. Things like that."

"Mom will totally freak out! I remember when you got that second LCB citation. You seemed unaffected, but I remember what a wreck Mom was—how much she cried and how scared she was. This seems much worse, no?"

"Unfortunately, it could be. Just hang in there for a while. Say some prayers and stay quiet until I can figure out what to do."

It was important to me to tell each of my "girls" myself—Kelly, my mother, and most urgently, Donna, and I fretted about how, when, and where to do it. This was difficult, but there was no way around it. I dreaded these conversations more than the possible legal consequences but dreaded even more that my family could hear something from the outside world before I could tell them. Two days later, I picked Kelly up after school, thinking this might be the best chance for me to explain what was happening.

Kelly was having a great year in high school; in addition to being a celebrated track star, her studies, friends, student council, and prom committee kept her busy. I hated to put a damper on her happiness.

After I summarized the state of affairs, Kelly asked, "Why is it a *criminal* investigation?"

"If you pay employees in cash, it is a violation of the law because you aren't paying into Social Security. If you underreport your income, it is another criminal charge."

"So what next?" she asked matter-of-factly.

"I'll meet with the lawyer and take it a day at a time."

"Your lawyer's good, right? Everything will be okay, Dad."

To my great relief, Kelly seemed unaware of the implications of the situation. Her innocent optimism and attempt to reassure me tore at my heart, so I wasn't going to say anything that could interfere with that naive confidence. She was used to her dad making everything better. Just so nothing interfered with her plans, she seemed to take it all with a grain of salt.

Before dropping her off at home, I added, "Kelly, I need time to tell your mother. She'll want to know every detail, and there's no way we can stop in the middle of this crazy-busy week. I'm going to have to wait for a chance to discuss it with her, so please don't say a word in the meantime. Maria knows because the Treasury guys went to our house first. You're the only other person who knows right now. Not a word. Promise?"

"Sure, Dad," she agreed as she bounced out of the car as though nothing had changed.

52

That was the start of elaborate scenarios forming in my head. Even though I knew these thoughts were counterproductive, I would let them play out in detail, feeling as though I were trying to leave a room but felt compelled to watch the end of a TV show.

We're all sitting around the dining room table on a Sunday at my sister's house. My mother, matriarch of the family, is putting together the finishing touches of her classic meal: a large bowl of pasta with her homemade marinara sauce and chicken breaded with Rice Krispies. I can smell the goodness wafting through the house.

As I try to joke around waiting for the feast, I can feel my nervousness growing. I know this has to be the day. In a couple of minutes, the secret that I've been harboring will be a secret no more. I am bracing myself to handle the consequences, but what if this sends my devoted mother off the edge? Even worse, what if she has a heart attack?

My mother walks in and joins everyone at the table. The omniscient storyteller in my brain knows that my mother suspects that something is going on. I had been too quiet . . .

You get the idea. But these scenarios seemed to have a life of their own; just as in a dream, I felt like I was watching them instead of creating them. I had never been one to ruminate, but these thoughts kept imposing themselves on me. Like a pesky fly, when I tried to shoo them away, they'd come right back. They would repeat but be a little different each time. In the above scene, sometimes Donna already knew, and sometimes she didn't. Sometimes Donna and the girls knew, and it was only news to my mother and sister.

In another of my anxious brain's recurring scenarios, we are in the courtroom:

It is winter, a deep chill in the air. I am re-entering the courtroom with my lawyer, followed by the defense attorney and the judge. The judge had told us that the verdict was in. My wife, daughters, and mother all have the same expression as our eyes meet, emanating both love and fear.

Everyone in the courtroom stands so still that you can hear the small creaks in the woodwork and the hiss of a radiator. The judge clears his throat and motions for the spokesperson of the jury to come forward.

A young woman nervously unfolds a piece of paper and reads, "In the case of Joseph Costanzo, Jr., vs. the Federal Government of the United States, we the jury find the defendant guilty of all charges."

The next day, I drove to Greenfield and told my mother. As supportive and devoted a mother as she was, she had never been an emotional person. She had many problems in her life and just dealt with them head-on, which is what she seemed to be doing when I told her everything. I don't think she understood the gravity of the situation.

Donna and I were on opposite schedules all week, and this wasn't the kind of thing to tell her in passing when either of us was on our way to work. We both had Sunday off, so that was when I planned to talk to her.

That Sunday, I picked Donna up from her shift at AirTran.

"Are you hungry?" I asked.

"Famished."

"I was thinking of a place I'd like to go, but it's in Midland. Are you up for a drive?"

"What kind of place?"

"It's a Sunday buffet that I've heard about from a few people." We enjoyed trying a new restaurant on occasion, where we would compare food, service, prices, and atmosphere, and maybe spark an idea or two for The Primadonna.

"Sure, let's try it."

At the buffet, Donna filled her plate and seemed to be enjoying the food. I started with just a cup of soup. Knowing what I had to confess, there was no way a meal could pass through the knot in my stomach.

"What's wrong, Joe? Aren't you hungry?"

"Not at all."

"What did you eat at home?"

"I had breakfast as usual. I'm just not hungry."

We made small talk for a while, and then Donna repeated, "What's wrong? It's very unusual for you not to eat. Why don't you take a walk over to the buffet table and take a look? There are a lot of good choices."

When I declined, she asked, "Are you okay? I mean—health-wise?"

"I'm fine," was my reply.

"I'd like to try some kind of dessert, but I'd enjoy it more if you'd eat something. It's just not like you, Joe. I'm becoming concerned."

"Please, Donna. Have something. I'm just not hungry. I just wanted to check out the place. I figured you'd be hungry."

When we got back into the car, I immediately said, "Love, I have to tell you something. The girls know about this already. It's not good news. Actually, it's really bad news."

"Oh, my God, Joe! Are you sick? Is that why you didn't eat anything?" Trying to collect myself first, I didn't answer right away, so Donna pressed on. "What is it, Joe? Do you have cancer?"

"I'm okay. I'm not sick, but these IRS agents came to the house, so that's how Maria found out. She sent them down to the restaurant, and they talked to me for a long time. It's serious, love, and I think I might have to do some jail time in a federal prison."

"*What?*" Donna was completely taken aback. "For what?"

I told her about the federal agents' visit, the questions they asked, and what I had done that would inevitably come out in an investigation.

"Oh, my God! What's going to happen to us?"

"It's going to be all right, Donna."

"*How?* How can you say that *this* is going to be all right?"

During our conversation, I had mentioned that Maria, Kelly, my mother, and my sister knew, but there hadn't been time in our schedules to discuss it between us.

As soon as we got home, Donna walked straight into the kitchen and called my mother. I could hear her saying, "Mom, Joe just told me about the IRS guys. Oh, my God! I feel like someone is inside my stomach punching me . . . What is happening? He might have to go to prison . . . It doesn't seem real; it feels like a bad dream . . . My husband? I don't understand."

It seemed like every time Donna and I would be in physical proximity, she would bring up a different hypothetical scenario. "How am I supposed to take Kelly to school and have the other parents looking at us, judging us for my husband being in prison?" Then, "How about the kids? What are people going to be asking them or telling them about you?" Donna couldn't get her mind off it.

I often hear people say you have to hit rock bottom before you head back up, whether they're talking about addiction, weight gain, or bankruptcy. I don't necessarily agree with that, but at the same time, I wanted to get everything out of the way that could take us downward any further, so I dropped the last bombs. I confessed that in 1995, I was depositing nine thousand dollars at a time for TV ads and that I had gotten a loan from the bank without Donna knowing about it.

Donna was seething. "If you touched the girls' college money, I'm leaving you. Just tell me straight."

"No, I didn't touch a penny of the kids' money." I hadn't.

Donna reached out to one of her best friends, Michelle, and they met for a long breakfast at a diner in Southside. "How will I tell my family? How will I tell my friends? Even though Joe's the one who did this, I somehow feel ashamed," she told Michelle.

I was giving Donna the space she needed and didn't pry. Feeling bad for both of us in different ways, Maria told me that Donna had said Michelle listened empathetically and shared with me a little of the exchange between them as told to her.

"Michelle told Mom that everyone has skeletons in their closet, but it's better to deal with situations openly. She talked about not worrying what other people think. I think she helped mom realize that if people say things that are judgmental or hurtful, it's a reflection on *them*, not on our family."

Michelle made it her mission to support Donna through this time. Michelle reminded us that not so long ago, Donna would say, "Wouldn't it be nice if people would start coming to the restaurant?" And they had! Over time, Michelle helped our family to see that there was much more to be proud of than to be ashamed of. She told Donna, "Even Mister Rogers sings, 'The very same people who are good sometimes are the very same people who are bad sometimes.' You and Joe are good people. We all know how hard you both worked for the restaurant. Politics can get really evil. Joe's rivals didn't want him in, and they destroyed him."

Looking back, the most difficult moments of the whole tax-related ordeal from start to finish were telling my wife and daughters. For my family, I only ever wanted to be a source of happiness, not disappointment or worry. I wish Maria wouldn't have known so I could have told her first myself, too, but the US Treasury beat me to it. That privilege was the first of the many things they stripped from me during that time.

53

The investigation that began right after Memorial Day in 2002 lasted until the trial—more than two and a half years of mounting pressure that never went away. People talked. Donna and the kids felt it. We tried to go on, but things were never really the same. We each suffered in multiple ways—anxiety, shame, fear, mistrust, and unknowing.

Rumors were swirling. People gossiped that I was an underworld figure. People gossiped that I laundered money. My staff was scared. As part of the investigation, the government informed me that they would be approaching people for information. I composed a letter explaining to my employees that I was under investigation. The IRS would be coming around, and they needed to be prepared. Once that letter got out, word spread quickly on the street.

After the letters were distributed, I talked to everyone and told them not to lie or try to second guess the investigators' motives. I said, "If they come to your house or come down here to the restaurant, just tell them what you think." It was just a bad situation that had nothing to do with any of these people.

A couple days later, investigators turned up at the houses of Anmarie and Hope, both servers, and questioned them in the late morning before they were due at work. They showed up unannounced and were ready to intimidate. They asked both women similar questions:

Does Joe live elaborately?

What kind of lifestyle does he lead?

Were there any poker machines in the restaurant?

Did he ever pay you in cash?

Does Joe have any underworld connections?

What are Joe's working hours?

Have you seen anything illegal?

The women reported that they kept their cool when interviewed, but when they came into work, they were quite shaken. Other employees were on edge about being questioned.

The agents went to all the businesses in the Rocks that I had affiliations with and did the same thing. They also went to my bank, to Wholey's, Pennsylvania Macaroni, Giant Eagle, and Theresa's Bakery. These people were not just business partners; they had become friends. I could feel them backing away from me, too.

One of my best vendors called and was livid. As soon as I answered the phone, he started screaming. "You got me in trouble with the Feds? What the fuck?"

I had to calm him down. He was a great guy, and I couldn't believe the investigators were bothering him. I said quietly, "I am sorry that this happened. I never mentioned you. Never. This is an investigation on me, not on you." The vendor then apologized. Since that time, I've heard that some agents like to go around to people connected to the person being investigated because it produces buzz and intimidation. It's a psychological tactic that shakes people up and helps their case.

Since I highly value loyalty, I expected others would, too. What I didn't anticipate was that although people showed concerned for me, the most common response was fear. Vendors didn't want to cooperate, as many were running mostly cash-based operations; they were afraid of being caught at their own game.

Although it was unsettling, I thought that the investigation would focus on the restaurant, and thus the people getting interviewed would include those who had worked in the restaurant, and maybe people with whom money had changed hands—suppliers and service workers. The investigation shortly went from a private to a public matter, however, as the government took liberties to interview anyone they wanted. We were all taken aback when I received a call from my mother on a Saturday afternoon.

The attorney had advised my mother not to open the door if investigators came around, and she was reminded more than once. She called to tell me that two men knocked on her door and showed their badges. She let them right in. As any decent Italian mother would do when someone comes to her house, she offered them a slice of her homemade apple pie.

The question that surprised my mother most was, "Does Joe ever give you money?"

She laughed and said, "No, he owes *me* money."

My mother was less naive than they gave her credit for. Although she had let them in, she at least had a sense that the less said, the better. When the men started asking too many questions, she blurted out, "Awww, c'mon. Why you want to know all this? I don't have the answers to your questions."

At that, the men thanked my mother and exited.

In her inimitable way, my mother remained unruffled as she relayed the incident. She has one mode: matter of fact. If she were annoyed at all, it would only have been because the men wasted her time when she could have been doing her chores.

54

Donna was with me when I visited my lawyer. The attorney lamented, "Joe, I can't help you. You need a criminal attorney."

"A criminal attorney?" I repeated, shaking my head in disbelief.

"This came down through a federal grand jury investigation—not on you, but on someone else. Someone mentioned your name, which was enough to implicate you in a criminal case. To make matters worse, there are new federal guidelines that (President) Clinton imposed that are related to this kind of situation—so you could be looking at some prison time here."

"You've got to be kidding me."

"Before the new guidelines, this probably would have been just a fine. I'm sorry, but the guidelines leave little room for interpretation."

The civil attorney's suggestion was to contact US Attorney Tom Farrell, a top-rated criminal defense lawyer in Pittsburgh. Government rules and tactics were no stranger to him.

Farrell also came at a high price. I started to realize why my father wanted me to be a lawyer. Every phone call or bit of correspondence was documented and to the tune of two-hundred-and-fifty dollars an hour. I was paying two-hundred-and-fifty dollars an hour for someone to be the bearer of constant bad news. To the best of my recollection, this is how it went.

Knowing the laws well, Farrell was nothing but pragmatic. Upon our first meeting, he told me that the government had a 99 percent conviction rate, so pleading guilty would be the way to go. If I pleaded guilty, the minimum sentence would be five months. If I pleaded not guilty and lost, the minimum sentence jumped to five years.

I treated Farrell like one of my employees and told him that this wasn't going to happen.

"Prison!" I shouted. "The federal government should be putting a statue of me in the Rocks for all I did for that town instead of trying to put me in prison!" I wasn't willing to be hit hard as a by-product of someone else's investigation. Farrell left the room speechless.

Donna and I talked through every facet of this dilemma when we were together. She pointed out, "Joe, you never documented any of the things that you gave away—gift certificates, sponsorships, zucchini, salad dressing, desserts, wine . . ."

"I know, I know," I acknowledged.

"You donated money to organizations and sponsored those kids to study abroad at a thousand dollars a piece. If you had documented the things you gave away, the government probably would have owed *us* money."

"I agree." Donna had been fighting a battle against my unchecked generosity from the start. I let her have the last word.

"The Primadonna is our bread and butter and was our miracle. You *did* lose your focus, Joe."

I'll never regret giving away anything, but I do regret not accounting for it. Looking back, accounting was one more thing that I didn't have time to think about.

Soon afterward I received a letter from the office of Tom Farrell saying that the choice was mine as to which way to plead, but I would need to live with the consequences. Perhaps Farrell recognized my resistance as a stage in dealing with trauma. For whatever reason, he was able to overlook my knee-jerk reaction and met with me again to further explain his recommendation.

The government used an archaic system of mandatory minimum guidelines. It worked like a grid—in the first row you would find the conviction, and then each column listed degrees of severity for each crime. The intersection provided information on what the punishment would be. By sacrificing my pride and pleading guilty, I would get approximately five months of prison time vs. three to five years for pleading innocent.

I was willing to take the gamble, but the rest of my family wasn't. My mother took the news hard, especially for someone known for keeping her cool. She called and asked me to come over.

"Joe, I want you to plead guilty."

"I don't want to, Ma. This is all overblown. Someone still wants to teach me a lesson for getting into the county commissioner race."

"Your attorney knows the law like you know the restaurant business. I want you to listen to him."

"If I had listened to everyone along the way, The Primadonna would have never existed. I would still be delivering mail."

I saw the emotion rise in my mother, a rare sight. She was as serious as I had ever seen her. "Now listen to me. I could stand it for five months if you had to go away, but I couldn't take it for five years. I guarantee you that by the time you come out, I will not be here," implying that she would likely die while I was in prison.

"I was a bad bookkeeper, Mom, not a bad man. I don't belong in prison."

But Donna was right—if I had documented everything I had given away, the IRS probably *would have* owed us money. That's why I didn't feel like I was cheating the government. I thought that maybe I could amend my tax returns or plead something along that line. Account for what I had given away. Make a payment plan to pay whatever they figured I owed plus the interest. At worst, it was more of a Robin Hood attitude, albeit an after-the-fact rationalization rather than a plan.

The Feds dug and dug for information, and just when we

thought they couldn't dig anymore, they did. They wanted all sorts of information—records, canceled checks, all financial matters from the past fifteen years. Anyone would have trouble gathering all that, but our lives had changed so much during those years and we had been so busy that our files were in far-less-than-perfect order. This put a tremendous amount of pressure on me, Donna, and my girls. That notice weighed heavily on us all. No one had any minutes to spare, but we also had no choice but to locate everything they asked for. The government was in it to win it.

The diabetes and its symptoms progressed to new levels. No surprise there. My ankles were always swollen, and I assumed it was because I was on my feet for seventeen hours a day all these years. I didn't realize that it was because of the disease that I was retaining fluid. In reality, it may have been an early sign that my kidneys were failing. My sight wasn't what it used to be, either, and changing prescriptions on the glasses didn't help much.

The financial pressure, the diabetes, the ongoing investigation, and the lack of any joyful family time collided. There was nothing but tension and exhaustion. One night Donna and I had a conversation that naturally led to the previously unthinkable—we considered selling the restaurant. John Welsh had been serving in the maître d' role at The Primadonna for about six months. Long before this, when he was a customer, he expressed interest in buying the place if I ever wanted to sell. Knowing that he now fully understood the responsibilities involved, I brought it up to him, and he was very interested. He planned to keep everything as it was. We quickly sealed the deal before I could change my mind.

Phone calls poured in from the media. The first call was from the *Post-Gazette*, followed by KDKA, WPXI, and the other TV stations. I talked to the callers, as these reporters were at least acquaintances if not friends made over the years though heavy media coverage of The Primadonna's successes.

The phone rang nonstop. The outpouring of love and support

from my friends and customers made the situation bearable. The most common reaction from people I spoke to was outrage at the investigation because I had done so much for my patrons and the community. Employees and customers were also missing me while I was missing them. The Masciola family said the mood in their house was like when their dog died. One of my younger customers, Sam Dines, had been coming in with his parents since he was a toddler. When I left, he said, "Joe's personality was the power generator for The Primadonna. It doesn't feel as warm now."

I submitted a piece to the *Post-Gazette*, "Joseph Costanzo, Jr. Retiring from The Primadonna Restaurant," that ran in their *Weekend* magazine in December 2002. In the *Tribune-Review*, Treshea N. Wade also wrote about my retirement in "Pushing Away from the table: Owner of McKees Rocks leaving the cooking up to others." Some excerpts from that article:

> After seventeen years as a restaurateur, Joseph Costanzo is hanging up his apron. Costanzo, owner of The Primadonna Restaurant in McKees Rocks, retired Thursday from his full-time duties. "But nothing will change. I'll just be gone. Like one of the busboys said—it will be just like the Rolling Stones without Mick Jagger," said Costanzo ...
>
> "It just kind of evolved into this monster. I got a couple good reviews that brought a lot of people in. It went from a small neighborhood restaurant to a regional thing," he (Joe) said, crediting marketing for his success ...
>
> Last year, Costanzo and his restaurant were selected separately as one of America's top 10 restaurateurs and top 10 Italian restaurants by the International Restaurant and Hospitality Rating Bureau ...
>
> The past seventeen years have brought troubles for Costanzo. Two years after the restaurant opened, he was diagnosed with diabetes. His health had gotten progressively

worse, and now he is dependent on insulin to control his blood sugar. He is also starting to go blind in his right eye.

Costanzo, 49, relates his life as a restaurateur to his declining health.

"There's a trade-off with everything. I had a good restaurant—but I would work 17-hour days seven days a week," he said. This (diabetes) was caused by stress, and as a result my health has gotten continually worse. That's why I decided to ease on out now ... I have missed out on a lot of family things. I've lost a lot of time working at the restaurant. That's the problem with being a hands-on restaurant owner..."

Many nights, Costanzo would be seen greeting customers. Famous people, including Jamie Lee Curtis, Danny Aiello, game show host Pat Sajak, former heavyweight champion Joe Frazier and former Los Angeles Dodgers manager Tommy Lasorda have visited the restaurant.

Costanzo has traveled from table to table to chat with his patrons. That's what he said he'll miss most.

"I am already going through withdrawal. I need this place. I will still have a vested interest and visit every now and then for therapy," he said. "This is my little baby. But the great thing is that it's not closing down—so it's still living on. My legacy is still living on."

When I wasn't tied up meeting with attorneys about the case or gathering things for the IRS, I would go out to lunch or dinner with friends, but to be honest, I wasn't myself. The stress of not knowing what was going to happen was worse in some ways than withstanding what actually did happen. It was a tough space to be in.

The first Saturday night that I didn't go into the restaurant still haunts me. I had wanted to go in and had even gotten dressed to do so as I had done for the past seventeen years, but I couldn't bring myself to leave my house. Even though the awning outside The Primadonna still bore my name, the restaurant was no longer mine. This reality held me captive and tormented me from the inside. The physical effects of my disbelief, disappointment, and anger that night were tangible, from the sweat that stained my professionally laundered shirt to the sound of my own blood swishing in my ears. I always said I didn't have time to think about the things that stressed me, but now I did. I paced and fretted and created out-of-proportion scenarios in my head until the clock struck midnight—too late to arrive as I had planned. I went to bed but lay awake ruminating on the end of my glorious Primadonna days until the sun came up.

Periodically I would go to The Primadonna for dinner with Donna, my girls, or my buddies, Jimmy Carr or Donnie Bernabo. There was a different air to the place, although it was hard to pinpoint. It was great to see everyone, but at the same time, it was disturbing. It was like visiting your own child at the adoptive parents' house. Little things like noticing that they changed the seating would irritate me. Seeing someone else running The Primadonna was a huge blow.

Still, I tried hard to be grateful when the restaurant was sold because most places don't get sold; they just close down and sell the equipment. I was happy it didn't happen that way. I still owned the salad dressing during that time, so I concentrated on keeping it in the stores, restocking, and distributing samples. It was good to have something to keep me occupied, something that was still mine.

55

On October 8, 2004, I pleaded guilty. Afterward, my family wrote letters and collected letters from folks who told stories of how I had helped them throughout the years and sent those letters to the judge. Then we waited.

When I received the official letter in the mail about the actual sentencing date being January 3, 2005, it was a relief in a way. For some strange reason, just knowing when something potentially awful is going to happen is much better than an undetermined wait.

I went downtown to the courthouse with Donna. Friends and family wanted to come for support, but I discouraged it because it would be a waste of their time. The decision had been made.

Never one to keep my mouth shut, even when silence is most important, I had a speech ready. I wasn't really supposed to say anything, but I did. The judge let me speak for several minutes, although he signaled to the US Treasury agent, who came up behind me when I was speaking. He was holding handcuffs in case I got out of hand.

I told the judge and those present about the good things I had done for the community and how much it had helped the entire area—things like paying an elderly woman's property taxes when she couldn't, paying for a young man from Greenfield to go to school and eventually become a state trooper, and feeding poor people in the back alley before and after business hours. I said, "I am more of a bad bookkeeper than a tax evader, but again, it's my fault. I ask you to please reconsider and give me probation."

From their expressions, I felt like the listeners couldn't have cared less. They were ready to go home for the day.

The judge said he took all that into consideration and did acknowledge that I was an honorable man who had made a mistake. He said I accepted the responsibility of my actions and apologized. That was why he decided to give me the low end of the prison sentence—five months at the Federal Correctional Institute in Morgantown, West Virginia.

I was able to go home for about two months after the sentencing. During that time, I called people who for one reason or another I felt I should tell personally that I was going to prison. I went out to dinner with my friends. My day-to-day didn't change much from the past couple years. Even when the date came close, it wasn't like I didn't sleep at nights. The worst had happened in 2002, and now it was 2005, so I just had the attitude, *Let's get this thing over with and move on with our lives.*

For a time, Donna fell into a depression. She found it hard to get out of bed in the morning. She lost weight and found little joy in anything. The doctor prescribed an antidepressant. I knew she was slipping away from me. I would try to cheer her up by saying things like, "Don, we are a family, and we are going to get through this," but I was unable to shorten her grieving process. I wanted so badly to help, but every time I opened my mouth, it seemed to make things worse.

In February Donna had fallen out of the underbelly of a plane while working at Air Tran. It was a bad fall, leaving Donna looking like a boxer who had lost a match as well as some teeth. She was able to return to work before long, but nevertheless, it added to the messy build-up of stress.

Later in February, I got the call telling me to report to Morgantown

Federal Correction Institute on March 3, 2005. We drove to the facility so I could see it. The prison looked more like a large school campus than the old, ominous penitentiary that we Pittsburghers were so used to seeing on the Ohio River, which eased my mind a bit.

We arranged for Donna's parents to move in while I went to prison. Cooking, cleaning, and driving them to lots of appointments kept Donna's mind occupied. Nanny was a spitfire lady with a positive outlook on life and a great sense of humor—just what Donna needed at the time. Her parents were getting older, and she got to spend some golden time with them.

About a week later, it was time for the real thing. Donna and her brother Russ drove me to the prison. During the drive, we kept the conversation light. When we got out of the car, Russ was quiet, Donna was crying, and I was just anxious to get this over with.

I hugged Russ and gave Donna a kiss. "Everything will be okay," I tried to assure her, even though I had no idea if that was the truth.

56

"Are you crazy? You can't bring anything in here." That was my greeting. Two administrators were waiting when I walked through the doors, and they knew exactly who I was. I had walked in with a bag of toiletries, and they confiscated the bag. I was led to a cell with a metal bench and told to strip. They gave me blue sweatpants and a blue t-shirt, which I learned was the uniform for newbies. Then one of the men opened a door and told me to report to the Girade Unit with a vague motioning of his arm and no further explanation.

Making friends with people was something I have always been able to do, so I headed into the "yard" and spoke to one of the first men I saw. He pointed up a hill, and I found my way to the Girade Unit. As I looked around, I was surprised that the population was about 90 percent minorities. I never understood the disparity between prisons but had heard that "white collar" prisons (a.k.a. "Club Fed") were "White people" prisons, but I was wrong. The disproportionate numbers of minorities say something about the system, though.

I realized very quickly that I was not going to get any help from the guards or the administration. The actual prisoners were helpful in telling you where to go, what to do, and how to do it. The guards seemed like they wanted you to fail. They gave no instructions, yet they had expectations. It was sink or swim. Make friends or stay lost.

I was assigned to a cell with three other guys who were easy enough to get along with. After a day or two, I was fitted for a regular uniform—a beige button-down shirt, beige pants, and work boots.

We were in the yard on the second day, and I was talking to a broker named Dwayne who was released soon afterward. He was answering my questions about the daily routine and where things were located. Slowly walking toward us was the biggest man in the yard. My acquaintance said, "That's Big Sexy. He's from the Outlaws."

"The band or the motorcycle gang?" I asked.

"The motorcycle organization."

I remembered reading an article in a magazine in the barber shop about the rivalry between the Outlaws and Hell's Angels. All I could remember from the article was that the Outlaws predated WWII. That surprised me.

Even though I was standing right there, Big Sexy looked at my new friend and asked, "What's he here for?"

"We didn't get to that yet."

Then Big Sexy turned to me. "What are you in for?"

I replied, "Tax evasion."

"Ha!" he burst out, and then laughed. "Tax evasion? That's a joke."

I asked the question back to him. He started counting off on his fingers. "Extortion, prostitution, meth, gun running . . . uh . . . you name it, I've been accused of it." Then he added, "You shouldn't even be in here."

I agreed, nodding. "Even the judge said that, basically. He said that I was an honorable man who made a mistake. They even printed that in the paper."

"Yeah? The judge said to me, 'Brian, you are the most dangerous man in Macomb County, Michigan.' And they printed *that* in the paper, too." We all had a good laugh. As different as we were, that was the start of a friendship.

It didn't take long for me to make friends. After all, that was my MO. It was how I built up the restaurant, and it was how I was going to get through prison.

After about a week, I was told I'd have to move to a different dormitory. It was a large room that reminded me of a warehouse with cubicles and bunk beds. We all got along okay at my end, but one night a fight broke out at the other end of the huge room. There weren't as many guards during the night, but after ten o'clock we were not supposed to leave our cubicles. I heard yelling and began to walk toward the argument. Two guys were starting to push each other. I jumped right in like it was a potential bar fight at The Primadonna.

"Stop! You're going to fuck this up for all of us," I demanded as I wormed my way between them. "Please. Whatever it is, it isn't worth it."

To my surprise, they slowly went back to their own areas, staring each other down as they retreated.

I met a superintendent named Bill from a Cleveland suburb. He got caught interfering with the bidding process on a big construction contract for the school district, rigging it so that contractors he wanted won the bid. The contractors were not even close friends; they were the ones he felt he could really trust with the job. Goes to show that the law is the law. I spent a lot of time with him. We usually ate together. We played cards. He became my mentor in many ways, navigating me through uncharted territory. We had a lot in common. He grew up in Greensburg, PA, so we were familiar with each other's hometowns. Even though he lived in Cleveland at the time, he was still a Steelers fan. We talked about our similar upbringing and all the foods we loved. At one point Bill said to me, "Your friendship really helps me pass the time in here."

I said, "Ditto, my friend. Ditto."

Another good friend in the prison was Norm, a neurologist from Erie who was doing time because he had his nurses giving injections that should have only been given by an MD or physician's assistant with special training and certification. One of the nurses made a big mistake, but when the patient sued, Norm was the one who did the time. I felt bad for him. He explained that a new health system took over the office, and they kept all kinds of metrics on how many patients the doctors saw. Forced to see more patients per day, he trained the nurses himself to free up more of his own time for the patients. He was a gentle person who didn't fit in well until I came. He was depressed, especially at first, and often woke with screaming nightmares. That annoyed other inmates. When I saw he was down, I would ask him to come out and take a walk, and we would talk. I even taught him how to play Spades so he could join in, although he rarely did. By hanging out with me, Norm got to know some of the other guys better. They started to come to him with medical questions because if you had a problem in prison that wasn't a 911-level emergency, you weren't seeing a doctor for at least a month. You had to get sick on their time, not yours.

One evening Norm was sitting by himself at a picnic table, reading, and motioned for me to come toward him when I walked by.

"Joe, if I ask you something, will you give me an honest answer?"

"Sure, Norm."

"Have you ever thought about committing suicide?"

"No, Norm, I have not."

Norm seemed surprised, like it was inevitable. "Never? Even after you were convicted?"

"No," I answered truthfully but gently.

"You laugh so easily. How can you still be happy?"

When he said this, I realized that Norm never laughed. "Life is still beautiful, Norm. I love my family and look forward to being with them again and getting back on track."

"I love my family, too, which is what bothers me most. I've messed up their lives as well as mine."

"In what way, Norm? In what way that can't be overcome?"

"Mostly, I've brought shame on my family. I was so blessed, and I let them down. I let God down. I can't get out from under the guilt."

"Yeah, I'm both Italian and Catholic, so I can allow guilt to get to me, too, but guilt is a useless emotion. When my mind goes there, I try to think of ways to make things better."

"I never used to have thoughts like this. My thinking was devoted to the science of making my patients well—academic thinking. I'd leave the house every morning at six forty-five and was lucky if I got home by seven thirty in the evening. My hours with my wife and kids were short but full. My wife always insisted that we have dinner as a family, which was a great way to stay close and share our days with each other. The kids would snack after school so they could wait for me to sit down to dinner each night. After this all happened, our former pleasant conversations turned to questions and fears about the future."

"Well, that's only natural, Norm. So use that academic thinking to figure out how to return to a good life when you get out."

"Joe, I lost my license to practice medicine! A patient was harmed because I let someone else do my job. My income is cut off, and two people in the office were laid off because of me. They did a great job and loved working there, but they were furloughed because they're not needed if I'm not working. I don't know how I'll provide for my family. I've let so many people down. Sometimes I feel like suicide would show everyone how remorseful I am."

My counseling experience from bartending came in handy. I showed no judgment. "How old are your kids, Norm?"

"Daryll is seventeen, Sam is twelve, and Sarah is nine. Daryll graduates from high school this year, and he's already been accepted into the bioengineering program at Carnegie Mellon in Pittsburgh. It's about thirty-five grand a year, Joe, without incidentals like books, a car, spending money, etc. We have savings, but now I'm afraid we'll need that money to live on, and at the same time, I don't want to let Daryll down."

"Okay. Let's break this down. You lost your license to practice, but you're still a doctor, right?"

"I guess so. They didn't revoke my degrees."

"Norm, you're a neurologist. You have incredibly valuable knowledge and can still contribute to society. Maybe you can't practice medicine, but how about being a researcher or a consultant or a professor?"

"With a two-year prison record?"

"Some people will judge you, but others will be thrilled to have someone with your knowledge. Someone will recognize the pressure you were under and will understand. Heck, my kids' pediatrician retired early in his fifties because he was so fed up with the way everything changed when his practice was bought out by a large health network."

"Yeah? You think I'll find work somewhere?"

"Of course you will. Rewarding work, maybe something you'll like even more than the work you were doing. Most importantly, is your family behind you? Do they understand why you did this?"

"They say they forgive me, but forgiveness is a *mitzvah* in the Jewish faith, Joe—a commandment. They're *obligated* to forgive me. I'm not sure what they say matches what they feel inside. I'm also obligated to forgive myself, but I can't. I feel completely broken."

"Norm, after any trauma—and this is a trauma—you have to go through some hard phases before you get to a place of acceptance and can move forward. It's different for each member of the family. Shock, betrayal, anger—they're all part of the process that needs to end in forgiveness. Like video game monsters that you need to beat before you can reach the castle."

"But I'm the monster, Joe."

"You're wrong there, Norm; I'm certain of that. You're a good person, but every person makes mistakes. Welcome to the human race."

"I feel like I've killed my family's joy." Norm broke into heavy sobs. I told him I'd be right back, grabbed some paper towels from the nearest rest room, and ran them back to him.

I thought while Norm tried to collect himself. Then I asked, "How long have you been in here?"

"Nine months. Fifteen more to go."

"What's your relationship like with your wife and kids?"

"Civil. Strained. Very strained."

"You need to bring them some love and hope, my friend."

"Love and hope? I'm dealing with despair myself."

"I see that, Norm. But I'm tellin' you—you'll start to heal yourself and help them along if you do this."

"There's a distance between us. Nothing's the same."

"If communication is difficult right now, there's an old-fashioned way to improve it."

"What are you talking about, Joe?"

"I'm talking about letter writing," I told him, like I had just invented something amazing.

"We talk a couple times a week, and they visit me. Why would I write a letter?"

"Because a letter is unexpected these days. Because you're totally in charge of the contents of a letter. Because you can say what you want, and no one will steer the conversation in another direction. Not just *a* letter, Norm—lots of letters. Letters to your wife. Letters to each of your kids. Letters to people who can help you when you get out of here. Nothing fancy, just heartfelt."

"I wouldn't know where to start," Norm said doubtfully.

He didn't look too excited about the idea, so I gave him my best sales pitch. "I have a box of stationery because I write letters all the time. I'll split it with you. I have stamps, too. They don't have to be traditional letters. You can write little 'love litanies.' Lists. Things you love about your wife or things that you miss about your kids or things you look forward to doing with them again. Restart the narrative—just focus on appreciation for each one. Drawings, even. Tell Daryll to start getting excited about Carnegie Mellon. You have years before your other two are ready for college. Let them know you're going to figure things out and lead your family back to a good place. Turn things around."

"When you put it that way, maybe it's worth a try. I think I could do that." For the first time, I saw Norm smile. Not a big smile, but a resolute smile that made me think he bought into the idea. A hopeful little smile.

57

I expected that there would be an unfamiliar "prison culture" to adapt to, but at this time in this prison, it wasn't all that threatening, at least not to me. People on the outside wonder about the rumors of inevitable rape that go around. I didn't see anything like that. I'm not saying it doesn't happen; I'm just saying I didn't see or experience anything like that.

I learned early on about currency. One can of tuna equaled one dollar. Lots of people also traded cigarettes because at the time, you could smoke (not anymore). I learned how and when to use tuna, cigarettes, or other currency to stay comfortable in prison. My feet ached because of the prison-issued shoes. There was this underworld figure named Moe who was in the middle of serving a ten-year drug sentence. He knew people in the laundry. They had some diabetic shoes, and I gladly paid twelve cans of tuna to get them. Moe was my go-to guy if I ever needed anything; if I had the tuna, he had the goods (or could get them). I still have the shoes to this day.

Guys who were in for drug-related crimes or an addiction would have their sentences cut up to half if they signed up for the drug rehab program. Of course, everyone wanted to get in. Who wouldn't? A big problem with the drug program, though, was that these men were also not allowed to smoke cigarettes, while the rest of us were. I never had a drug problem and was never a smoker, but man, giving up drugs and cigarettes at the same time had to be hard. I used to buy cigarettes and would give them away to the people who were in the drug program, sometimes as a trade but mostly as an act of kindness.

They would say to me, "Joe, are you packin'?"

I would say, "Yeah, I'm packin'. Meet me behind the gym."

I'd give them cigarettes and they would give me M&M's, and everyone was happy.

Everyone had to work at the federal facility. Hank was the only guy who didn't have a job. I had no idea how. I had heard that the best job in the place, highly coveted, was duck chaser. Just chasing the ducks off the lawn. By the time the weather got brutal, I'd be out, so I wrote to the facilities manager and somehow landed the job of duck chaser, making eighteen cents an hour. It was big money.

One time I was trying to help someone, but as the saying goes, no good deed goes unpunished. I was supposed to be chasing the ducks. There was a guy from Detroit who owned a car dealership. He needed something from the laundry. I think it was extra socks. He asked me if I could get them for him. I said, "Yeah I know some people in the laundry," and I went to see my friend Moe. Then I was going to hurry up and meet this guy up in the dorm. In the meantime, there was a count, and I was missing from my post.

The one thing in prison that you don't want to hear is your name coming over the loudspeaker in the facility, and I heard, "Joseph Costanzo, report to the office." I hurried down to the office, and they shut the door. The assistant warden said, "You were not at your job."

I said, "I'm sorry. I'm diabetic, and I went to check my sugar."

He said, "That's bullshit."

"I went to my dorm to check my sugar, and then I went back down."

Ignoring my excuse, he said, "I'll throw you in the fucking hole."

I replied contritely. "I love my job, sir, and I really apologize."

The guard said, "I don't believe you, but you are catching me on a decent day. I should throw you in the fucking hole."

The "hole" was slang for isolation. I had heard only bits and pieces about what happens in the hole. Guys seemed hesitant to even talk about it, like they had signed a disclosure agreement. Any references to the place, however, indicated that it was hell.

Another time, I was on my duck post, and a guy I knew asked me to hold a box while he went to eat lunch. He said he was going to mail it home right after lunch, but we weren't allowed to bring anything into the mess hall.

There was a rule about holding things for other prisoners, like the recording in airports about reporting anyone who asks you to hold or transport something. Since I knew the guy, though, I didn't think anything of it. A guard came by and immediately pulled me over.

With a stern look, he demanded, "What's in the box?"

I shrugged. "I don't know."

"You don't *know*?" The guard dragged out the words, suggesting disbelief.

"I really don't. I'm just holding it for someone while they eat lunch."

"You know you aren't allowed to hold anyone's personal items. Come with me."

I followed him to the assistant warden's office. He put the box down on the desk and asked again, "What's in the box?"

Again I replied, "I don't know."

The guard reported, "He was holding this box while on duty. He says someone gave it to him while they went to lunch."

The assistant warden said, "You can't hold people's property. We are going to open this box, and if there's contraband in here, you are going into the hole. I don't care if you knew what was in it or not. You understand?"

I nodded, holding my breath and saying my silent prayers as he opened the box. Thank God, there was nothing except what looked like a letter and some old pictures. He gave me the box back.

The assistant warden warned, "Take it back to your friend, Costanzo, and don't ever hold anything for anyone again. Do I need to remind you that no one is above the laws here?"

"No, sir. It will never happen again."

I put the box down on the lawn and went back to chasing ducks.

The guy came back and said, "Where the hell did you go?"

Pissed, I told him, "The guard grabbed me and took me to the assistant warden's office. I almost went into hole because of you. Understand?"

"What the fuck do you mean? I *don't* understand, Joe. Because of me?"

"We're not allowed to hold things for each other; looks like you and I had both better review the fuckin' rules."

The prison had all kinds of regulations you'd never think about unless you were in there. Another one was that you couldn't look any woman who worked at the prison directly in the eye. It was called "reckless eyeballing."

There was this lady who was always too dolled-up for her prison job. Rumor had it she was sleeping with one of the guards, so a way to pass the time if they happened to be together in our line of vision was to see if there were any signs of a relationship between them. I never saw anything, but one day Big Sexy was staring her down with an emerging sly smile on his face, enough to let her know he liked what he saw. He was looking her right in the eye.

I watched the exchange and walked over to Big Sexy, smacking his arm with the back of my hand. "Hey, Big Sexy! You are reckless eyeballing."

He answered, "I don't care, man," never taking his eyes off her.

I advised, "Seriously, it's not worth it. She's nothin' but trailer trash."

Big Sexy turned to me and said, "Joe, I *love* trailer trash."

Speaking of love, knowing how I love food, people were always asking me what the food was like in prison. Short version: nothing good.

One day I asked the guys at the table, "What are we eating here? Chicken or some kind of cheap veal patty, or what?"

They said, "Fish sandwich."

"*Fish*? How'd they take the fish taste out of the fish? Mine's two pieces of cardboard with cardboard in between."

We'd have spaghetti for dinner, and the next day for lunch they'd serve "tomato soup," which was just the leftover sauce from the previous night. If Primadonna sauce were in the dictionary, the prison's sauce would be listed as an antonym.

We talked constantly about what we'd eat when we got out and the great food we had known. We'd get so into it that we could've published a food review magazine.

I quickly became multicultural. I was invited and attended the Muslim service, the Jewish guys invited me to the Jewish service, so I showed up there, and I went to the Catholic service that I was used to. I was everywhere. There wasn't anyone who I would turn down because it was all interesting. I even did some yoga. Picture that!

58

Once I found my social niche, which didn't take long, life in the prison wasn't too bad. The corrections officers, guards, and administrators were never friendly; their sole purpose was to intimidate. They all had attitudes, but there was nothing I could do about it. The only sense of community to be found was among the prisoners. I was the only guy in there solely convicted of tax evasion. Everyone else was in for extortion, drug running, gun running, armed robbery—deeds I had only seen in movies.

To illustrate how the guards could antagonize, I'll tell you about a time Donna, Maria, and Kelly tried to visit. All three of my girls drove to West Virginia on a hot Saturday afternoon, arriving well before the limited visiting hours to maximize our time together. When it came their turn to pass through security, one of the guards immediately declared, "You are not dressed appropriately for a prison visit."

Dumbfounded but forewarned about remaining polite and compliant under any circumstances, Donna said, "I really thought we were dressed modestly, sir, for a ninety-five-degree day." Maria was wearing cropped pants and Donna's top had a v-neckline, but it wasn't low.

"You can return if you change into appropriate clothing," said the guard off-handedly.

"I understand, sir, but we live in Pittsburgh and don't have other clothing with us."

"Then we'll see you next time," replied the guard. Dismissing them with a wave of his hand, he called out, "Next!"

They drove down the road until they found a gas station, and then asked an attendant where the closest place was to buy clothing. He told them there was a Super Kmart about eight miles away. They repeated and followed his directions, but they didn't end up at the Super K. They drove for another mile or so before asking a man who was getting out of his car in a driveway, and he redirected them. They hurried into the store and quickly decided on sweatshirts and sweatpants—cheap, useful around the house, and definitely not revealing.

By the time my family returned to the prison and went through security, there was little visiting time left. Donna and the girls sweated profusely, having hurriedly put the sweat suits on over their clothing. They were not allowed to hug me or have any physical contact. We were ushered into a large room with cafeteria-style folding tables. There was a speaker high up in the cinder block wall that we had to assume could work both ways. That visit was awkward and uncomfortable.

In the prison I was surrounded by criminals, but like anywhere else, I was able to adapt. I think we were reading Aristotle way back in high school when I read that every one of us is a mixture of good and bad. That was a relief to learn, different from the guilt-inducing quest for holy perfection that my Catholic schooling inflicted. Aristotle wasn't Jesus, but he was a pretty credible figure. Maybe these guys did some bad things, but I saw a lot of good, too. A lot of frustration endured through patience, resentment endured through forgiveness, loneliness endured through new friendships, and hardships endured through humor.

One night while playing cards, everything was funny. We were laughing so hard that one of the guys left the table, feeling sure that laughing like that was somehow against the rules.

Toby, serving fifteen years for armed carjacking, asked, "Hey, Joe, what do you tell people back home when they ask what it's like in prison?"

"I tell them it's horrible. Just like Shawshank." The crowd erupted!

Vince added, "Yeah. If we only had booze and women in here, we'd fuckin' never wanna go home!"

I noticed my friend Norm was becoming more sociable and seemed less nervous. He sometimes joined in playing Spades. Other times, though, he reminded me with a wink that he had letters to write.

We had one more memorable serious conversation. One cool evening in the yard, we sat on the ground and had a long talk.

"I think those letters are working," Norm confided with a smile. After two months and about a dozen letters to my wife, I got one back with a few pictures enclosed. She said they're all looking forward to having me back home. She wrote, I think maybe jokingly, 'Don't worry—I still love you.' She hasn't said that in earnest since this whole mess began, but it's a step. I write to my kids, too. Sarah wrote back right away and sends me pictures she draws. She likes to draw butterflies. I got a funny card from Daryll, and Sam wrote a letter that Daryll put inside the card. Although I call home, these letters are different, deeper. More about the good times than the day-to-day. I feel like the ice is broken and my wife might even begin to forgive me."

"That's the best news I've heard in a long time," I gushed.

"I'm still not doing too well in the guilt department, though. God gave me so many blessings, and I blew it."

"We're in the same boat there, Norm. God forgives us, though. You know the psalms, don't you?"

"Yes. I read them daily."

"In Bible study the other night, the chaplain focused on Psalm 103: 'As far as the east is from the west, so far has he removed our transgressions from us.' He had us repeat it with him three times. He talked about how God forgave David for murder and adultery."

Norm seemed truly baffled. "How? How can God keep forgiving us?"

"After we had the girls, I could understand it better. There's nothing I can think of that I wouldn't forgive them for if they were sorry and tried to make amends. From when they are born, they poop all over you, and you understand."

"Do you have people you have a hard time forgiving?"

"Me?" I chuckled. "You want a list?"

Norm pressed on. "Were you able to forgive them?

"I have no choice. We have to forgive if we want to be forgiven."

"That's what we believe, too, Joe."

I added, "Just so I never run into those dirty lowlifes on the street." We laughed hard.

On my last night at Club Fed, there was a big party for me organized by my friends Bill, John, and Vince. The guys pitched in and planned creatively. There were not only snacks and drinks from the vending machines, but also sandwiches, pizza, and foods they could heat in a microwave. There were quesadillas, spaghetti, chicken, as well as cookies—all likely stolen or traded from the kitchen. Two guys with guitars provided music. They wrote a song that we all sang along to called, "The Warden Don't Want No Marijuana in Here," based on the old "Mama Don't Allow" song. We had a blast! At one point two officers came down, but they seemed to look the other way, as they knew it was my last hoorah. Everyone had a great time in the spirit of appreciation for each other.

Don't think for a blink that I took my time in prison lightly. There are people who were treated so inhumanely in prisons and hated it so much that they risked their lives, and some lost. We've all seen Shawshank. I'm just saying that at that time in that prison, it wasn't so bad. I knew I was only in for a few months, my new friends and I supported each other, my family still cared for me, and it turned out to be great hands-on diversity training that gave me a new appreciation for people I might otherwise have judged from afar.

I got out of prison in late summer of 2005 but was under deep supervision and on probation for two years following my sentence.

59

The simple worn-out phrases "There's no place like home" and "Home is where the heart is" suddenly seemed like profound truths. Donna had visited me every weekend the entire time I was in prison, but it was so good to be home with her now. It was a huge relief to have not only prison, but also the entire ordeal, behind us.

My mother had moved into my sister Diane's house, where we celebrated my homecoming with a small feast. The women prepared the Costanzo family favorites—pasta, meatballs, Rice Krispies chicken, chunks of beef, fruit, salad, and a dessert buffet. If felt like Christmas in August, a summer version of what we do for holidays.

Diane gave a toast "Glad to see Joe home. To brighter times ahead!"

Another silver lining from the prison experience was that it forced Donna and me into a separation that made us realize how much we had missed each other. The roughest patch in our marriage happened in the '90s when I had used our savings for the political campaign, but the more recent stress of the investigation and sentencing inevitably put a damper on our romance as well. When we were apart for those five months, though, we both came to the same conclusion—we belonged together.

That weekend Donna and I escaped to the Sheraton at Station Square for a romantic getaway. We were walking downtown, hand in hand, when a stranger stopped us. The woman said, "Excuse me, but I have to say that you two look like you're so happy and in love."

Almost in unison, we said, "We are."

And we were. My heart was no longer fearful that Donna would leave, and her heart was no longer angry. We had unexpectedly traveled through the looking glass back to that place where we first fell in love—that place where your heart tumbles and your hands tremble when you connect. That place where everything else is subordinate.

The big celebration for my coming home, organized by my friend Mitch Galiyas, took place in August of 2005 at the pavilion in Fairhaven Park in Kennedy Township. We called a mix of people from the past and said we are having a party—childhood friends, family members, staff and customers of the restaurant, and everyone in between who had been a part of my life. The extensive buffet included fried chicken, pasta, cold cuts, hamburgers, hot dogs, potato salad, tossed salad, beer, and pop—a huge spread for a picnic—catered by Marge's Place, a great little coffee shop just a few doors away from The Primadonna.

A couple hundred people showed up for this festive event. Hufty, resurrecting his role as DJ, kept playing Steve Winwood's "Back in the Highlife" while shouting over the microphone, "Joe Costanzo, back in the high life again!" People were dancing, and laughter abounded. Mitch proposed a toast: "Glad to see Joe home!" and the crowd cheered vigorously. Larry Gregg interrupted his vacation in Hawaii to be there. With all the food, drinking, dancing, and mingling, it reminded me of a wedding.

It felt so good to be able to talk to everyone and know that I meant something to the people who meant so much to me. I again felt their positive energy, the force that kept me going throughout our years at the restaurant. People were genuinely supportive, and it was the perfect way to come back. That celebration erased all my misgivings about being judged or ostracized when I returned, and it put my mind and heart at ease. Sartre is famous for "Hell is other people," but I have to take the opposite stand and say heaven is other people, too.

I know I have a great group of friends because that support

continued beyond my initial homecoming. I called Giant Eagle one day, and the guy answering the phone said, "Giant Eagle. This is Erv. How can I help you?"

I recognized the voice. It was our former college-degreed dishwasher, Erv.

"Hey, Erv! This is Joe Costanzo."

"Joe! How the hell are you doing?"

"I'm okay, Erv. You?"

"I've got to tell you this story. Got a minute?"

"Sure."

"When you got into trouble, I was sick over it. I went home and said to my wife, 'Joe is in some trouble. Someone mentioned his name in a grand jury investigation. He is in trouble. I want to tell you something. I want to let you know that if they ask me to testify against Joe Costanzo, I'm probably going to jail. I could never testify against Joe Costanzo. If anyone asks me any questions, I'm going to say I take the Fifth Amendment. I think that would put me in contempt of court, so that means I would be doing some jail time.' You know what my wife said? She said, 'Erv, I understand. I think you would be doing the right thing.'"

So I said to him, "Erv, Jesus Christ wished he had a disciple like you."

60

I was out of prison, but it wasn't out of me. I was under probation and scrutiny for the next two years. My every move had to be monitored and reported to my probation officer, which will be important to the story later. Whatever I did, I had to tell him.

Maria was slated to graduate with a master's in psychology from Pepperdine University in Malibu. She really wanted us to be there, and after all we'd been through, I agreed that we could use some family time centered around something happy.

Before I bought my ticket, I had to alert my probation officer who then issued me a convicted felon ID that I had to carry with me, alerting the airline that a felon would be on the plane. It was post-9/11, everyone was fearing terrorism, and it didn't seem fitting that I warranted an alert. Not long before I had been the one who people flocked to when they needed something—a job, a meal, some reassurance, you name it. Now my ID was warning the public that I was someone to be wary of. Something was not right about the situation.

It's so easy to beat yourself up after making a mistake big enough to land you in prison. The regrets can kill you. You can spend your days thinking about how things could have gone differently, how quickly one move changed your life, how it all could have and should have been avoided, etc. Or you can move on and spend your thoughts on the silver linings. Prison had a number of silver linings.

I had never been to California and didn't know much about it. Aside from my daughter and her fiancé, I thought I didn't know anyone on the West Coast. Then on the plane it dawned on me that I *did* know another person from California. His name was Franco Vitale, and he was about Maria's age. I met him at Club Fed where he was serving time for some type of online money fraud. We met because I fulfilled a need for him. Franco was in the drug program and desperate for nicotine. He heard that I might be able to help, and I was happy to provide. He was one of the guys who used to ask, "Hey, Joe, you packin'?"

We had a little gap in our schedule, so I gave Franco a call. "Hey, man, I'm comin' to California. Where do you live?"

"No way, Joe! I'm in LA. Where are you going?" He sounded so happy to hear from me.

"My daughter's graduating from Pepperdine. We'll be staying in the Beverly Hills area."

"Great! That's only about an hour from here. You've gotta come over to my mom's house. She makes the most legit Italian food."

"Franco, I'd love to see you, but I don't want to invite myself to your parents' house. Let me know when you are free, and we'll take you out to dinner. Maybe there's a good Italian place where we could meet up?

"Joe, this ain't no Pittsburgh and this ain't no New York City. Italians are few and far between around here, and the absolute best food is right here at my house. Besides, man, we are both on probation, and technically, we're not supposed to be in touch. We can't meet up in public. Get my drift?"

"Ah, yes. Well, I'll call you when I get there. Maybe we can just stop by and say hello, but if we do, please tell your mom not to fuss."

I knew all too well there was no telling an Italian mother not to fuss. At my house, there would have been no stopping my mother. It didn't matter whether you just had a full seven-course dinner. When company came, my mother was like a magician backstage cooking up some magic in no time. Food would just keep on appearing—antipasto, cheese, bread, crackers, shrimp, fried zucchini—well, you get it. I had a feeling we were going to be in for much of the same at Franco's house.

I felt bad imposing on his family, but at the same time, I wanted to see Franco (and I have never turned down good food).

A couple days later, Donna, Maria, and I headed north on the 405 to Franco's parents' place to visit with Franco. Set in the Agora Hills section of Los Angeles, the modern-day art deco houses looked perfectly placed. The houses were similar, yet each had modifications in the architecture that made it unique. We slowed down, taking in the lovely neighborhood as we searched for the house.

We arrived and rang the bell, prepared with a gift bag of goodies—wine, burrata cheese, and Caffarel Gianduia chocolates with hazelnuts—that we were able to secure from the only Italian store in the city that Maria knew. When we walked in, we were greeted with warm hugs and love all around. You'd have thought we were related to these people.

Our hosts could not have been nicer, ushering us in and showing us around the house. When we reached the kitchen, we met Franco's grandmother, Nonna, who was cooking away, just like my own mother would have been doing.

"We heard you're a great guy. I never thought I'd have the chance to meet you in person," said Franco's dad, Gino, as though I were a celebrity instead of Franco's fellow inmate.

Although she introduced herself as Lisa, I remembered Franco telling me his mother's name was Elisabetta. "Thank you for helping to look after our baby while he was away back East," she gushed.

It remains funny to me that former inmates rarely refer to our time in prison as our time in prison. We are gone, away, on hiatus, taking a break. Maybe it just sits better this way.

As I suspected would happen, we were led to a fully set table in the dining room. The smells that were emerging from the kitchen reminded me of my own home growing up. First came the antipasto, then the wine and a toast.

Franco started, "To Joe, one of the best guys I've ever known!"

All mumbled their affirmations and drank. I thought about the irony of Franco calling me "one of the best" when our relationship started with my *breaking a rule* in a *prison*. In truth, though, I had stuck my neck out to ease an acquaintance's stress, so our cigarette capers were more acts of kindness than violations. Things are not always what they seem.

Conversations stirred, switching naturally from one-on-one to small group to whole-table exchanges. After a while, Lisa got up but soon returned with Nonna, placing a bowl of wedding soup in front of each of us. Lisa returned to her seat, but I noticed that Nonna never sat down until the main course had been served. So like my mother.

There were a few seconds of silence while we all started on the delicious chicken soup with tortellini and sausage. Then Franco asked Maria, "What do you do for work?"

Maria explained, "I work for a for-profit university in Marina del Rey. I mainly give presentations in schools that will help students in some way. You know—topics that aren't in a normal curriculum, like how to utilize your personality to the best of your ability or how to avoid credit card fraud."

My heart dropped. I never thought to tell Maria why Franco had "gone away." It had to do with credit card fraud. While my mind raced for a way to transition to another topic, my silence was overpowered by others' laughter as Franco's face turned beet red with embarrassment. Then his sister Mia blurted out, "Franco knows a thing or two about credit card fraud. Ask him for some pointers. Or maybe he can be your guest speaker."

The Vitales howled! Their sense of humor surprised and impressed me. Maria seemed flustered, but Franco continued candidly. "Talk among yourselves. I'll explain to Maria."

I was curious about what Franco had to say, but I picked up the lead to save either Franco or Maria from further chagrin. Maria later told us how Franco explained the ins and outs of how people can protect themselves from fraud. He also told her about phishing online, which was a very new concept at the time. Maria was amazed at the valuable first-hand information that would enhance her credit card fraud talk.

Lisa got up again and addressed Maria and Franco. "Are you two finished with your lesson? It's time for the main course."

Maria replied, "Yes. I really learned a ton just now." Then turning to Franco, she said, "You're really smart."

Franco laughed and said, "Listen, most people get to prison because they are smart. Actually, we are too smart. We outsmart others—unless or until we get caught. A lot of us are the best of the best at what we do. We really should work for the FBI, but the prison record is an obstacle."

The room erupted with laughter, and in came more food. Lisa and Nonna brought manicotti followed by some cavatelli that I had noticed Nonna was making as we entered the kitchen earlier. Those delicacies were followed by veal, meatballs, and *baccalà*, a traditional dried salted cod fish that is a part of every Italian celebration. Although we were already stuffed, an array of homemade Italian cookies was set on the table. To top off the night, we were served shots of Sambuca with three coffee beans for good luck. I declared another toast:

"To friendship!"

Franco added, "And unique ways of meeting!"

I looked at Nonna as I declared: "To fantastic food!"

That last toast garnered a loud, collective, "Here, here!"

I'm sure our families were hoping for the kind of luck that would not land either of us "away" ever again.

It was such a wonderful night for all of us.

61

While I was in prison, many people checked in with Donna. Larry Gregg was like family by this time, helping me as much as I had helped him as a kid. And guess who else offered his support? Remember that fight during the "Bar Era" where I intervened in the Curt and Toby fight and ended up street-fighting Curt? Curt not only had been a great customer afterward, but he contacted Donna and asked if he could be of help while I was gone. Chuckie Richards checked in on my family and asked how I was doing, too. He took homegrown tomatoes to Donna and told her if she needed anything financially, just let him know. He was such a loyal friend; I missed him and wrote him a couple letters from the federal correctional institution.

When I came home, Chuckie and I went to lunch at the Sheraton Station Square, the same place he, Danny Cannon, and I had lunch before I went to prison. We talked about how that was then and this is now. When I asked Chuckie how he was feeling, he said the Agent Orange was taking effect, resulting in growths on his body that he said were "just bad." He said it casually, motioning with his hand that he'd rather move on to other topics. He looked a bit thinner to me, but basically the same. That was the last time I saw him alive.

The executor of Chuckie Richards's will called me at home to tell me that Chuckie had left me money, which is how I found out he passed away. I felt horrible; I knew he was sick, but I did not think his death was imminent. Chuckie named twenty-one people in his will, but he left me the greatest percentage of his assets.

There was a small, informal memorial service at the funeral home for Chuckie's buddies and relatives, which Father Regis Ryan attended. Fr. Ryan was Executive Director of Focus on Renewal, known as the FOR, a far-reaching organization with multiple programs and services intended to improve the lives of residents of McKees Rocks. Beloved throughout the Pittsburgh area, Fr. Ryan was known for his tireless efforts for the poor and his personal connections to the people of the Rocks. Because of those connections, he frequently ended up celebrating people's life events at The Primadonna.

Fr. Ryan spoke about Chuck's dedication to his country, saying he was a good human being, "a great guy who loved his Budweiser beer." He really was. Chuckie's death affected me deeply as I began to realize how much I had learned about being a good person and a loyal friend from his humble example.

I wasn't told how much Chuckie left me; I assumed it wasn't much. When I received a large envelope containing the details of the inheritance, it included two IRAs totaling around thirty thousand dollars and another thirty thousand dollars in assets, adding up to around sixty thousand dollars. I couldn't believe it. The gesture made me cry like a baby. I imagined Chuckie denying his own wants repeatedly so he could leave something behind for the people he loved. I still get choked up when I think about it.

In celebration of the relief I felt from this lucky break, I bought two bottles of Budweiser and went up to Calvary Cemetery. I popped the cap off one and poured it over the graves of Chuckie and his mother. I talked to Chuckie as I enjoyed my beer. "Thank you so much, my friend."

Then I looked over at Chuckie's mother's grave. "Mrs. Richards, you did such a fine job of raising such a wonderful son."

When I finished my beer, I stuck the bottle into the ground upside down between the graves, as Chuckie and his mother were both big Budweiser fans. The ground was wet from the rain, so it was easy. I let the rain fall on me, feeling somehow that I was really visiting with the Richards family.

That same day, I played ten bucks on #105 in the lottery in honor of Chuckie's birthday, and it hit straight for five thousand dollars! No one will ever convince me that was a coincidence.

62

When I was ready to start another venture, my original idea was to open a coffee shop with coffee, upscale desserts, and a liquor license as well. I thought it was a great idea because there was nothing in the city quite like that.

I saw an ad in the newspaper for a modest-sized space—about a thousand square feet—uptown in Washington Plaza, right across the street from the Civic Arena, entertainment venue and home arena for the Pittsburgh Penguins. A new venue (the Consul Center, currently PPG Paints Arena) was being built just across the other side of the street. Rent was only five hundred dollars a month, utilities included, seeming too good to be true. I looked at it and liked the space, but thought it probably wasn't the location for what I wanted to do. The upscale dessert idea might be better for the theater district.

Real estate people told me what I wanted to hear, though—that the clientele would be 50-60 percent professionals and that the Washington Plaza tenants would provide a daily customer base. I started to rethink the menu and decided to give it a go. Café Costanzo opened in the spring of 2008.

True to the saying, "If it seems too good to be true, it probably is," the clientele was about 90 percent students from Duquesne and a few other schools. Washington Plaza tenants rarely came into the restaurant, and people who worked or ate downtown didn't travel that far uptown. If there was an event at the Civic Arena, we were busy; otherwise, we were not.

The situation worsened when a new company took over the building about a year after we opened. My lease was null and void, and they tripled the rent.

After proving everyone wrong about The Primadonna thriving in the Rocks, I probably underestimated the importance of the location for Café Costanzo. I should have held out for the right place and time, but I was anxious to get back into the business. I cut my losses and closed the restaurant before the new Consul Center ever opened. There wasn't much during that time that's worth sharing except for one final story—Big Sexy came to Pittsburgh.

63

Big Sexy called because he was coming to Pittsburgh for a family reunion. He didn't tell me that he was going to Burgettstown (about thirty miles west); he said that the reunion was in Pittsburgh. I agreed that he could stay with me.

On the day he was to arrive, Big Sexy called from Penn Avenue in Wilkinsburg (about twenty miles east). He told me that he was with his buddy, and they were on their motorcycles. They were "lost and pissed," so they stopped their bikes, and they were lying on someone's lawn. He said he "wasn't fucking leaving" and wanted me to pick him up. This was the first I had heard that he was bringing a friend, and the first inkling that I might have bargained for more than I was expecting in having him as a house guest.

I knew that I needed to go retrieve Big Sexy and his friend, or I would probably have to retrieve them at a local police station.

I announced, "Donna, I have to go to pick up Big Sexy. Want to come?"

Donna, being the good sport she always is, came along for the ride.

This was the first time I had met Big Sexy's buddy; all I knew about him was that he was a fellow Outlaw and that they were also in the bar business. They opened a speakeasy for the Outlaws in their town. Here's how Big Sexy put it: "Yeah. The cops said as long as we don't bother any of the citizens, they are okay with it."

They ran a bar without a liquor license? All I could think was that the police must have been picking their battles for that one to have passed.

Big Sexy first wanted to stop at Café Costanzo for some drinks. As soon as we got to the Café, Big Sexy's buddy was trying to hit on girls, and I knew that the best way to diffuse this situation was to leave as quickly as possible. We suggested that we go back to our house. I lured them by saying that we had drinks and food there.

When we got to my house, Big Sexy's buddy was snapping photos of our house and texting his "old lady," telling her that he was livin' large in Pittsburgh.

Next, they wanted to go to The Primadonna that night for dinner, which I was more than happy to oblige, but that would only take a couple of hours, and I had these guys all night. I was thinking, *What can I do with these guys?* Then I remembered another famous McKees Rocks destination they would surely enjoy, and conveniently for me, it was open late.

I told Donna, "Right after we eat, I'm going to take Big Sexy and his buddy down to Club Erotica. I'm going to drop them off. It's open all night, and they can drink for free and hang out with naked women and hopefully stay out all night. I can pick them up in the morning, and everyone will be happy." It had the workings of a great plan; however, sometimes my plans don't go as expected.

We were eating at The Primadonna when Big Sexy turned to Donna and said, "We are going to the strip club after dinner; would you like to join us?"

Donna said, "No, I definitely don't want to do that. No. No, thank you."

Big Sexy really didn't understand, "Donna, why? This is going to be fun. C'mon!"

Donna followed with, "I will pass. Thank you, Big Sexy."

After dinner, I drove them to Club Erotica in my car. The plan was to drop them off and go back home. When we got to the parking lot, I kept the motor running and said, "Have a great time, guys. They're open all night. Call me when you're ready to come home; I don't care what time it is."

Showing his surprise by stopping abruptly and knitting his bushy eyebrows, Big Sexy said, "What do you mean by 'goodbye,' Joe? We just got here. You have to come in for at least one drink."

I really didn't want to, but I said, "Okay." I parked the car, and we stood in line. I had the sixty dollars ready to give to the bouncer for our cover charge. Big Sexy's friend had his hat on backward. The bouncer took one look and said, "Turn your hat around."

Big Sexy's friend cast a deadly stare at the bouncer, and I started to understand why Big Sexy proudly boasts that he is a "one percenter," which in layman's terms means that the Outlaws are proud to be the "baddest" 1 percent of people in the world. I had to think quickly on my feet, so I said, "Look, man; please don't do this. You want to have a good time drinking and looking at the girls."

He looked at me and didn't say one word, but he did turn his hat around, and I breathed a sigh of relief. We went into the club—a most unlikely trio with me in my button-down shirt and nicely pressed pants next to Big Sexy and his buddy dressed in full Outlaw biker apparel.

The stripper saw these guys and recognized that they were real-deal Outlaws, so she went off the stage and came back out wearing an Outlaw hat. My guests were going crazy! They went up to her and put twenties in her G-string.

Big Sexy shouted over the music, "Joe this is great! The best night ever."

His friend added, "Free booze and naked girls."

I was relieved that it looked like my plan was working. I said, "I have to go."

Big Sexy said, "What do you mean? It's heaven here."

I said, "Listen, I'm happy that this is the place for you, but this ain't for me. Give me a call at two or even four—whenever you are done. They are open all night."

Driving home, I was somewhat relieved that it looked like everything was going to turn out okay. Still, I went upstairs and told Donna and Kelly to lock their bedroom doors. I realized we could be in for a crazy night.

In less than thirty minutes, the phone rang, and it was Big Sexy. He ordered, "Come on down and get us. We have a couple of girls here, and they want to go on the bikes." The bikes were parked in my driveway.

I went back down to Club Erotica and picked up the two ex-cons plus two strippers. They jumped into the car, and when we got to the driveway, I thought my job was done. Big Sexy called me aside as I was walking towards my front door.

"Joe, we need to borrow your downstairs for a couple hours."

I said, "Big Sexy, this is where I have to draw the line. Donna has been more than understanding. She is letting you stay here. She let me take you guys to the strip club, but I can't let you bring two strippers into the house. I'll give you the money, but you need to go to a hotel."

In the meantime, Big Sexy's friend was all over his stripper, who was currently dating a Hell's Angel—a big NO for everyone involved. They got on the bikes and revved their engines, which at one o'clock in the morning in my neighborhood sounded as loud as fireworks. I said, "Look, you can't do this here. Everyone is sleeping. You can't wake these people up. They work in the morning. Please. You have to get the hell out of here. Someone is going to call the cops."

Before Big Sexy's friend took off, he said, "I'll just ring your bell when I get back."

I said, "You can't do that, either, because people are going to think you are trying to break in. If anyone looks out, they will immediately call the cops. We all know each other around here. I am going to sleep on the couch in the living room. If I don't hear you coming, knock gently."

After they got a couple of drinks, they came back. I was so paranoid that I waited outside for them. There was no chance I could convince law enforcement of my innocence while chauffeuring and housing ex-cons. By five o'clock, all was quiet, and Big Sexy and his friend were asleep downstairs.

As I went back upstairs and relocked the bedroom door, I looked and Donna and said, "I owe you one, Donna. I owe you one."

She looked back and me and said, "You owe me *one*? This is absolutely the most ridiculous thing I've ever unwillingly been a part of!"

And you know what? Once again, Donna was right.

64

As I reflect on all that has happened to me, I am in disbelief that I lived this life. When I read the words on the paper, my life reads like a work of fiction. What reasonable person would choose to live life the way that I did? As I look back now, I ask myself, *What the hell was I thinking*?

So where did it all go wrong? In my opinion, it was the moment I decided to throw my hat into the political arena. I was a successful restaurateur and believed that I would be an even better politician, which is why I decided to enter the race for county commissioner in 1995. Donna said from the start, "You only have one miracle in life, and that miracle for us is The Primadonna." I should have listened.

Tell me, what logical person would:

- run for political office with no political experience, no party backing, and no organization?
- make the jump believing that his name recognition, synonymous with his beloved restaurant, would be enough to propel a new political venture?
- spend fifty thousand dollars on TV ads in the final week of a campaign?
- take his wife's retirement funds to do so? (Yes, my intention was to replace the money, but that never happened).
- So why did I do it? Just as I had no restaurant experience yet made it all happen with hard work and sweat equity, I

felt I could do the same in the political arena. I thought the marketing algorithm that I had created for The Primadonna would easily cross over to the voters in Allegheny County. I thought wrong.

I was devastated watching the results on election night; however, I had no idea at the time what lasting effects this decision would have on my life and the lives of the people I love the most—my family. I've been reminded of these consequences every day since. The hurt that I caused can never be erased, and it remains one of my biggest regrets.

There is a quote that resonates with how I chose to live my life. I share it with my family often, helping them to understand me. I want to share it with you as well, as you are now part of this journey, too. "The intangibles that enabled me to achieve my greatness, also contained the seeds to my destruction." Whether you choose to call it blind ambition, determination, risk-taking, or any other name, it rings true.

Was it all worth it?

HELL, NO!

To this day, it is hard for me to absorb all the losses that resulted from my decision to run for county commissioner. I lost the election. I lost the financial security that I had once enjoyed. I lost the ability to provide for my family. I lost my beloved business. Eventually, I lost my freedom.

I also secondarily lost the dream house that I built to create memories for my children. I lost my health due to the stress and poor food choices. I lost one of my greatest joys as a person—the ability to help people. I could no longer help the kids hanging out on the corner by giving them a job at the restaurant. I could no longer help local charities that provided people with food and other essentials. I could no longer be a part of the special memories that my customers entrusted to share with me for so many years. This hurt then, and it hurts now.

What have I learned since? I have learned the power of having the unconditional love and the support of an amazing family. I have learned the power of forgiveness. I see this power every day, in my wife especially. My actions directly put her in precarious situations, but over time, whether through counseling, a change in perspective, or belief in me, she always found a way to not only forgive me, but also to understand me. She was and is my number one fan, and she continues to elevate me. She also wasn't afraid when the tables turned, forcing her to be the breadwinner of the family.

After we lost everything, Donna started working for minimum wage at a convenience store and was driving a Jeep that had two hundred thousand miles on the odometer and no heat. Wrapping herself in a wool blanket, she drove back and forth to work in that cold vehicle just to keep us on health insurance that I so urgently needed, as my own health had taken a dive. We were struggling, but no one knew it. About a year in, my blood pressure pills became too much for us financially, and I was consequentially diagnosed with congestive heart failure. Donna once again had to rise to the occasion and try for a management role. When she got the news that she had gotten the job and would be making fifty thousand dollars a year, you would have thought we won the lottery. What a change in perspective, right?

However, the final chapter of my life has also been one filled with joy and surprise. Although it had been nearly a decade since I walked away from The Primadonna, my heart leaped when I opened the *Post-Gazette* on December 20, 2012, to *The Server's* full-page spread of twentieth century restaurant awards. The Primadonna had garnered more awards than any other restaurant. Four of our maître d's made the list of "Western Pennsylvania's Top Maître D's of the 20th Century"—David Rigo, Chris Singel, Mark Kautzman, and Theo Giannoutsos. The list only contained fourteen names in total. The honor of "Western Pennsylvania's Restaurant of the 20th Century" was shared between The Primadonna (Ethnic) and Park Schenley

(Continental). In the list of "Western Pennsylvania's Restaurateur of the Decade in the 20th Century" (which started with the 1930s), I received the honor for the 1990s. On July 6, a separate full page listed more than fifty restaurants under the title "The Best Restaurants in Western Pennsylvania History." On the bottom of that page, under "The Best Overall Restaurant in Western Pennsylvania History" was The Primadonna—with my name right underneath.

Seeing our names in print among the most legendary restaurants and restaurateurs in the history of Pittsburgh was a surreal experience. I was so happy to see Mike Kalina named "Western Pennsylvania's Most Influential Person in the Restaurant Industry in the 20th Century," albeit posthumously.

I am so grateful for the support and love of Donna, the true "Primadonna" (first lady) of my life. I also am so thankful for our two greatest blessings, Maria and Kelly. Maria is not only the coauthor of this book, but she is out there trying to help others with a hand up, not a handout. She is a grant writer for a nonprofit, St. Paul's Community Development Corporation, in Paterson, NJ, an area strikingly similar to McKees Rocks, Pennsylvania. Kelly is the owner of Sharp Hair Boutique in Pittsburgh, PA, where she styles the hair that I have left. I am so proud of my daughters and their beautiful families. Our grandchildren—Helena, Josephina, Rocco, and Adia—are the joys of my life. My cousin Pino and I have reconciled and see each other occasionally.

As you can tell from the story, Donna is rarely wrong. She *was* wrong about one thing, though. Remember the line about only getting only one miracle, and The Primadonna was that miracle for us? Well, I actually was lucky enough to get a second miracle. After struggling on dialysis for four years, I received a new kidney in September of 2019, which stopped working less than a month later. As distressing as that was, we never gave up hope. On September 22, 2020, I received the gift we were all praying for—a lifesaving second kidney transplant. Donna and I can now look forward to our retirement years.

As hard as I worked toward my dream of bringing fine dining to the Rocks, my mind's eye could never have foreseen the details that can only unfold in real life—the two-hour waits down the block, my two-hour sleeps in a booth around dawn, the fifty-thousand-dollar-a-year linen service bill, Frank Sinatra eating Primadonna takeout, or the family of employees and friends that would emerge in a *Field of Dreams* build-it-and-they-will-come manner. Words cannot capture the wild velocity of the Primadonna experience. I can barely think about it without getting emotional, but as Robert Frost wrote, "Nothing gold can stay."

In that interview for *Robinson Community Magazine*, where I first stated publicly that I'd like to get involved in politics, another question asked of me was this: *What have you always wanted to tell your clients?* The same answer I gave at the time now goes for you, too, who have taken time out of your own life to allow me to share mine:

      Thank you for coming by;
      I really appreciate your patronage.
      With love and gratitude,
      Joe

ACKNOWLEDGMENTS

FROM MARIA AND RUTHIE:

To the Buffalo Dog Ears Writers' Group: you helped us figure out that this book had one voice—the voice of Joe Costanzo—and you pressed us to explore the pieces of the story that we had not originally included.

To our beta readers (in alphabetical order) Sandra Burley, Mike Conturo, Gigi DePascale, Samuel Dines, Kathryn Hurdman, Stefanie Kratter, Joseph Palmer, David Perritano, and David Rigo: You all left your mark on this story with every correction, question, or typo, and you helped to refine the manuscript prior to submission. Joe and Dave, your Hollywood knowledge and sense helped us to keep driving this story forward and to fill in the narrative gaps that once existed.

To our content advisors, Maria's parents Joe and Donna, her sister Kelly, and her Aunt Diane Hulings: You helped us remember things that we forgot and added your experiences to enhance the story.

To our agent Leticia Gomez at Savvy Literary: From the moment Maria met you, you were the one we wanted to represent us and the book. Receiving your offer email will forever remain one of the most wonderful moments of our lives. Thank you for believing in us and for giving us a chance.

To our web designer Ter Dines: your artistic sense and technical expertise have given us a beautiful means by which we can share this story and connect with readers everywhere.

To our team at Koehler Books: To Danielle Koehler for your amazing cover design. You were able to capture the essence of the story from a small conversation after Maria had been up all night tending to a sick daughter; to our editor Becky Hilliker: Your objectivity and expertise made this story a little better with every suggestion. We are blessed to have been paired with you. And last but not least, to John Koehler: You saw potential in this story from the start, and you believed in it enough to offer us our very first book deal. We will always be grateful.

To the staff and senior management at the Senator John Heinz History Center: We appreciate you all and the attention you have given to this project. It is an honor to launch this book at the Smithsonian's home in Pittsburgh. In particular, we'd like to extend extra gratitude (in alphabetical order) to Sandra R. Flower, Allison E. Herrmann, Cassandra C. Horrell, and Brady M. Smith.

To The Primadonna staff, customers, and social media followers: You supported us from the very start, and this story is as much yours as it is ours. Thank you for sharing your lives with us. We hope that this story sparks warm memories for you.

FROM MARIA:

My mom always says, "There's a lid for every pot. Sometimes it takes a while to find the ones that fit." This could not be truer with the seventeen-year journey of *On the Rocks*. Here are my proverbial lids:

To my early helpers, Lisa Tener, Dan Blank, and Kim Meisner, whose classes and mentorships helped to lay the foundation for what followed.

To my boss at the St. Paul's Community Development Corporation, Richard C. Williams: You have been my supporter since I became your first hire back some ten-plus years ago. Thank you for helping to give this project an extra push in NJ!

To my parents, Joseph and Donna Costanzo, Jr., my sister Kelly Costanzo Argirakis, my in-laws Thomas and Alice Palmer, Claudia "Gege" Homer Slusser, all my brothers and sisters-in-law, nephews and nieces, aunt, uncles, cousins, and friends: thank you for following along on this insane journey for the past seventeen years and for being my support system through all the good and the bad.

To my husband, Joseph Palmer: Thank you for being the amazing soul that you are and for the support that you've given me, our family, and this project. Your brilliance and kind nature are two things that I cherish most. God had his hand in bringing us together, and I'm grateful for you every day.

To my children, Helena and Josephina Palmer: You both are the true lights and blessings in my life. If you've learned anything from watching me go through this project, it's that you should never stop following your dreams. I love you both so very much.

To my father, Joseph Costanzo, Jr.: Thank you for trusting Ruthie and me with your story. I know it is difficult to be vulnerable and to show all sides of yourself, even through the worst times. Thank you for being honest, looking beyond, and helping us take back the pen to tell the story that needed to be told!

To my coauthor, Ruthie Robbins: You always found a way to help me find my voice. I am forever grateful for the impact you have and continue to have on me. There is no one else who could have ever been a more perfect writing partner for me. What a blessing it has been to be on this journey with you!

FROM RUTHIE:

Writing a book is an incredibly time-consuming endeavor, and so are the publishing-related tasks that follow. Maria and I collaborated nonstop during the height of the pandemic when nobody could do much else anyway. Now that the world has opened up again, however, I am most grateful for the patience and understanding of my family and friends from whom this project has taken much time that could have been spent together.

To my husband Jay: I am so blessed to be reunited with you, as your zenful spirit has transformed my world. Thank you for unconditional love and for letting me share your qi that energizes me. It is because of you that I understand and believe "the best is yet to be."

To my sons, Terrill, Christian, and Sam, to my daughters-in-law Shelby and Krystle, to my grandchildren Naomi, Tasha, and Isaiah, and to my stepsons Brad and Kyle, their wives Gayle and Ashley, and our grandchildren Harper Lee, River, and Cash: beaches, concerts, and roller coasters await us!

To my sweet sister Gigi DePascale: thank you for being the sounding board who listens to my rants, proofreads my writing, and supports me without judgment when in reality, we'd much rather be shopping in Chicago.

To my wonderful friends: You are such blessings in my life, and I look forward to making up for lost time.

To author Nick Flynn, William Condeluci, and the late Sister Rita Anne, OP: you showed me the power and the pleasure that come from reading and writing.

To my coauthor Maria Costanzo Palmer: There can be no denying the uncanny connections that led to our working together on this book. Luckily for me, you might be the easiest person in the world to get along with. It was wonderful to be able to work closely with someone without any drama or tension. You are a beautiful person.

To God: I give praise and gratitude "for allowing me to participate in this life," a prayer I learned from my son Christian.

Photos by Joseph A. Colucci, Jr.

Photos by Joseph A. Colucci, Jr.

Dick Butkus,
Former NFL Player Chicago Bears

Danny Aiello,
Actor

Tommy Lasorda,
Former LA Dodgers Coach

Joe Frazier,
American Boxer

THE PRIMADONNA RESTAURANT

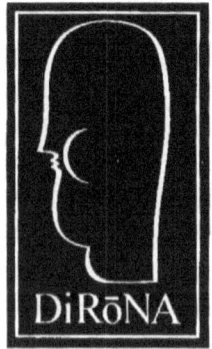

801 Broadway Ave
McKees Rocks, PA 15136
412-331-1001

Winner of "The Most Coveted and Most Prestigious Restaurant Award in America" -

The DiRōNA Award -
Given by Distinguished Restaurants of North America

Joseph Costanzo, Jr.
Owner

2002 AMERICA'S TOP TEN
RESTAURATEURS

JOSEPH COSTANZO, JR.
PRIMADONNA-Pittsburgh, Pennsylvania

JOHN FOLSE
LAFITTE'S LANDING-Donaldsonville, Louisiana

DANIEL FORGE
BEAU RIVAGE-Malibu, California

WAYNE FRICKS
STOCKYARD-Nashville, Tennessee

LEON GREENBERG
LG's PRIME STEAKHOUSE-Palm Desert, California

LEONARD LOGAN
ELIZABETH'S CAFE & WINERY-Duck, North Carolina

CRAIG & SCOTT PETERSON
RINGSIDE-Portland, Oregon

WAYNE PIERCE
BON TON CAFE-New Orleans, Louisiana

RON WEISS
JEFFREY'S-Austin, Texas

RON WOODSBY
CHARLEY'S STEAK HOUSE-Orlando, Florida

International Restaurant and Hospitality Rating Bureau
Serving The Hospitality Industry Worldwide Since 1949

Photo by Joseph A. Colucci, Jr.

Photo by Tony Tye, Pittsburgh Post-Gazette

www.ingramcontent.com/pod-product-compliance
Lightning Source LLC
LaVergne TN
LVHW091625070526
838199LV00044B/940